In Praise of the Ancestors

BORDERLANDS AND TRANSCULTURAL STUDIES

Series Editors:

ROSLYN LAPIER
RUDY GUEVARRA
PAUL SPICKARD

| Susan Elizabeth Ramírez

In Praise of the Ancestors

| Names, Identity, and Memory
| in Africa and the Americas

University of Nebraska Press | Lincoln

Portions of chapter 4 first appeared as "Historia y memoria: La construcción de las tradiciones dinásticas andinas," *Revista de Indias* 66, no. 236 (2006): 13–54.

The University of Nebraska Press is part of a land-grant institution with campuses and programs on the past, present, and future homelands of the Pawnee, Ponca, Otoe-Missouria, Omaha, Dakota, Lakota, Kaw, Cheyenne, and Arapaho Peoples, as well as those of the relocated Ho-Chunk, Sac and Fox, and Iowa Peoples.

Publication of this volume was assisted by the Department of History and the AddRan College of Liberal Arts, Texas Christian University.

Library of Congress Cataloguing in Publication Data
Names: Ramírez, Susan E., 1946– author.
Title: In praise of the ancestors: names, identity, and memory in Africa and the Americas / Susan Elizabeth Ramírez.
Other titles: Names, identity, and memory in Africa and the Americas
Description: Lincoln: University of Nebraska Press, [2022] | Series: Borderlands and Transcultural Studies | Includes bibliographical references and index.
Identifiers: LCCN 2021058268
ISBN 9781496230256 (Hardback: acid-free paper)
ISBN 9781496231475 (Paperback: acid-free paper)
ISBN 9781496232069 (ePub)
ISBN 9781496232076 (PDF)
Subjects: LCSH: Names, Personal—Luba-Lulua—Case studies. | Names, Personal—Iroquois—Case studies. | Names, Personal—Andean—Case studies. | Onomastics—Africa, Sub-Saharan—Case studies. | Onomastics—Andes—Case studies. | Onomastics—Americas—Case studies. | Oral tradition—Case studies. | Lulua (African people)—Social life and customs. | Iroquois Indians—Social life and customs. | Incas—Social life and customs. | BISAC: SOCIAL SCIENCE / Ethnic Studies / African Studies | SOCIAL SCIENCE / Ethnic Studies / Caribbean & Latin American Studies
Classification: LCC CS2305 .R36 2022 | DDC 929.4—dc23/eng/20220209
LC record available at https://lccn.loc.gov/2021058268

Set in Sabon Next LT Pro by Mikala R. Kolander.

For Helen Elizabeth McCartney de Ramírez, a mother whose support, generosity, and love were never lacking, and Fernando Arturo Siles Quesada, my partner and husband, for his quotidian love and encouragement

Swear now ... that thou wilt not cut off my seed after me, and that thou will not destroy my name.

—I SAM. 24:21, KJV

History consists of a series of accumulated imaginative inventions.

—VOLTAIRE

History is a myth that men agree to believe.

—NAPOLEON

El mundo al reves ... y no hay remedio
[The world upside down ... and there is no remedy]

—FELIPE GUAMAN POMA DE AYALA, *NUEVA CORONICA Y BUEN GOBIERNO*, 1609–12/1980, 1128 [1138]

Contents

Illustrations

Maps

Tables

Acknowledgments

This book has been a long time coming, in part because of my own need to familiarize myself with two cultures that I had not studied in detail during my formal schooling. Colleagues helped me by recommending bibliographic sources, and the anonymous donor of the Neville G. Penrose Chair gave me the time to delve into Thwaites's seventy-two volumes of documents on the Ho-De'-No-Sau-Nee, the reports of the first explorers and travelers to South Central Africa, and the hundreds of other primary and secondary sources that provide the substance of this book. Texas Christian University also furnished the travel funds for trips to the archives and libraries of Spain, Peru, and Bolivia. The archivists and librarians are the unsung heroes of many studies, and I owe them my gratitude as well. Family members, most notably my mother and my husband, offered enthusiastic support and assistance.

In Praise of the Ancestors

| Chapter One

Alternative Ways of Remembering and Knowing

For millennia, the invention of writing has been heralded as a characteristic of civilization. Standard world-history texts name it—along with monumental architecture, occupational specialization, and central governance—as definitional. The new technology that associated symbols with sounds and numbers enabled specialists to record, communicate, and govern more efficiently. Ethnologists who have studied societies going through the process of adopting writing in modern times, such as the Cuna of the San Blas Islands, discuss how writing facilitated census-taking, tax collection, the codification of law, governmental elaboration and centralization, and communication over long distances. Literacy became the basis for the transmission of the past and the development of modern historical consciousness in general (Howe 1979).[1]

Written records, then—such as those in cuneiform, inscribed on clay tablets; those left on a stone stele like Hammurabi's Code; and the first to be written on papyrus or paper—became in time the bedrock sources for fixating memories and constructing histories. Without a written record of events, recollections might, it was assumed, be abandoned to oblivion (Burke 1989, 97). Time and dates became the convention that societies used to order actions, resulting in a linear sequence of events and the organizational principle for much of the historical accounts. This also meant that for most of the document-ed past, historians dealt with the stories of leaders, elites, and heroes, which only in the last few decades have been supplemented with attention to the experiences of common people and everyday life.

Memories and identity link dialectically. Recollections of the past, be they of individuals, families, lineages, ethnicities, or nationalities, learned or experienced, help fashion identities, and the construction of identities forces the sorting, sifting, and winnowing of reminiscences to fit the present context and needs. Apart from the collective memories of lived experiences, much of the modern world's historical sense comes from written sources stored in the libraries and archives of the world. Selections from these sources are conveyed to various publics through such institutions as movies, documentaries, commemorative monuments, museums, parades, ceremonies, and schools.

Accepting this posture in the not too distant past, scholars described preliterate peoples as societies without history. Archaeologists' use of the word "prehistory," though now slowly disappearing from academic publications, defined people who left no written records and whose past they reconstructed from the mute material record. Eric Wolf's famous book title, *Europe and the Peoples without History* (1982), referred to societies on the periphery of Europe, distant and at least partially isolated.[2] Angel Rama's (1984/1996) influential essay on the "lettered city" restricted the written record to urban centers, largely beyond the reach of the vast majority of the rural, largely unlettered populace.

In partial reaction to such pronouncements, recent scholarship has focused on alternative ways of recording and remembering the past. There are, in fact, many ways that preliterate societies accomplished this. Chapters in Elizabeth Hill Boone and Walter Mignolo's edited work, *Writing without Words: Alternative Literacies in Mesoamerica and the Andes* (1994), draw attention to visual documents and the messages they convey. Following this lead, Joanne Rappaport and Thomas Cummins's book (2012) includes analyses of drawings (on pottery, for example) and a discussion of paintings as alternative means of communication by peoples without a written language. An example of this emerging trend on the topic is Chilean anthropologist José Luis

Martínez Cereceda's (2009) insightful article on the scattered petroglyphs of northern Chile, which, after an exhaustive survey, he characterizes as a recognized system of early communication.

Oral tradition[3] is another alternative way of communicating (Thompson 1978).[4] Among the Greeks, the time-honored tradition of oral storytelling conveyed knowledge to both young and old at family and community gatherings. Some orally transmitted memories were of the Trojan War era. The Greek epic poems, the *Iliad* and the *Odyssey*, both attributed to Homer, were orally conveyed (Edwards 2003) before appearing in written form in the eighth century BCE. As in the case of the Greeks, the Norse oral culture passed from generation to generation in long poetic sagas. One scholar described these as characteristically "complex narratives exhibiting sophisticated portraiture and realistically detailed events" (S. Mitchell 2003, 203). Topics were historical, legendary, and religious and revealed attitudes toward the past. Skalds, or Scandinavian bards,[5] recited epic poems, recounting with details the deeds of heroic Viking kings and lords. Anonymous Icelandic family sagas (*Íslendingasögur*) retold the tales of real people who lived in Iceland from its settlement in the 980s until about 1030 (Byock 1984–85, 153).[6] Like their Scandinavian counterparts, medieval Gaelic and British professional storytellers added music to the verses they composed. They were typically employed by a monarch or noble patron to commemorate one or more of the patron's ancestors or the patron's own deeds. Irish bards are one example of these. They formed a professional hereditary caste of highly trained and learned poets, familiar with the history and traditions of clan and country. As chroniclers in the court of kings or chieftains, they celebrated their employers and condemned those who opposed them until their gradual disappearance in the seventeenth and eighteenth centuries.

These experts on the past of their societies also had counterparts in Africa, the Andes, and Australia. In West Africa, a griot or *jali* (also *jeli*) served as a historian, storyteller, praise singer, poet, and musician (or both of the latter). As a living library of oral tradition and a leader, he advised royalty.[7] In Niger, praise singers sang "old words" to music and the "patter of dancing feet" (Stoller 1994, 634). The African bard or griot, in this case, is an oral historian, "the custodian of tales that speak to the greatness of empire, the valor of past battles, [and] the courage of past kings." They sing of the non-Islamic magical capacities of Songhai kings and the glories of the Songhai elite (Stoller 1994, 641).

In the Andes, some Inca kings founded lineages, whose members dedicated themselves to preserving the king's deceased body and mummy and his memory. Chroniclers of the Andes relate how singers, poets, and musicians learned songs and performed them to recall a group's history and instruct successors to power, much like the griots, bards, and minstrels did in Africa and Europe. They used songs, quipus (knotted strings) (discussed below), and paintings to this end (Hernández Astete 2008). One incoming king spent time listening to bloodline songs to learn about his named predecessors' reigns and accomplishments (Ramírez 2005, 73; Betanzos 1551–57/1996, 167). According to Spanish chroniclers, assembled on the main square (Haucaypata) of the City of the Cuzco, the mummies of dead emperors and their songs recreated for the assembled the religio-political history of their civilization, stretching back to the ancestral gods (P. Pizarro 1572/1978, 89; Guaman Poma de Ayala 1613/1980, 318 [320]; MacCormack 1991; Estete 1534/1924, 54; Lorandi 1995, 86).[8] Likewise, for the initiation ritual of adolescent males to adulthood (*warachiku*), lineage specialists sang the epic chants recounting heroic deeds and life stories. The lyrics encouraged the initiates to mirror their ancestors' exemplary lives (Yaya 2015, 646, 651). The royal epics, writes Isabel Yaya, "presented a selective appraisal of the political accomplishments attributed to individual kings so that altogether these narratives embodied a repetitive programme for dynastic success" (2015, 652). But, since no one dared utter the personal name of a king except with profound awe (Garcilaso de la Vega 1609–12/1959, 53), these songs would have used his praise name or the title of "the Cuzco." If the latter were the case, the living "Cuzco" would have been attributed with the past heroics of his like-named predecessors.

In a similar manner, North American natives chanted the history of their predecessors' distinguished deeds (Le Petit 1730 [Thwaites vol. 68], 161). The historian and lawyer Marc Lescarbot (1612–14/1896

[Thwaites vol. 2], 135), who wrote a history of New France published in 1609, describes the customary dances and songs of praise around the corpse of the famous chief Membertou (Memberton). Similarly, the Jesuit missionary Pierre Biard mentions the funeral dirges (*nae-niasck*), which could last day and night for as long as a week (Biard 1616/1897 [Thwaites vol. 3], 129).

Finally, native singers in Australia sang of their ancestors. The late Geoffrey Gurrumul Yunupuyŋu, also known as Gudjuk, from the Gumatj nation of North East Arnhem Land (Australia), sang of his forefathers: Wititj, the ancestor Rainbow Python who gave birth to the people; ancestor boss ladies Dhuwandjika and Daylulu who can still be seen at Gunyaŋara; and ancestors Batumaŋ, Djarrami, Djeŋarra, and Gurrumulŋa. He sang, "I am Batumaŋ, I am Djarra-mi, I am Djeŋarra, . . . I am Barrupa, I am Dhukul̲ul̲, I am Maral-itja, I am Ŋunbuŋunbu. . . ." In other songs he chanted of other predecessors: mother Baywara, who is the creator; and mother an-cestors Gun̲djul̲purr I Buliyaŋu Dhawu-Minydjalpi; Guwarruku; Gu-warruku Balpal̲una, Mämbila; and Wandjudupa Gapu-wal̲kal̲mirri Nuŋguritjmarra. His songs mention other ancestors: Loli, Galpar-ra, Gurrumulŋa. His "mind," his lyrics continued, "has gone back, to Bekul̲, Galupayu, dhärriŋ [*sic*] and Mayaŋ-ŋaraka" (Gurrumul CD notes, www.skinnyfishmusic.com.au).

Dance added movement, illustration, and intensity to the sung nar-ratives (Castro-Klarén 1993, 164). In fact, in the Andes, dance was al-most always accompanied by song (Jiménez Borja 1946). Augustinian missionaries in the 1550s described these songs and dances (*taquies*) as praises to native heroes and gods (Agustinos 1550/1992, 16). Simulta-neously, officials of the Catholic church labeled the content of com-memorative enactments as pagan and idolatrous. Colonial secular authorities shared such sentiments and joined the religious to repress them during colonial times (Estenssoro 1992, 13–19, 26–27, 30–32, 35, 38; see also Rostworowski 1984 and 2003, 3). Luis Capoche, describ-ing Potosí (Bolivia) in 1585, wrote that "many men and women gath-er together to carry out great dances, in which they practice the old rites and ceremonies, bringing to memory through their songs the gentile [non-Christian] past" (1585/1959, 141).[9] Another dance, called the *huacón*, involved Andean participants who wore masks that were "venerated objects because they represented the indigenous communities' founding ancestors (*malquis*) [objetos de adoración debido a que representaban a los ancestros fundadores de las comunidades indígenas]" or valiant cultural heros, which when worn conferred upon the dancers the *camac* (*fuerza vital*, vital force) of their predecessors (Barraza Lescano n.d., 1, 13; Taylor 2000, 4–7 on *camac*). Such performances kept memories alive.

Ancestral lives reenacted in African ritual and related in stories and songs likewise preserved social memories, conveyed meaning, legitimated authority, and helped construct history (Kelly and Kaplan 1990, 123, 125). African funerary rituals for a member of a royal family in Zimbabwe include singing and dancing and much recalling of the Lunda tribe of old. Ian Cunnison, a mid-twentieth-century ethnographer of the tribe, wrote: "Talk on these occasions regularly turns to Lunda history, the ancestry of Kazembe [the chief], and the victories of the past; slogans (*nkumbu*) are beaten out in the old *kampokolo* language on the talking drum, the *mondo*. They resurrect the past in all these ways and are thus conscious of their unity" (1951, 1).

Rituals for the Andean dead, and especially the *purucaya* ceremony, during which his followers transformed a dead Inca ruler into an honored and revered ancestor, elicited memories that reinforced the hegemony of the king. The ceremony began after fifteen days of recalling the deceased's deeds in the locations where they occurred and saying prayers, asking him to protect and favor the living. The ritual itself, according to the Spanish chronicler Juan de Betanzos, was a "ceremony of canonization" that converted a deceased Inca ruler into a "saint" and represented his becoming a "semidivine ancestor" (Danwerth 2013, 74). Rituals within the characteristic monumental architecture constructed by the Inca in the Andes transmitted their cosmology, history, and ideas, especially to visitors or prisoners (Acuto 2005, 218).[10]

But not all rituals involved dancing and singing (Ramírez 2005; Estenssoro Fuchs 2003). The ethnohistorian Thomas A. Abercrombie

(1998) analyzed "memory paths," one form of ritual performance that involved a memorized sequence of names, practiced by the K'ulta of modern Bolivia. These, like the Inca *purucaya* ceremonies, fostered a form of historical consciousness linking the living, the dead, and the places they frequented (114, 319). The libations and the sayings that accompanied these gatherings were offerings and sacrifices to the ancestral gods that carried individual memories back in time and out across the landscape (349–60).[11] Pilgrimages and processions with their shared personal experiences and observations also sometimes ended with rituals and ceremonies where participation heightened feelings of belonging and integration. Such often-historical enactments recalled important events in society's past and welded participants into the wider group.[12]

Recent research has also highlighted the omnipresent indigenous voice in traditional societies. Some toponyms (that tie places with associated stories), whether in dictionary form or linked to narratives, also relay native memories, thus becoming windows into past peoples' worlds (Basso 1984; 1988, 101; 1996; Ramírez 2014b; Vellejo 1957; Pawlik 1951; Barnes 2002; Urton 2002; Krazanowski and Szeminski 1978). They may be commemorative, relating stories of significant people and events associated with place. Keith H. Basso's anthropological work on the Apaches (1988) is a good example of how these sometimes ancient toponyms can summon ancestral images and voices, of how ancestral wisdom resides in places (especially 114; 1996).

Félix A. Acuto's work (2005) on the construction of landscapes and the symbolism of the built environment demonstrates how it is "loaded with meaning and ideological connotations" and, in short, could act as a "memory aid." He details how cultural space suggests meanings and transmitted messages about social and political relations. He states that "experience and routine allow any social actor to know her or his role in this context, the actions that he or she can and cannot perform, and the class of relationships he or she should and could establish with other agents" (213–14). The City of the Cuzco embodied imperial history and made it visible through monuments, shrines, and objects "principally oriented to remember, glorify and diffuse

Fig. 1. Textile (manta) showing the drawing and quartering of Tupac Amaru II, 1780s. Photo from Ramírez Textile Collection.

Inka ancestors' achievements, gods, emperors and victorious battles" (217). It thus communicated native "worldview and legitimacy" (213). Acuto agrees with Susan Niles (1999) that the surrounding landscape "was a propagandistic tool that emperors used to assert their power and the centrality of the Inka, to depict ancestors in a flattering light, and to inscribe their names in history" (Acuto 2005, 217). In the rural areas, military fortresses, ritual centers, way stations, roads, and production and storage enclaves reminded provincial peoples of the Inca presence and might.

The absence of alphabetic writing does not preclude the existence of artifacts that also conveyed information. Textiles are such artifacts that often transmit messages about the past. Spanish chroniclers agree that the dress and other insignia of a visitor allowed the king to immediately recognize his ethnicity and lineage (Gutiérrez de Santa Clara c. 1600/1963, 3:211). Andean peasant women still weave stories and imagined scenes, such as the drawing and quartering of the famous Andean rebel Tupac Amaru II of the 1780s, into their shawls (mantas).[13] Gail P. Silverman's study of contemporary weavings and weavers around the modern southern Andean city of Cuzco shows

Fig. 2. Close-up of manta figure. Photo from Ramírez Textile Collection.

Fig. 3. Dumbarton Oaks tunic, showing *tocapus*. Courtesy CreativeCommons.

how certain motifs are "read" by native viewers. Each motif has a specific name and meanings, creating pictograms and ideograms, thus becoming "a true graphic lexicon" (1994, 171–72). She concludes that the textile is a way to preserve and communicate Andean knowledge.

Similarly, scholars debate the meaning and significance of 294 square designs on certain high-quality textiles, called *tocapus*, but agree that they are a system of communication (Gentile n.d.). Spanish chronicler and friar Martín de Murúa wrote in the early seventeenth century

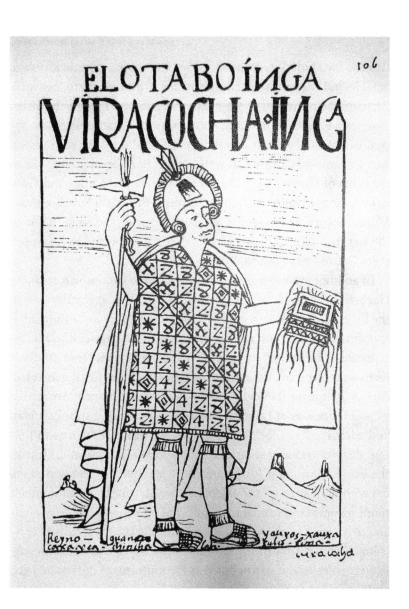

Fig. 4. Inca clothed in a tunic adorned with *tocapus*. Felipe Guaman Poma
de Ayala, *Nueva corónica y Buen Gobierno*, Facsimile Edition of the circa 1613
manuscript (Paris: Institut d'ethnologie, 1613/1936, folio 106).
(Hereafter Guaman Poma, c. 1613/1936.)

that the Inca king Viracocha instituted the *tocapus* (Murúa 1613/1986, 72). He and his ministers communicated through them, but after his reign the meanings of the square designs were lost. Art historian Margarita E. Gentile, however, notes that such square designs also appear in rows and columns on Inca ceremonial drinking cups or beakers (*queros*) and clothing, as well as on certain items going back to the times of Moche (1–800 CE), Paracas (800 BCE–100 BCE), and Tiwanaku (c. 200–1000 CE). Although the meanings might have been lost, Murúa, according to Gentile, wrote that during the reign of one of the last Inca kings, Guaina Capac, they still appeared to have used them (Murúa 1613/1946, 78).[14]

In addition, the chemist and student of pre-Columbian art Joerg Haeberli believes that the border band of a Paracas textile, now in the Brooklyn Museum, served as a "mnemonic device for the timing and duration of various ritual/ceremonial and/or agricultural/socio-economical functions" (1995, 123).[15] Anthropologist R. Tom Zuidema likewise interpreted the designs of Chuquibamba textiles as calendars. A male tunic (belonging to the Peabody Museum of Archaeology and Ethnology at Harvard University) presented a solar calendar, and a female shawl (belonging to the Museum of Fine Arts in Boston) showed a sidereal lunar calendar. Another Chuquibamba textile, the Kosok shawl, now lost, represents a standardized sidereal calendar within the solar year (Zuidema 2011).[16] Martínez Cereceda wrote a more encompassing and most significant book (1995) on the symbols and decoration of clothing and personal objects, the regalia of early colonial native Andean authorities that conveyed nonverbal messages on their roles and status, much as the uniforms of nurses, soldiers, and the police do today.[17]

Rolena Adorno, a student of the humanities, interprets the illustrations of native chronicler Felipe Guaman Poma de Ayala, although drawn after first contact with Europeans, as another means of relating to the past. She writes that the approximately four hundred full-page drawings "convey more and different information than the verbal narration" on about eight hundred additional folios. These drawings "can be read as a self-contained narrative independent from the writing."

She maintains that the visual texts offer information on native and colonial society that the "text does not always provide" (1981, 52).

Mnemonic devices supported traditional narratives in some societies. Notable are the different knots of quipus (also *khipus* or *quipos*), devices made of colored strings that recorded information that was received by the Spanish as reliable and sometimes read and transcribed as testimony into the records of court cases all over Andean America (Urton 1998, 2003, 2006; Urton and Brezine 2005; Mann 2005; Salomon 2004; Ascher and Ascher 1981; de la Puente Luna 2014, 2019; Zuidema 1989). The priest José de Acosta, author of the *Historia natural y moral de las Indias*, wrote:

[Los quipus] significan diversas cosas . . . [y] cuanto los libros pueden decir de historias, y leyes, y ceremonias y cuentas de negocios, todo eso suplen los quipus tan puntualmente, que admiran. . . . para diversos géneros, como de guerra, de gobierno, de tributos, de ceremonias, de tierras, había diversos quipus o ramales; y en cada manojo de estos ñudos y ñudicos y hilillos atados, unos colorados, otros verdes, otros azules, otros blancos, y, finalmente tantas diferencias, que así como nosotros, de veinte y cuatro letras, guisándolas en diferentes maneras, sacamos tanta infinidad de vocablos, así éstos de sus ñudos y colores sacaban innumerables significaciones de cosas. . . . Yo ví un manojo de estos hilos, en que una india traía escrita una confesión general de toda su vida, y por ellos se confesaba, como yo lo hiciera por papel escrito.

[The quipus] mean diverse things . . . [and] all that books can say about histories, and laws, and ceremonies and business accounts, all this the quipus can precisely supply. . . . For different categories, like war, government, tribute, ceremonies, [and] lands there were various quipus or strings; and in each handful of these knots and little knots and knotted little strings, some red, others green, others blue, others white, there were finally so many differences, that thus as we, from twenty-four letters, combining them in different ways, get an infinity of words, so these [natives got] from their knots and colors innumerable meanings of things. . . . I have seen one handful of these threads, in which an Indian woman had inscribed a general confession for her

Fig. 5. Quipu and its creator and interpreter. Guaman Poma,
c. 1613/1936, folio 360.

entire life, and by them she confessed, as I would have done with a
written piece of paper. (Acosta 1590/1979, l. 6, c. 8, 189–90)[18]

Natives continued to use the quipu after the Spanish arrived into (at
least) the mid-twentieth century (Salomon et al. 2011, 354).[19]

In addition to stories, songs, and dances that praised rulers, the
Luba of northern Shaba region (formerly the Katanga Province) of
Zaire in Central Africa used a *lukasa* (claw or "the long hand") as an
esoteric memory device that was manipulated and protected by the
Bambudye, an old and formerly powerful secret sect that operated
in the eighteenth and first half of the nineteenth centuries. Thomas
Reefe (1977) designates the object as integral to the oral literature and
the political and religious system of these peoples. Holes, lines, and
beads transmitted information on (1) mythical heroes and early rulers and migration routes that gave legitimacy to the Luba royal line;
(2) the organization of the Bambudye society; and (3) divine chieftainship. These devices guaranteed that there would be an "'official' version of the [origin] myth in which the heroes of the Luba would be
described correctly and in which the storyline would be recited in its
proper sequence" (50). They also helped in remembering deities and
ancestral spirits (49–50).

The Iroquois or Ho-De'-No-Sau-Nee had two mnemonic devices to "prop up their minds" (Jennings et al. 1985, 17) and aid memory: the canes[20] used to guide the roll call of the fifty hereditary chiefs
(discussed in chapter 3, following Fenton [1950]) and founders of the
League and strings of shell beads or belts, called *wampum* (a word
meaning "word" or "voice").[21] Two important and related functions
of the latter were to transmit and affirm messages or seal treaties (Jacobs 1949; Snyderman 1954, 469; Becker 2008, 2; Michelson 1991).[22] In
the latter case, groups exchanged wampum as a means of communicating, recording, confirming, representing, and recalling agreements
so that the parties were assured that the words were truthful, "acceptable, correct, and binding" (Snyderman 1961, 571). Each of the belts
designated an important item of business and reinforced a statement
before it changed hands at conferences. If the wampum's message was

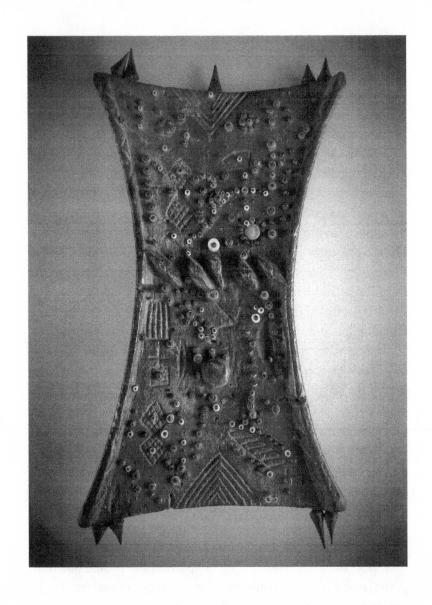

Fig. 6. An African (Luba) *lukasa* (memory board).
Courtesy Wikipedia Creative Commons.

acceptable, the receiving party would retain it and might reciprocate with its own wampum. Such reciprocal gifts helped support close relationships (Snyderman 1954, 474). Elaborate belts carried color-coded pictorial symbols and designs of figures, villages, nations, and paths. For example, war was symbolized as a war kettle or a hatchet; while white belts symbolized peace and life (Snyderman 1954, 477, 487; Jacobs 1949, 598; Muller 2007; Prince 1897, 880). Also, a wampum belt dyed red or smeared in a red substance usually meant war. Thus, in 1841 a Potawatomie war party dipped a belt in blood and the recruited warriors were thereby "invited to come and drink the blood of their enemies" (Father De Smet as quoted by Snyderman 1954, 473). Other figured belts conveyed messages. Jacobs reports that in 1748 a belt of almost seven thousand beads showed a design of seven figures holding each other by the hand with two rows of black wampum beads underneath. He writes that the first figure represented the governor of New York or the king of Great Britain, his superior; the other five figures represented the five nations and the seventh, the Wyandotts. The parallel rows of black beads signified the road from Albany into the territory of the Five Nations to the Wyandotts. The belt commemorated the alliance with the English (Jacobs 1949, 600).

One member of the Ho-De'-No-Sau-Nee delegation committed to memory the significance of the belt and the item or transaction it stood for so that the belt and its message could be recalled and "read" in the future. The "reading" of the wampum belts was possible as long as there was a person who could recall and teach their meanings (Jennings et al. 1985, 17–18, 85–91, 99, 104–10, 122–23; Prince 1897, 480; Muller 2007, 135; Converse 1895, 343–45; Jacobs 1949, 598; Becker 2008, 2). An archive of wampum belts was kept at Onondaga by a chief with the title Ho-No-We-Na-To (Snyderman 1954, 477; 1961). Thus, figure 8 would be read, from left to right: Seneca Nations, Keepers of the Western Door; Cayuga Nation; Onondaga Nation, Keepers of the Central Fire and the Heart of the Five Nations Loyal to the Great Law; Oneida Nation; and Mohawk Nation, Keepers of the Eastern Door.

Some preliterate peoples had an additional means of recalling their past, which remains mostly overlooked and understudied: a naming

Fig. 7. Condolence cane. Used by permission of Rhonda and Ben Maracle, owners of the Wampum Shop near Bantford, Ontario, Canada. The cane was made by Haohyoh (Ben Maracle), a faith healer of the Lower Cayuga Longhouse, Deer Clan.

Fig. 8. Wampum. Courtesy Wikimedia Creative Commons.

system, identified by Cunnison in the late 1940s and labeled "positional inheritance" (1951, 1956).[23] Positional inheritance was a system where names were passed from one individual to another. Most names disappeared after three or four persons took them. The names that were always inherited were those of important people, like that of the founder or leader of the group. Each individual who inherited a name also inherited some of the previous holder's possessions—a belt, a kettle, a bracelet, and even a wife or wives. Each name was associated with accomplishments of all the individuals who had taken the name in the past, to the extent that the present holder of the name claimed credit for all those significant historical events (e.g., using the same logic, President Harry S. Truman would have taken George Washington's name at his inauguration and be attributed with founding the country and winning the Civil War). These names and titles, inherited from one generation to another, link present memory to the past and through commemoration and ancestor veneration contribute to the formation of collective consciousness and a group identity.

Since reading about this practice, I have found evidence of the same practice among the natives of sub-Saharan Africa back to the eighteenth century; the indigenous populace of the North American Great Lakes regions in the seventeenth and eighteenth centuries; and Andean ethnicities from the sixteenth century right up to the present.[24] This study compares the working of this institution among multiple unlettered native societies on three continents from the sixteenth to the mid-twentieth century, with additional references to peoples who still practice it in one form or another today.

My focus on positional inheritance does not deny nor ignore the huge corpus of scholarly literature devoted to names and naming. The few studies reviewed here fall into three overlapping genres. The first includes studies that collect, count, and categorize names. One is Charles A. Cooke's article, published in 1952, in which he lists 6,200 Mohawk personal names and then classifies them with their representative counts into such divisions as occupational, animal, plant, religious, calendrical, food, and status names, among others. For example, he found that 616 names referred to geographic features, while he associated 56 male and 43 female names with divisions of time. Percy Valladares Huamanchumo presents a similar but much later study (2013) in which he lists surnames in a long-lost language, Quingnam, once spoken on the northern coast of Peru, that he located in archival sources, published Spanish chronicles, secondary materials, and oral histories, quite a feat in and of itself. The well-known historian Mario Góngora (1980) likewise presents a compilation of colonial-era names from baptismal records in two parishes in the city of Santiago: Sagrario and San Isidro. His tables then tabulate the incidence of the names by the social standing of the parents. In group 1, he includes the children of high royal officials, members of the town council, *encomenderos* (persons granted native labor in return for service to the Spanish king), notable wholesale merchants, military authorities of the rank of captain and higher, and all individuals with the title of "Don," denoting respect and status. The names of all other reportedly Spanish children are listed as group 2. Group 3 is restricted to the names of the offspring of everyone else: Indians, blacks, mestizos (children of Spanish and native parents), mulattoes (children of Spanish and black parents), *zambos* (children of black and native parentage), and other *castas* (mixed-blood peoples). A sample finding is that the name Juan was the most popular boy's name from 1581 to 1589 in the Sagrario parish, but especially favored by parents of children in group 3. Not surprisingly, María was the most common girl's name in that same parish from 1633 to 1638, also concentrated among the non-elites.

Beyond mere collecting and counting are works that center on classification. A good example is Patricia Galloway's (2006, 206) chapter on Choctaw names, including personal names, war names, political names, and genealogical names. Theodore Holland (1995) posits a typology of Navajo names that includes secret war names, terms of endearment, and descriptive names, noting that an individual might be known by different names and nicknames throughout a life. Frank Exner Little Bear (2007) catalogs the names and translations of native North American names in general and adds a discussion of the effects of colonization on traditional naming practices. Finally, Wendy Schottman (2000) groups the names of Baatɔnu (or Bariba) (from northern Benin) into three categories corresponding to birth, youth, and adulthood, which she then subdivides further. The result is a minutely detailed overview of tribesmen's names.

A transitional work that carries the discussion from collecting, counting, and categorizing studies into the broader works on naming practices and meanings is the ambitious and important book by Ximena Medinaceli (2003) on the Sacaca peoples (of Bolivia), based on a census of 1614. Among her findings is that individuals change names during their lifetimes, a common practice as will be detailed in the following chapters. She also includes sections on practices and the translated meanings of individual appellations. Thus, the name Chira means "chile pepper seeds" and Toco means "only son." On the basis of these translations from the Aymara into Spanish, she then groups the names into such categories as kinship terms, plant and animal names, and the like.

A wide range of authors examine the practices of name-giving and name-taking. Margarita E. Gentile, in a 1999 article on the *rituchicuy* or name-giving ceremony for Inca adolescent males, notes that their newly given names refer to ancestors, key personages in "lineage" history, and their religious beliefs. Likewise, Ovid Vickers (1983) documents the naming practices of the Mississippi Choctaw. Among them, men take successive names after completing a worthy deed or hazardous task, a practice also shared among the Ho-De'-No-Sau-Nee (of chapter 3) and Andeans (of chapter 4). John Thornton's excellent 1993 discussion of the naming patterns for the peoples of the Angolan region of West Central Africa found that the kings (after the 1509 contact with the Portuguese) took the surnames of their father, grandfathers, and great-grandfathers. In one case, a royal's full name was "Mobemba am-Camga, à-Mubîca, à-Zumba, à-Mobemba, à-Mozinga à-ncu-à-Mutino," which equates to Mobemba son of Canga (sic), grandson of Mubîca, great-grandson of Zumba, and so on (733). Genealogies of kings could go back one and a half centuries to Nzinga à Nkuwu, the first Christian king of the Kongo. Thus, a name referring to descent for the royals gave them legitimacy. Female names also followed the paternal line.[25]

Of wider interest here are the works that deal with names as texts—that indicate something more than the designation of a person at a given time and provide information on the sociopolitical context of its use. The multiple names of the Mashona peoples of southern Rhodesia (now Zimbabwe), the object of research by Heinz Wieschhoff (1937), reveal the context of one's birth and the behavior of the person (497).[26] Susan M. Suzman (1994) examines traditional Zulu names, noting that they referred to or recalled a family event or an ancestor. Jill Grant and Martin Zelenietz (1983) mention that the people of Kilenge (Papua New Guinea) in the late 1970s and early 1980s had names that referred to a person's status or reputation. Names could be as straightforward as birth order or be a "built" name that acquired status through ceremonial sponsorship and acts of generosity and hospitality (179–80). Since names in this society, like those among the Ho-De'-No-Sau-Nee, were the preserve of particular social units, the name alone identified an individual with the group to which he or she belonged. Joan Bamberger, who studied the Kayapó of Brazil, similarly learned to "read" names as part of the tribal kinship system. She found that the system of name-bestowal among these people can be comprehended only as part of a genealogy. She states that "names, representing both kin connections as well as avenues of access to positions of social prestige in general ritual, constitute a form of symbolic representation which link [*sic*] generational succession with individual social statuses" (1974, 363).

Similarly, the South African names studied by Robert K. Herbert (1997) were commemorative and were passed on. They often drew attention to social position or marked links to other individuals, a statement that could easily hold for the Kilenge of Papua New Guinea (Grant and Zelenietz 1983, 180, 189). Naming practices of the Sanumá or Yanoama, who live between the Orinoco and Amazon Rivers, resemble these. In this regard, Alcida R. Ramos (1974) documents how a Sanumá child received a first name after a ritual hunt during which his father killed an animal. The name of the animal designated the youngster until he took names that referred to a physical or behavioral characteristic, commemorated an event, or referenced a place of residence or place of birth. The child's name usually located him within the group's social structure. David Maybury-Lewis (2009), writing about the inhabitants of Central Brazil, likewise mentions that names are bestowed in sets that are taken sequentially. Persons enter and leave each name. He interprets his data to mean that names do not identify individuals but instead transform them into persons by linking them to society and reinforcing or replacing descent (6–8). The names of the Ilongot of the Philippines and the Kodayan of Borneo also revealed biographical knowledge (Rosaldo 1984; A. R. Maxwell 2009, 25–26, 36–37).

Two studies use an innovative analysis of onomastics over a person's life cycle. Martha B. Kendall's 1980 article on the Yuman (the Yavapai, Hualapai, and Havasupai) peoples of Arizona is one of the few studies with such a longer diachronic perspective that allowed her to record a sequence of individual names that revealed the person's biography and individuality. Sequences of names became histories, indexes of changing statuses, or marked changing social affiliations. Names and nicknames, she writes, were evocative of episodes of a person's life history (262).[27] As Robert K. Herbert (1997) later showed, names reveal values, interests, hopes, fears, and the complexities of social relations, roles, statuses, and the distribution of power. Thus, when studied chronologically, names served as abbreviated texts, often understood only in their historical contexts. Such a conclusion mirrors Peter Whitely's writings on Hopi names, which he called a form of oral literature with rich connections that served as "tiny imagist poems" (mentioned by Moore 2007, 289).

Some data reveal a repeating cycle of bestowal and name-taking. T. O. Beidelman (1974), studying the Bantu-language-speaking peoples of Kaguru of Tanzania, discusses the names of the dead that were given to an infant. Among these people, names of the dead and the living repeat one another in a perpetual cycle (286). Another study by Patrick Moore (2007) of the Dene Tha and Kaska (two Canadian Athabaskan groups) mentions the neighboring Tlingits, who hand down personal names within matrilineal lineages. Names are handed down to the newborn who, they believed, inherited the spirit of an individual when he died. These names represented the reincarnated. In contrast, the Dene Tha believed in reincarnation but did not normally give the newly embodied their previous names. Other names referred to personal predisposition or potential (289). Among the Baatɔnu the inheritance of the name of a defunct individual did not indicate reincarnation; according to their traditions, the name represented a social and spiritual replacement. The memory of exemplary members of the family was thus perpetuated in younger members with such namesakes (Schottman 2000, 90). Finally, F. Niyi Akinnaso (1983) writes of three types of Yoruba names that transmitted values and experiences, that is, cultural knowledge and worldview. Of comparative interest are the names given to children believed to be reincarnations of a revered, venerated, and worshipped ancestor (especially 151–52). As such, these recycled and reembodied names enshrined the past.

The diachronic approach is elemental to the documentation of positional inheritance. Three works raise the possibility of unrecognized positional inheritance. The first is by Gabriela Sica and Sandra Sánchez (1994) on the possible meanings of an ethnic lord's name, (Cacique) Viltipoco, of the Jujuy region of modern Argentina in the seventeenth century. Their discussion suggests that the name referred to a composite, which represented more than one person. Patricia Galloway (2006) also includes material on the Choctaw names that functioned as titles. She, like Sica and Sánchez, does not develop this point, but the practice where more than one individual would eventually hold the name might indicate the phenomenon. Bamberger (1974) also mentions "great names" and inherited ritual positions (365).

Methodologically, the recognition of the institution of positional inheritance reminds us of the communication difficulties inherent in cultural contact and confrontation. Such initial encounters involved peoples with disparate cultural traditions who spoke a multitude of different languages. Europeans were not culturally attuned to understand that members of some societies, like the Mississippi Choctaws, the Incas, and many other groups, used more than one name during a lifetime (Vickers 1983). The Portuguese, English, French, and Arabic explorers, traders, and missionaries in Central Africa of the seventeenth and eighteenth centuries met peoples speaking a wide variety of languages. Custom dictated that Kampocolo be spoken at the court of the paramount chief in Central Africa, while the commoners spoke other tribal or ethnic languages. The Spanish in the sixteenth-century Andes encountered peoples using such languages as Mochic, Sec, Tallan, Colle, Quingnam, Quechua, Aymara, and Puquina, to name a few. Instances when one interpreter did not understand one of the languages of the peoples Europeans encountered are enumerated in the primary texts. Translation, as will be illustrated in the chapters that follow, was not only literal but also cultural and was extremely challenging. Early observers in Central Africa, for example, assumed for at least the first eighty years or so after contact that the names of the chiefs were inherited from father to son. This was not always the case; it was customary among some groups but not in others. Thus, contexts and assumptions colored what was conveyed. Such difficulties and the differences in rank and standing of those relating oral traditions contributed to manipulations of the stories, misunderstandings based on culture and language, and the incomprehension of the listeners (Pearse and Heggarty 2011; G. Ramos 2011; M. Sahlins 1983, 524; Ramírez 2006b).

Because the Europeans possessed the technology of writing, their interpretations of what they saw and heard came to predominate.

Status differences among the native peoples themselves often determined what they told the foreigners and what they left out. European bias confirmation also worked to reshape oral tradition and fixate it as "history." Thus, in the face of confusion and contradiction in oral testimonies, the standard (see Juan de Betanzos, cited in chapter 4, below) was to select some remarks and omit and silence others; to simplify and to systematize, according to one's own cultural conventions, into a narrative of what the invader expected (Lamana 2008; Szeminski 2001). Thus, language barriers, cultural filters, and lack of knowledge of context brought into the historical narratives mistakes, errors, and falsities, with consequent misunderstandings. This process created in time an archetype or stereotype that through repetition and portrayal set collective memories of those who did not experience the process personally. Andrew Roberts writes cogently on this situation with regard to precise dates, but his words hold for any writings—especially those that codify oral tradition: they are transmitted without scrutiny, and even without acknowledgment, from one writer to another "in literary 'traditions' that are quite misleading as any tradition can be" (1967, 129).

The three case studies analyzed here also address a wider point, namely, the generation and use of knowledge as fundamental to understanding and evaluating the knowledge itself. This is the underpinning concern of this reexamination of these three early histories of preliterate native peoples on three continents. It is born of a review of early colonial accounts and other sources that reveal incongruities in accepted knowledge. Such contradictions encourage a reassessment of this information, especially the native practices for the creation, transmission, and preservation of memory; the experience of collecting and recording these stories after contact; and the construction of social narratives and identities in general.

The book consists of three case studies and a final consideration of these last, more theoretical concerns. In the first, "'Positional Inheritance' in Africa," I outline (following Ian Cunnison) the concepts of "positional inheritance" and "perpetual kinship" from the eighteenth to the mid-twentieth century in Central Africa (i.e., Zambia) as a key to remembering the past. I use Cunnison's ethnographically based model from the 1940s and reports and journals of English and Portuguese travelers for details. The discussion will specify how major political titleholders became known by the name of their symbolic ancestor (J. C. Miller 1979, 78), emphasizing how changing and inherited names and positions chronicled the Lunda past across time.

From Central Africa the analysis moves to the next chapter, "The Narration of Ho-De'-No-Sau-Nee (Iroquois) History." This chapter focuses on the several native groups that made up the Iroquois Confederation and their practice of using names to memorialize notable leaders in the seventeenth and eighteenth centuries, based on French and English sources. Positional inheritance proved key to structuring and maintaining their memories.

The last case study and the most detailed, given my training and longtime interests, focuses on naming and "The Making of Andean Ancestral Traditions." This chapter surveys naming practices in Andean ethnicities that occupied territory from what is now Ecuador through Peru and into Bolivia in the sixteenth and seventeenth centuries, based solidly on sixteenth-century manuscript sources and later testimonies found in Spanish and Andean archives. Here, my familiarity with the sources enables me to question colonial narratives and the standard Inca king lists by documenting the use of this alternative system of memory perpetuation that was initially unrecognized by the Spaniards. Significantly, I write that the traditional list of ten to twelve Andean kings is telescoped and shortened and was devised by early Spaniards because they did not understand what their informants were telling them. Several, therefore, admit that they invented what they wrote, ultimately putting their information into a dynastic form, so as to help European readers better understand their observations by using a familiar paradigm easy for their audience to comprehend.

I conclude with general remarks on oral traditions as history. This chapter discusses the "politics of memory," theorizing on the experience of these three examples. It includes views on how oral histories keep the reputations of heroic names and events alive in the memories of the living; and on the relationship between myths and history (in the traditional European sense), following Marshall Sahlins. It further connects the societies under discussion to Claude Lévi-Strauss's conceptualization of hot and cold societies and the related cyclical and temporal aspects of native historical consciousness. Unlettered peoples did not conceptualize time in a linear fashion. Rather, they purposefully constructed a "heroic" or mytho-historic view of patterned change, which was cyclical and correspondingly ritualized in scheduled and repeating ceremonies. Indeed, in the absence of writing, I argue that natives' sense of history is expressed in cosmology, narratives, rituals, and ceremony.

These remarks emphasize the multiple historicities of societies around the world. Raymond D. Fogelson summarizes this recognition when he states that "events may be recognized, defined, evaluated, and endowed with meaning differently in different cultural traditions." He urged ethnohistorians to make a "determined effort to try to comprehend alien forms of historical consciousness and discourse" (1989, 134–35; Kan 2019, 171). Correspondingly, I join him in advocating a relativistic and pluralistic approach (1989, 189). I question the "authority" of the written word and query the nature of knowledge itself. My findings challenge historians, anthropologists, linguists, and archaeologists to escape their own confirmation of biases and cultural-specific expectations, definitions, and paradigms. Unless we can think culturally unthinkable thoughts we will be condemned to looking only for information that confirms our own preconceived notions, thus perpetuating a Europeanized version of the history of others.[28] I call for a concerted effort to escape the present scholarly echo chamber for "decentering" and a rethinking of both the history of the other and our own.

| Chapter Two

"Positional Inheritance" in Africa

In the race to reach the so-called Spice Islands in the fourteenth and fifteenth centuries, the Portuguese led the Spanish, preoccupied until almost the end of the fifteenth century with the last remnants of the Moorish troops, by exploring routes southward along the coast of Africa. Eventually, they rounded the Cape of Good Hope in 1488 and sailed on to India and beyond. It was, therefore, the Portuguese and their native contacts who introduced Europeans to the societies inhabiting the African coast and interior. Once established along the eastern and western coasts, the Portuguese, responding to native emissaries from the interior, encouraged and later sponsored their own expeditions into Central Africa, hoping to open a transcontinental overland trade route to secure the ivory and slaves coming out of the remote hinterlands.

This chapter provides an overview of these expeditions, the interaction of the explorers and traders with local leaders, and the expanding knowledge about these Central African societies and their naming practices from the eighteenth through the mid-twentieth century. It ends with an outline of an institution, described ethnographically by Ian Cunnison based on research among the Lunda (also Luunda, Eastern Lunda, and Cazembe Lunda) peoples who lived in the Luapula area (in modern Zambia).[1] His description of what he calls "positional

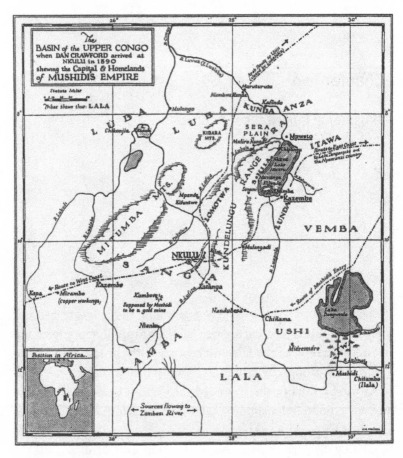

Map 1. Luapula country. From G. E. Tilsely, *Dan Crawford: Missionary and Pioneer in Central Africa* (New York: Fleming H. Revell, 1929, opposite p. 134).

inheritance" serves as a model for the analysis of other naming practices in North and South America that follow.

First Encounters

Prominent in the first reports of the Central African interior by intrepid travelers, traders, and missionaries are the names of the kings and headmen of the peoples they encountered on their marches. The ruler of the Lunda peoples who settled in the Luapula River Valley and the adjacent lands, the object of this first case study, was referred to as Mwata[2] Kazembe (Casembe, Cazembe),[3] a word that with time came to refer to the tribal king or paramount chieftain. It is translated by different writers as "emperor" (Gamitto/Cunnison 1831–32/1960, 2:109; Travassos Valdez 1861, 2:174), "king" (Velasco/Burton 1805/1873, 164 and Cunnison 1956c, 134; Gordon 2006a, 36; 2006b, 23), "general" (Livingstone 1874, 2:247),[4] and "paramount chief" or "lord."[5] José Maria Corrêa Monteiro and Captain Antonio Candido Pedroso Gamitto, travelers in 1831–32, note that it is from this name and title that the various tributary tribal peoples and the lands over which this sovereign dominated took their name (Gamitto/Cunnison 1831–32/1960, 2:109).[6] David Livingstone (1874, 1:161) wrote in the 1860s that he arrived at Casembe, thus territorializing the word. Francisco Travassos Valdez (1861, 2:212) used "Kazembe" to refer to the king's jurisdiction, eventually the territory where his subjects lived (2:225), and the tribe itself, that is, the Kazembes were Lundas (2:148, 213, 229). Cunnison seconds these remarks, stating that "Kazembe" referred to the chief's "own" people and the lineage itself (1951, 38; 1957, 24).

This succession of rulers all with the same name exercised military, administrative, and judicial powers through subchiefs and headmen and were regarded as the highest-ranking religious representative, although priests assisted them and shared in the ritual and worship of their ancestral spirits in return for their blessings and favors (de Lacerda/Burton 1798/1873, 102; Pinto/Burton 1798–99/1873, 115; Cunnison 1954; W. H. Whiteley 1950, 25, 27). The name itself became synonymous with power and, ideally, with respect, goodness, generosity, and compassion (Kazembe XIV/Cunnison 1948/1961, 66; Cunnison 1954, 20), although some Kazembes could also be greedy and cruel. Boundless liberality and hospitality exhibited a ruler's greatness of wealth and spirit and often cemented the loyalty of his subjects to his person.

A few contemporary and later writers sketch the history of the establishment of the Kazembes in central Africa. They write that from c. 1740 to 1860, the Lunda tribe that occupied the territory of present-day Democratic Republic of Congo and Zambia was mostly under the sovereignty of two powerful monarchs, Mwata Yamvo[7] in the west[8] and Kazembe in the east. Their common border was the Lualaba River. Mwata Yamvo[9] traced his predecessors back a century or more. A simplified and shortened version (one of several) of the history of the Kazembe dynasty begins when Kazembe's ancestor, a captain (*quilolo*) and noble named Chinyanta, left Yamvo's capital in the early eighteenth century to seek slaves, colonize the reportedly rich lands to the east, and gain control of the salt marshes east of the Lualaba River (Cunnison 1961, 62; de Lacerda/Burton 1798/1873, 38).[10] He departed with one of Yambo's sons, known for his cruelty and insubordination,[11] and a Kampocolo-language-speaking fighting force. After Chinyanta discovered the son's plot against him, he returned to Yamvo to report his successes. When he returned a second time to the interior, he was drowned by the prince in the Lualáo or Lualaba River. The Yamvo, in return, executed this son (de Lacerda/Burton 1798/1873, 104; Travassos Valdez 1861, 2:258–61).[12]

The Mwata Yamvo then sent Chinyanta, the son and namesake of the murdered man, into the east to subdue any lingering resistance by the natives and invested him with the title Kazembe (de Lacerda/ Burton 1798/1873, 104; Coxhead 1914, 3; Travassos Valdez 1861, 2:258; Livingstone 1874, 2:252, 295; Cunnison 1957, 26; Gordon 2006b, 23), thus becoming a tributary chieftain of Yamvo (Macola 2002, 43). These forces gradually established their hegemony over the autochthonous, matrilineal native lineages through conquest and marriage.[13] In memory of their origin and founder, all the other successor rulers took the name of Kazembe. Later Kazembes established a measure of independence from Muata Yamvo (de Lacerda/Burton 1798/1873, 104; Travassos Valdez 1861, 2:261). In about 1740 Kazembe established his capital near Lake Mweru in the lower Luapula Valley (Kazembe XIV/Cunnison 1948/1961, 37; Cunnison 1961, 61–62; 1956c, 134; 1957, 22).[14] It slowly became a vital entrepôt in the trade between the Angolan Portuguese in the west and the Portuguese in Mozambique to the east (see also de Lacerda/Burton 1798/1873, 33; Pinto/Burton 1798–99/1873, 126).[15]

Most of the modern knowledge about precolonial Central Africa and the Kazembe dynasty comes from European traders, official expeditions, and missionaries. The first Portuguese to personally contact Kazembe and his successors was Manoel Caetana (or Gateano) Pereira, whose father, Gonçalo, was an established trader and gold prospector in Central Africa, originally from Goa. Manoel Pereira informed Governor and Dr. Francisco José Maria de Lacerda in 1798 that his father lived five days north of Tete (a trading town and entrepôt in Eastern Africa) and traded with Bisa tribesmen, from whom he had heard that their lord, Kazembe, would like to contact him. Manoel's testimony added that Kazembe had already received goods (such as plates, cups, and cloth) from his "father" Mwata Yamvo in the west in return for slaves. Presently, the Kazembe sent emissaries to Tete (1797 and 1798) who reiterated his desire to trade (Cunnison 1961, 64; de Lacerda/Burton 1798/1873, 55).

In the next four decades, three Portuguese expeditions traveled inland to make the connection: those of Dr. Francisco José Maria de Lacerda e Almeida (1798–99); the Pombeiros[16] (i.e., P. J. Baptista and Amaro José [1806–11]); and Major José Maria Corrêa Monteiro and Captain (and later Major) Antonio Candido Pedroso Gamitto (1831–32). These were the first literate observers of the Kazembe Kingdom (Gordon 2006b, 26). Reports from these expeditions and other documents gradually relayed a picture of the various Kazembes as successive dominant authorities.

The abovementioned mathematician, astronomer, and explorer, Dr. Francisco José Maria de Lacerda e Almeida, a Brazilian by birth, took up his post as governor of the Sena River in January 1798. He was also appointed by Donna Maria I of Portugal (reigned 1777–1816) to lead an expedition to explore and trade in Central Africa with the object of opening an overland transcontinental route between the east and west coasts. The diary of his march, which left from Tete on July 3, 1798, for the capital of King Kazembe, describes his first contact with the ruler to the time of de Lacerda's death near the ruler's capital on October 18, 1798 (de Lacerda/Burton 1798/1873, 59, 106; Burton 1873, 3–4; Cunnison 1961, 66), when his chaplain Father Francisco João Pinto assumed command and the writing of the journal. De Lacerda regarded the Kazembe as grave and inspiring respect and also as generous at times, giving away slaves and cloth to his vassals as well as to strangers and whites. He ruled over a widely dispersed population of fisherfolk and farmers who lived in small villages, which occasionally relocated.[17] He had many wives, which was the native sign of wealth and dignity. Dr. de Lacerda's request to meet with the ruler required him to leave grave offerings to the spirits of previously deceased rulers, who, he noted, the natives considered to be gods (de Lacerda/Burton 1798/1873, 102; Gamitto/Cunnison, 1831–32/1960, 2:13, 116) and were consulted regularly as oracles (de Lacerda/Burton 1798/1873, 103; Pinto/Burton 1798–99/1873, 128).[18]

After Dr. de Lacerda's death, Chaplain and Commander Fr. Pinto continued the relation. He, too, had to send "gifts" of cloth and beads with his request for an audience since, with the exception of close friends, natives did not speak to each other nor send messages without a gift (Pinto/Burton 1798–99/1873, 107–8). Pinto pressed the Kazembe for safe passage to Angola to the west, but the ruler, after wavering back and forth, ultimately denied the expedition permission to go on (107, 121, 135, 142). With that decision, the de Lacerda expedition to establish a transcontinental trade route failed.

The diary contains other information on Kazembe's peoples' customs and history. Pinto remarked on the king's illness, thought to have been caused by sorcery, and the sacrifices made for his recovery. He noted his multiple wives and many children; his generosity; his severe punishments for witchcraft, adultery, theft, and other infractions of custom; and his council of notables who helped him rule. He also collected a few notes on the peoples' history. Subjects told him that they came sixty years ago (c. 1738) from the west (Pinto/Burton 1798–99/1873, 117, 121, 125–29).

Subsequently, copies of de Lacerda and Pinto's records arrived at the office of the captain-general of Angola who directed a new effort to establish intercontinental trade. He delegated command to the director of the "Fair of Cassange,"[19] Lieutenant-Colonel Francisco Honerato da Costa, who sent two half-caste members of his staff—Pedro João Baptista and Amaro (elsewhere also Anastacio) José—and merchants to attempt the crossing, this time originating in the west (Baptista/Burton 1806–11/1873, 169).

The route journal and other reports and documents of the two staff members, pertaining to the route between the farm belonging to one of Muropue's (Muata Yamvo's) sons and Kazembe's court, reveals that they arrived in the ruler's presence on December 31, 1806 (Baptista/ Burton 1806–11/1873, 169–88, 203–40, especially 224). They were forced to remain at the Kazembe's capital until 1810 and only achieved their transcontinental goal, arriving in Tete, in February 1811. They wrote that the present Kazembe was feared by all the great chiefs and ruled over a great many peoples. Baptista is the first to note, in passing, that there had been several Kazembes over the years. He described the king seated in the public highway, where he customarily delivered justice to his people in the company of the members of his council (169, 187, 223, 227, 230, 232).

Major Monteiro and Captain Gamitto (Monteiro and Gamitto/ Burton 1831–32/1873, 245–57) traveled from the west and through the area in 1831–32. Their poorly outfitted and provisioned expedition was characterized by sickness, death, and privation (Cunnison 1961, 73, 75). In their reports, Monteiro and Gamitto added ethnographic observations about the Kazembe. In general, they confirmed that the ruler acted as the supreme religious authority (Gamitto/Cunnison 1831–32/1960, 2:117; Travassos Valdez 1861, 2:241–42) in charge of ancestor worship. He had four hundred wives (Gamitto/Cunnison 1831–32/1960, 2:19) and was considered wealthy in that respect as wealth was reflected by the number of wives a man had and their fecundity (1:89). They recorded that the number of people subject to an authority proved an index to his power. The more hospitable and generous a chief, the more subjects he attracted and the bigger his court and the stronger his forces (1:72). They noted that Lukesa (also known as Muata Cazembe Lekéza) was the first Kazembe who had seen and spoken to whites (Dr. de Lacerda) (2:13, 31) and that his spirit still watched over and protected his people (Beke/Burton 1831– 32/1873, 250).They also established that people and strangers remembered and revered the old Kazembe, the father of the present one, for his many "estimable qualities" (Beke/Burton 1831–32/1873, 248), specifically for his virtue and munificence (Gamitto/Cunnison 1831– 32/1960, 2:83).[20] The present reigning Kazembe was the opposite and was "detested by his own relatives" (2:83).

After these three expeditions, the Arabs and the Yeke tribal traders succeeded in establishing more frequent trade with the Kazembes
(Cunnison 1961, 76). Their influence extended from c. 1840 and ended
about 1890 (Cunnison 1966, 227). Arab traders, for example, Tippu Tib
(also Tip, according to Roberts [1967], 123), interacted with the Kazembe. But this trader could not even remember his name after he drove
the Kazembe from the country for making threats of terrible punishment for the Lunda. After 1890 Arab and Yeke influence diminished
with the "almost simultaneous arrival of British and Belgium [sic] official expeditions, the end of the Yeke kingdom and the Arab caravans,
the eclipse of [the successive] Mwata Yamvo[s] under pressure from the
Chokwe, and the beginnings of European rule" (Cunnison 1961, 227–28).

Other visitors followed. Travassos Valdez, appointed arbitrator at
Loanda on the west coast of Africa (1861, 1:ix), mentions a Mr. Freit-
as who arrived in 1853 to write a work on African languages and dia-
lects (2:213), and Travassos Valdez himself visited "the very important
and almost unknown country of Lunda, called Cazembe" in which
the potent emperor Mwata Cazembe reigns in 1861 (2:212–13). He adds
that the ruler's mother also inherited her name and title (2:219).[21] Interestingly, too, he writes that the Kazembe considered himself im-
mortal; his person was sacred and was protected by sorcery (2:251–52).
The death of previous Kazembes was explained as due to a neglect
of their sorceries, not the consequence of a human's mortal nature.
A Kazembe died only from the negligence in the work of the sorceries, the chief assured Travassos Valdez, who quoted one ruler who informed him that "I don't die, I am only transformed" (2:193). Indeed,
the chieftain was sacred and permanent and exempt from death, living on through ritual reincarnation (K. B. Maxwell 1983, especially
120).[22] Cunnison, in describing the initiation ceremony of Kazembe
XV, reported that he was told: "Now, Mwata, you are changed, you
are Mwata Yamvwa," as if his spirit was reincarnated or embodied
by the individual being installed (1952, 5).[23] People believed that, in
death, the various Kazembes continued to communicate with the living from their graves, to experience the same passions and necessities
as the living, and to walk about at night (Travassos Valdez 1861, 2:243).

Dr. David Livingstone visited the Kazembe's compound and town in the late 1860s and 1870s (Cunnison 1966, 228, 233; Kazembe XIV/Cunnison 1948/1961, 88). In 1867 the Kazembe was awaiting Livingstone's visit, having been kept abreast of his advance by runners (Livingstone 1874, 1:242, 246). His "town" or "rural village," as Livingstone called it, had a population of a thousand souls who lived scattered over a square mile of cassava fields (1:262). The Kazembe himself resided in a gigantic hut inside an enclosure roughly 200 by 300 yards in size (1:262). But Livingstone noted that this town was not the same one entered by de Lacerda, the governor of Tete on the Zambesi, for each of the seven previous Kazembes had built a new town in a different location (1:264). The town visited by Major Monteiro in the 1830s was at the same spot as the one in 1868, but the Kazembe's enclosure (*mosumba*) was 500 yards southeast of the present one. Because of this itinerant pattern of residence, he concluded that "it is useless to put down the names of chiefs as indicating geographical positions, for the name is often continued, but at a spot far distant from the dwelling of the original possessor" (1: 304).

Livingstone is the first European traveler to include in his journal a list of the previous Kazembes, as related by an elderly native informant (see table 1). He may have been able to collect and verify these names because the Kazembes still venerated many of the dead chiefs buried in the graves in the vicinity (Gordon 2006a, 32).

Livingstone notes that each Kazembe had a different character. Manoel Caetano Pereira, the first visitor to the Kazembe's capital in the 1790s, said that the Kazembe (Lukwesa, according to Cunnison) had twenty thousand trained soldiers at his command, watered his streets daily, and sacrificed twenty humans per day. The Kazembe of Livingstone's day (1867) could not muster even a thousand soldiers. He had usurped power five years earlier and his severe, mutilating punishments (e.g., cutting off ears and hands) and the practice of selling children into slavery for any infraction had sent his people fleeing to the protection of surrounding chiefs (Livingstone 1874, 1:254). "This is the common mode," Livingstone wrote, "by which tyranny is cured in parts like these, where fugitives are never returned" (1:265). Another

Table 1. Livingstone's and Cunnison's lists of Kazembes

Kazembe	According to Livingstone	According to Cunnison
I	Kanyimbe	Ng'anda Bilonda (Vironda)
II	Kinyanta	Kanyembo Mpemba (Mukanso, Kanyimbe)
III	Nguanda Milonda	Lukwesa (Lequéza) Ilunga
IV	Kanyembo	Chibangu Keleka (Kanyembo, Mayi)
V	Lekwisa	Kapumba (Muonga)
VI	Kiréka	Chinyanta Munona
VII	Kapumba	Muonga Sunkutu
VIII	Kinyanta	Chinkonkole (Kafuti)
IX	Lekwisa	Lukwesa Mpanga (Ilunga, Mabote)
X	Muonga	Kenyembo (Kanyembo) Ntemena (Chipepa, Muvanga)

Sources: Cunnison 1951b; Livingstone 1874, 1:295.

reason that this Kazembe lost population is that he refused to share the profits from the ivory trade with the elephant hunters, who eventually left or stopped hunting. Therefore, without ivory tusks to trade for the items he wanted, Livingstone and other foreigners labeled him "poor."[24] Another of Livingstone's informants thought that this Kazembe had poisoned his predecessor (1:277) and poisoned his wife's mother, a queen, when he feared that she might oppose his securing her daughter (1:277). But Livingstone judged the Kazembe as "reasonable and fair" in April 1868 and a month later noted him to be a gracious host, though very poor in ivory (1:292, 297, 299). A later native account noted that because he[25] was unloved by his people they failed to inform him that an enemy approached. Without a stockade or other refuge, he was taken and killed. His enemies put his head and his regalia on poles (2:253).

Some years later (in 1893), the missionary Dan Crawford met the Kazembe after passing the king's extensive cassava plantations (Tilsley

1929, 266–67). Crawford described a middle-aged Kazembe dressed in a tall headdress and much "bulky native jewelry" who sat on a throne carried on the shoulders of about forty men (268).

Name-Taking

Although some of these researchers wrote cursory notes on succession, few were interested in the details of the custom and of always assuming the predecessor's title. Monteiro and Gamitto's report is one that included a few general remarks. They note that (Gamitto/Cunnison 1831–32/1960, 2:111) a man ruled a village either because he founded it or because he inherited the chieftainship (1:92–93; 2:111). They further wrote that the successor of the Kazembe had to be the son of a Kazembe and a woman (one of his first four wives), who was a subject of Mwata Yamvo all of whose people were called the Kampokolos. The eldest son with the woman was "the one to whom succession rightly belongs." If there were no son with the needed qualities, custom dictated that the sovereign's closest Kampokolo relative be elected. If there were none who were apt, then a subject of Mwata Yamvo was nominated to be the next Kazembe (2:111, 123; Travassos Valdez 1861 repeats these rules, 2:232). Monteiro and Gamitto flesh out these rules with examples. The successor of a ruler took the same name, "in honour of the first one whose memory is held in great veneration" (Gamitto/Cunnison 1831–32/1960, 2:129–30). An African chief called all his people his "children," perhaps thus accounting for the "son" designation and notion of primogeniture that colored previous accounts (1:165; 2:130).[26]

The ethnohistory of these African peoples is complicated and confusing to outsiders, given the proliferation and repetition of names across the various reports (see Roberts 1967, 123).[27] European confusion led to some of them noting the Kazembe's personal names as a means of distinguishing between them. Singularly, Livingstone recovered more than the names of the present Kazembe and his predecessor and began to number them and list them as a dynasty. A comparison and contrast between Livingstone's list and a modern list elaborated by Cunnison illustrates the confusion (see table 1 above).

There is a coincidence in the order given for six Kazembes: from Kazembe III to VIII on Livingstone's list and Kazembe I to VI on Cunnison's list. There are also two Lukwesas named on both lists, although the second Lukwesa on the modern list appears at a date after Livingstone collected the names. Thus, Livingstone's informant named ten kings, while the modern list shows only seven for the same period. The missionary Dan Crawford (perhaps following Livingstone) wrote that Chinyanta (also Kinyanta) was the second chief of the Kazembe dynasty (who was the sixth according to Cunnison [Gordon 2006b, 32]).

Cunnison devoted an entire article to the information and discrepancies on the different Kazembes mentioned in the historical accounts, comparing them to a modern account by Kazembe XIV (Cunnison 1956c, 133–34), who he judges represents the native voice and is the most authoritative. Cunnison noted (132) that Baptista named Mutanda (i.e., Mutanda Yembeyembe), whom Cunnison identifies as the leader of the first expedition east, as the first Kazembe and Ng'anda Bilonda as the second. Kazembe XIV's account places Ng'anda Bilonda in the first spot. Although Ng'anda Bilonda was not the first leader, he was the first to bear the name Kazembe; and "it is this name that all the Mwata Kazembes who have succeeded have been called after" (Kazembe XIV/Cunnison 1948/1961, 21, 118–19). Cunnison concludes that there is no important divergence in Baptista's account; the chieftainship preceded the Kazembeship by one reign.

A comparison of Kazembe XIV's Lunda account with Gamitto's shows confusion between the names of Kazembe and Kanyembo.[28] Cunnison explains this by remarking that the name of the chief when Gamitto arrived was Kanyembo (Keleka) and the name of the chief preceding Lukwesa was also Kanyembo (Mpemba). Gamitto's list names five chiefs including the one reigning during his stay; while the Lunda version gives four for the same period. But the first chief considered by Gamitto was probably Chinyanta, the father of Ng'anda Bilonda. Even in 1956 Chinyanta rather than Mutanda Yembeyembe is sometimes named as the first chief, as the father of the first Kazembe and someone they still venerate (Cunnison 1956c, 133).[29]

Adding to the causes of such confusion is the fact that personal names were also inherited, something that was not always explicitly recorded by the on-the-spot historical observers. One man may have used four or five different names in a lifetime or held several names at once (Cunnison 1957). Furthermore, lesser chiefs were known to use the same names and titles as the paramount chief. Thus, the missionary Crawford mixes up Chinyama, a chief of the Aushi from further south, with the Lunda Chinyanta (Tilsley 1929, 137). Livingstone also mentions a stream called Casembe (1874, 2:250).[30]

Positional Inheritance

Resolving in part such confusions, in the mid-twentieth century ethnologist Cunnison scientifically analyzed and described the subtleties of a naming system that preserved the names of the founders of a lineage and retained them as the names of their positions. His description provides a nuanced context in which to place the observed data on the Kazembes as practiced by the native lineages of the Luapula Valley in the late 1940s. Simultaneously, it sheds light on the information in the accounts by explorers and traders. Formerly, the valley peoples responded to the paramount lord or king Kazembe, the Lunda conqueror from the west. Kazembe's subordinate but still important chief in his own right was Nkuba, an earlier Shila conqueror (Cunnison 1951b, v) who occupied the lower Luapula Valley before Kazembe's Lunda invaded (Cunnison 1952, 7). These peoples organized themselves into clans, subclans, lineages, and houses.

Thus "there is no detailed history of the present land of Kazembe, or of the conspicuous geographical unit of the Luapula Valley. . . . [It is rather] the personal history of Kazembe, incorporating his political relations with the generals who bore the brunt of his conquests and political action" (Cunnison 1951b, 5).[31] As noted above, Cunnison called the naming practice he observed "positional inheritance." Since then, scholars have found it or a variation of the practice operating in other African societies, like the Yao of Nyasaland (Malawi), the Bemba of northeastern Zimbabwe, the Wambugwe of Tanganyika (Tanzania) (Cunnison 1956b, 29), the Kaguru of eastern Tanzania (Beidelman 1974), the Mbundu (J. C. Miller 1976) and the Imbangala

of northwestern Angola (between c. 1620 and 1912) (J. C. Miller 1972).[32]
As outlined in the next two chapters, the same institutionalized naming system was operative among the Ho-De'-No-Sau-Nee (or Iroquois) and the Andeans.[33]

We turn now to how Cunnison portrayed the functioning of the system among the Luapula lineages of fisherfolk and farmers, based on fieldwork conducted from 1948 to 1951. In brief, positional inheritance or succession is a system of inherited names within a kinship group. The inheritance of a name means that successive holders of it are usually known by that name and no other. Thus, all the Nkubas (Cunnison 1957, 22) of the eighteenth century are "Nkuba." The same pertains to village headmen and the headmen of clans, subclans, and lineages (Cunnison 1952, vi, 3). In practice, a boy received a name from either father's or mother's lineage at birth, known as a "spirit name" and representing the essence of a deceased senior relative. At about age six, the boy entered adult society and assumed his own position in it. From that point forward, his position should be succeeded to and his name inherited by a junior member of the lineage. The older a youth who died, the more important the succession became. Once married, succession was essential. Thus, during youth, a male might assume different names. After the birth of children, he was addressed teknomymously, that is, as the father of a specific child (Geertz and Geertz 1964). The name by which he finally was known could be any of a succession of his names, although it was usually the one by which a man went at the moment that he died. Theoretically, within a year, another man took the deceased's name. For the successor, the taking of a new name signified a promotion to a senior status, that of the man who had died. He adopted the name, the role, the position, and the responsibilities that his predecessor had held and he was often called by the kinship terms that were addressed to his predecessor. He also received the deceased's wives and at least one object that belonged to him, usually a bracelet, a kettle, a pot, or a belt (Cunnison 1951b, 294; 1952, 3).[34] Society deemed succession complete once the successor and the principal wife of his predecessor spent two nights together and consummated the union (Cunnison 1957, 23; Cunnison

1959, especially 93–94, where he also mentions variations in the succession customs without details). The Kazembe ratified the decision of the lineage and formally installed the successor's new title by bestowing upon him special insignias, which held magical powers (Macola 2002, 88; Kazembe XIV/Cunnison 1948/1961, 6; J. C. Miller 1976, 24).

Over time, it was the name rather than any particular incumbent of it that achieved fame and gained currency in traditions. Every man occupied a named position, and, ideally, after he died, the position and its name survived. One name came to be inherited by someone who already had a position of his own, marked by a name. The man who inherited, thus, embodied two names. Of these the inherited name, being senior and more prestigious, overrode his original junior name, which, if not itself inherited, might be forgotten in time. The more important the deceased, the weightier was the choice of a successor. Among the Luapula, the ideal successor was considered to be a "brother"—a full brother or a maternal half brother or "any" brother or male relative of the same generation.[35] Among the Luapula, most names died out after two or three holders. Those names that endured were important ones, those to which historical traditions were attached or those whose holders had played a part in forming the lineage.

"Perpetual kinship," a second and related concept, arose as a consequence of this system of positional succession. A sustained relationship existed between a pair of positions whose names had been inherited through the generations. Cunnison gives an example: if, for instance, A was mother's brother (uncle) to B some generations back, and both names had been continuously inherited, the position of A was still in the relationship of mother's brother to the position of B, and the present-day incumbent of position A was still "mother's brother" to the present-day incumbent of position B.[36]

Cunnison's information suggests that the name of the founder of a lineage is the name that is always inherited and maintained so long as the group is known as the clansmen of that name. If the lineage later divides, then the headmen's names are both regularly inherited and a perpetual relationship between them continues. If the members of the lineages are nearby, contact is likely to be maintained. If they set-tle at a distance, the junior group in time may gain its independence. "But independent as they may be in practical affairs, the known quasi-kinship link of their leaders subsists and prevents a lineage formed in this way from becoming isolated. It remains part of a wider group" (Cunnison 1956b, 39). In Cunnison's example, which particular lin-eage in a group was the original from which the others segmented was remembered. Junior lineage leaders could respect the leader of the senior; "but the respect does not include acceptance of the senior leader's authority" (42). Kin did not always remember all the incum-bents of the positions. In recall, informants dropped some of these (usually the oldest) out, a practice known as "telescoping" in genealog-ical circles.[37] Therefore, determining the temporal distance between founder and junior segmentations is usually impossible.

Cunnison gives another example that shows how political hierar-chies are established between groups and names. A group of kinsmen immigrates, perhaps seeking protection or offering military aid to a chief. The chief grants the leader permission to settle on unoccupied land. From this settlement, various leaders and their followers might break off and move elsewhere. The new headmen would have their relationships—whether brother, son, or brother-in-law with the origi-nal headman—perpetuated as they were succeeded. This relationship establishes a hierarchy by fixing the relative genealogical positions of the villages through their leaders and outlines settlement history.

Such a structural connection between one generation and anoth-er affects the group's memories. The known association between two headmen is a testament to the historical events that brought the re-lationship about; and, conversely, the historical events recounted in an almost identical form year after year vouch for the expressed re-lationship and for the superior political position of the original lin-eage in relation to the other. Cunnison further noted that the events recounted on these occasions appeared, from the way in which they were told, to have happened only yesterday; the association becomes retrospective, and any incumbent of a line of older, superior chiefs is described as father to any incumbent of a later one (1951b, 34; 1956b,

44). Moreover, the chief who tells the history does not distinguish between the various incumbents of his name but refers to them all in the first-person singular. The chief inherited the name of all of his predecessors along with their identities and kin relations. The kinship terminology collapses the whole lineage into two generations and takes no account of the passage of genealogical time. According to Cunnison, in these histories the incumbents of the names belong both to the present and the past. They belong to the present because, in the histories, they recount in the first person to their listeners the actions of all the incumbents of the name without distinguishing one name-holder from another; and they belong to the past because they speak not only of themselves but also of the persons whose actions created the present situation.[38]

J. D. Y. Peel takes the analysis a step further in his article on the Yoruba town of Ijeshoin southwestern Nigeria. His research led him to the concept of "stereotypic reproduction," and in that context he describes how the Yoruba say "Baba ni jungi" (or "Your father is a mirror") (1984, 113). The physical appearance, aptitudes, spiritual affinities, and social position of a father are expected to be echoed in his sons. Marshall Sahlins argues that the same is true of the Polynesians. In his studies, aboriginal heroes (who also stand for abstract cultural categories) are archetypes: to quote Sahlins, "just as the father is to his sons, so the ancestor stands to his descendants as a general class to its specific instances" (1981, 13) Among the Yoruba and the Polynesians a reigning chief used the first-person pronoun to describe the doings of a remote ancestor. Sahlins quotes a subclan headman of the Luapula kingdom of Kazembe, first recorded by Cunnison, as follows:

> We came to the country of Mwanshya ... I killed a *puku* [antelope]. ...
> We gave some of the meat to Mwanshya. He asked where the salt came
> from and he was told. So he sent people who killed me. My mother
> was angy and went to fetch medicine to send thunderbolts. She de-
> stroyed Mwanshya's village. ... Lubunda ... heard about my strength.
> He came to see us and married my mother. They went away and I re-
> mained. (Cunninson 1959, 234; 1951b; 1957)

"All these events," Sahlins wrote, "including the narrator's death, transpired before he was born" (1985, 147). Peel cites M. Eliade (1954) as believing that the phenomenon is universal among preliterate peoples. Activities are "real only to the extent that they are replications of archetypes" (85–86, quoted by Peel 1984, 113). Such an argument undermines the pursuit of historical sequence.

The lineage histories are often recounted—both then and now—in a seemingly shallow generational narrative, starting at the point of fission from the clan to which the group belonged before their fairly recent migration from surrounding areas. The relationships between groups are constant, as in the segmentation of a lineage whose secession is frozen into a past and present, superior and subordinate rankings by the adopted and preserved use of kinship terms. Cunnison further observes that lineages may have genealogies up to seven generations in depth. More often only three to four generations are recalled from the founder of the lineage to its present-day leader, suggesting that telescoping has taken place in the course of the last two centuries since the Lunda invasions (Cunnison 1957, especially 22–23).[39] According to a lineage leader who inherited the name of the founder and is the repository of its history, and the only one to relate lineage history of conquests and secessions in the context of royal succession, when speaking the names of the past, a successor may be referred to as "brother" to the person whose place he has taken. He is reckoned to be of the same generation, even though he may be two generations removed. This accounts, writes Cunnison, for the long strings of "brothers" who are mentioned as having been successive holders of one name in the history of many lineages. The kinship terminology tends to place all members of a lineage, dead and alive, into two generations (23, 27). "Histories," according to Cunnison, "refer only to the generations of the founders, and these are compressed through identification of the founder and his successors . . . histories remain vested in lineages and a history comprising a wider kin group does not emerge" (24, 26).[40]

Kazembe dynastic history, in contrast to the shorter and more parochial and personal lineage accounts, defines a royal sequence that is relatively easy to verify and recall when associated with graves, cultural landmarks, shrines, and references, after the end of the eighteenth century, in chroniclers' accounts.[41] Cunnison did not believe that there was telescoping in this sequence. The history of the kingship since the time of Livingstone also lists kings by name and sometimes includes details on their parentage and the events that took place during their reign. Cunnison concedes, however, that aristocrats related royal history often to the benefit of their own hereditary names. The incumbent is the repository of the name's history and the name itself was the hero of the stories (Cunnison 1957, 27).

But there is no consensus on the accuracies of either dynastic or lineage histories.[42] The study by Joseph C. Miller about three decades after Cunnison's pioneering research underscores the fact that such dynastic sequences may be filled with "spuriously regular father-to-son successions," commonly with telescoping in remoter periods (1979, 51).[43] Miller went on to note that listing may be a habit characteristic only of literate societies. He contends that preliterate people with only oral tradition to rely on did not make lists. He warns that "what appeared to African historians to be sequentially-ordered lists of rulers may in fact have been no more than conceptual 'chunks' of royalty possessing little or no internal order" (51, citing the work of Goody 1977, 74–111). He suggests that what "chronophiles" have established may be "diachrony"or "the artifical ordering of essentially unsequenced elements in a myth structure that is produced spuriously by the necessity in a non-literate culture of realizing them orally, in time." He raises the possibility that king lists elaborated by anthropologists and historians, giving them order and chronology, are "in fact synchronous unordered categories" (51).[44] Miller's study comparing orally related Kessanje king lists of the Imbangala[45] with Portuguese, Dutch, and Italian written records leads him to conclude that the oral dynastic chronicles possess "reliable sequence, if not chronology" (52).[46]

In a study of the Luo of Kenya, Ben G. Blount found that in trying to reconstruct the genealogy of a clan "individual initiative and ability [of an elder] was the central factor in establishing as correct any portion of the genealogy"(1975, 117–18). Initiative and ability were based

on speech prowess, knowledge of Luo history and folklore, and social positions among participants at the meeting where history was
discussed. The result was a negotiated genealogy. It was "partially dictated and a partially arbitrated synthesis. In effect, the genealogies as
history were created by the elders in competition, cooperation, and
occasionally by fiat within a framework of Luo social interaction"
(118). This research underscores the manipulability of oral tradition
(Peel 1984, 115).[47]

Despite these shortcomings in the details and sequence from a Western historical perspective, Cunnison (1956b) sees these two institutions—
positional inheritance and perpetual kinship—as creating a customary
symbiotic relation between the social groups. Historically, they told
a story, an oral tradition, of conquest and the establishment of kin
ties between conquerors and natives. Politically, they set up perpetual relationships between groups that used kinship terminology to
grace interaction "in favour of overall peace" (48). Robert F. Gray
(1953), who conducted fieldwork in 1950–51, adds that positional succession among the Wambugwe allowed the substitute to assume the
kinship relationships of the dead person and in the case of a married
person, his affinal relationships. It recompensed the surviving relatives for the loss of the deceased, much as similar customs did in Ho-
De'-No-Sau-Nee society. The system he described affects inheritance
of property, preferential marriage of widows, the guardianship of or-
phans, and adoption customs (233). These, however, are beyond the
scope of the present study.

Living Memories

In short, the defining features of the naming system and the memories they generate as described by Cunnison for mid-twentieth-century
Africa are:

1. A hierarchy of named positions

2. The importance of perpetuating names, especially those that refer
   to the first person to have held or created a position

3. The practice of taking on more than one name during a lifetime

4. The desirability of moving into vacant, senior named positions

5. The perpetuation of relative positions based on kinship or quasi-fictitious kinship relations between the original holders of the names

6. The collapsing of history into the then and now

7. The absence (at least to the mid-twentieth century) of any institutional history of a wider tribal group or region[48]

Thus, the keys to the memories of the peoples of the Luapula Valley were the names and titles of their leaders. Individual names had "content." Names became the repositories of lineage and group knowledge. As individuals succeeded, they claimed the position, status, and accomplishments of their predecessors. Name-taking was important because it secured respective ranks and bestowed rights and responsibilities. It also confirmed relationships with other nearby groups, underscoring their identities.

The inhabitants of the Luapula Valley constructed their past in a patterned, cyclical way that conserved what they considered important. Positional inheritance preserved the relationships that gave meaning to collectivities of various sizes through kinship ties. Consequently, it organized memory and power.

Ideally, history was repeated and society, at first glance, might seem unchangeable. Yet ethnographic studies of the Kazembes and other African tribes, mentioned above, show discrepancies in the telling of tales and their performances. The transmission of the past was manipulated, negotiated, distorted, telescoped, and possibly lengthened to fit current designs. Oral traditions facilitated this refashioning and variation until they were supplanted and fixated by the persons who would record them in writing.

| Chapter Three

The Narration of Ho-De'-No-Sau-Nee (Iroquois) History

Across the Atlantic Ocean and thousands of miles to the northwest, another preliterate population employed naming conventions to recall the past. The Ho-De'-No-Sau-Nee and the Hurons of North America shared an analogous system of naming with their African counter-parts.[1] Names among these peoples evoked memories of their origins. In these northern societies, positional inheritance assured that some individuals took the most important names generation after gener-ation, thus keeping alive the stories and reputations of those who had preceded them. This means of reembodying their history, all the way back to the founding events of their sociopolitical system, is ev-idenced at the clan and nation levels as individuals were resurrected both by kin and nonkin adoptees. The resuscitation of a chief or *sa-chem*[2] is the best documented of these native renaming traditions, as will be discussed below.

This narrative is restricted to the Ho-De'-No-Sau-Nee, also known as the Haudenosaunee (also Hodenosaunee) or People of the Long-house,[3] a matrilineal multifamily residential unit (Kapches 1990, 50), and the related but non-League members, the Huron-Wyandot who shared a language and culture.[4] The first formed a League or Con-federation, built on kinship loyalties, of five and later six nations or tribes[5] (Beauchamp 1895a, 217; Morgan 1851/1962, 60) to guarantee a peaceful future among them.[6] The five original tribes or nations were the Seneca (or Genundewah, Jo-No-Do-Van-Gan, Non-Do-Wan-Gan, or Great Hill People[7] and guardians of the western door of the tribal longhouse); the Cayuga (People of the Marsh); the Onondaga (People of the Hills and keepers of the central fire); the Oneida (People of the Border or of Standing Stone); and the Mohawk (People of the Place of the Flint and keepers of the eastern door of the longhouse).[8] In the early eighteenth century, the Ho-De'-No-Sau-Nee incorporated the Tussaroras (also Tuscaroras or Hemp Gatherers) as a sixth confederate (Jennings et al. 1985, 18; Perrot c. 1700–1720[9]/1911–12, 1:85).[10] Charles A. Cooke (1952) adds the Cherokees (427). Originally, each of the tribes was known by the name of the tribal chief (Tooker 1970, 95).[11] Commemoration through naming among these peoples and the Iroquoian-speaking Hurons was most evident in the customs of individual name changes, adoption, and resuscitation of the dead, especially of the chiefs, as the sections below will detail.

Table 2. Ho-De'-No-Sau-Nee names

The Ho-De'-No-Sau-Nee (People of the Long House)

Nation's name	English translation	Commonly known as
Gä-ne-ă'-ga-o-no'	People Possessors of the Flint	Mohawk
O-nun'-dä-ga-o-no'	People on the Hills	Onondaga
Nun-da'-wä-o-no'	Great Hill People	Seneca
O-ná-yote-kä-o-no'	Granite People	Oneida
Gwe-n'-gweh-o-no'	People at the Mucky Land	Cayuga
Dus-ga'-o-weh-o-no'	Shirt Wearing People	Tuscarora

Source: Morgan 1851/1962, p. xxi.

Ho-De'-No-Sau-Nee oral traditions,[12] as reconstructed and synthesized from the written versions of anthropologist and adopted Seneca Lewis H. Morgan (1851/1962, x) and historian and student of religion Christopher Vecsey (1986, 82–94), on both of whose writings, in part, I depend here, traced their origins back to ancient times. Briefly, a legendary being named Tarenyawagon saved the Five Nations from giants and monsters and ordered their world. He gave five families the means of making war for expansion; these families, however, went their separate ways. Subsequently, a child, named Da-Gä-No-We'-Dä (also Deganawida,[13] Deganawi'dah, Dekanawidah, Dehayenhyaawa"gih, or Tarenyawagon [the "sky rememberer"]) (Hewitt 1944, 70; Fenton 1949, 144), was born to a virgin who lived among the Hurons near the Bay of Quinte.[14] Because the child was fatherless, the grandmother was upset until she dreamed that the baby was the incarnation of a spirit with an important mission to fulfill. He grew up honest, good, generous, beautiful, and peaceful. He eventually left his mother and journeyed to the Mohawks who were engaged in intertribal warfare with the sorrow, destruction, starvation, and death that such activities brought. He admonished them to cease killing each other, promising to protect them and organize a government. He subsequently traveled about explaining three principles: righteousness, peace, and power. Among the laws that he established, Deganawida mandated that venison feed the people and its antlers be worn on the head to symbolize authority. Because of this activity, his name is preserved as the League founder and its first lawgiver (Morgan 1851/1962, 61). Eventually, the natives moved from near Montreal on the northern bank of the Saint Lawrence River[15] south to what is today the state of New York to continue their horticultural, hunting, and fishing way of life (Morgan, 1851/1962, 5). They lived dispersed or in small villages that were moved from time to time (Thwaites 1649/1898 [Thwaites vol. 34], 251; Brébeuf 1636/1897 [Thwaites vol. 10], 275).

One of those who accepted Deganawida's preaching was Hiawatha, who became an Onondaga chief.[16] After Hiawatha's family was killed by a wizard and chief, possibly Hiawatha's half brother, named Tadadaho of the Onondaga, he continued his journeys, spreading his message to the Oneidas, Cayugas, Senecas, and Mohawks. Eventually, these all joined in a procession to the Onondagas, where they recruited a transformed Tadadaho and began a new era of peace and tranquility.

The formerly squabbling Five Nations joined into one people or family and created a confederate government with local autonomy, based on the three principles of: health and peace (*Ne skenno*);

righteousness and justice (*Ne gaiihwiyo*); and authority and spiritual power (*Ne gashedenza*). To instill and propagate these principles, they established permanent and hereditary sachemships or chieftainships as protectors and guides of their people. Their power was equal and joint, "co-extensive with the League" as Morgan wrote (1851/1962, 62–63). League members agreed that the Onondaga nation, being situated in a central position, would be the keepers of the wampum,[17] in which the structure and principles of the government and the laws and treaties were symbolically recorded.

The founders instituted a roll call of the fifty[18] League chiefs, naming them by nation and clan. The founders divided sachemships among the nations: nine each to the Mohawk and Oneida nations, fourteen to the Onondaga, ten to the Cayuga, and eight to the Seneca (see table 3 for their distribution and names in the Seneca dialect).[19] Together they constituted the Council of the League, the ruling body that exercised legislative, executive, and judicial authority (Morgan 1851/1962, 63). They mandated that the council meet to declare war or make peace, send and receive embassies, enter treaties, regulate League affairs, and extend protections over weaker tribes, besides "raising up" sachems (chiefs or captains) to fill vacancies (66–67). The founders also established the ceremonies for installing the chiefs, which will be described below.

Table 3. Roll call of the fifty chiefs

	Native name	Translation	Tribe
Gä-ne-ä'-ga-o-no or Mohawk Nation			
1	Da-gä-e'-o-gä	Neutral, the shield	Turtle
2	Hä-yo-went'-hä	Man who combs	Turtle
3	Da-gä-no-we'-dä	Endless	Turtle
4	So-ä-e-wä'-ah	Small speech	Wolf
5	Da-yo'-ho-go	At the forks	Wolf
6	O-ä-ä'-go-wä	At the great river	Wolf
7	Da-an-no-gä'-e-neh	Dragging his horns	Bear
8	Sä-da'-gä-e-wä-deh	Even tempered	Bear
9	Häs-dä-weh'-se-ont-hä	Hanging up rattles	Bear

O-na-yote'-kah-o-no or Oneida Nation

1	Ho-däs'-hä-teh	A man bearing a burden	Wolf
2	Ga-no-gweh'-yo-do	A man covered in cat tail down	Wolf
3	Da-yo-hä'-gwen-da	Opening through the woods	Wolf
4	So-no-sase'	A long string	Turtle
5	To-no-ä-gǎ'-o	A man with a headache	Turtle
6	Hä-de-ä-dun-nent'-hä	Swallowing himself	Turtle
7	Da-wä-dä'-o-dä-yo	Place of the echo	Bear
8	Gä-ne-ä-dus'-ha-yeh	War club on the ground	Bear
9	Ho-wus'-hä-da-o	A man steaming himself	Bear

O-nun-dah'-ga-o-no or Onondaga Nation

1	To-do-dä'-ho	Tangled	Bear
2	To-nes'-sa-ah		
3	Da-ät-ga-dose	On the watch	Bear
4	Gä-neä-dä'-je-wake	Bitter body	Snipe
5	Ah-wä'-ga-yat		Turtle
6	Da-ä-yat'-gwä-e		
7	Ho-no-we-nǎ'-to		Wolf
8	Gä-wǎ-nǎ'-san-do		Deer
9	Hä-e'-ho		Turtle
10	Ho-yo-ne-ä'-ne		Turtle
11	Sa-dä'-quä-seh		Bear
12	Sä-go-ga-hä'	Having a glimpse	Deer
13	Ho-sa-hä'-ho	Large mouth	Turtle
14	Skä-no'-wun-de	Over the creek	Turtle

Gue'-u-gweh-o-no or Cayuga Nation

1	Da-gä'-ä-yo	Man frightened	Deer
2	Da-je-no'-dä-weh-o		Heron
3	Gä-dä'-gwä'-sa		Bear
4	So-yo-wase'		Bear

5	Hä-de-äs'-yo-no		Turtle
6	Da-yo-o-yo'-go		
7	Jote-ho-weh'-ko*	Very cold	Turtle
8	De-ä-wate'-ho		Heron
9	To-dä-e-ho'		Snipe
10	Des-gä'-heh		Snipe

Nun-da-wah'-o-no or Seneca Nation

1	Gä-ne-o-di'-yo	Handsome Lake	Turtle
2	Sä-dä-gä'-o-yase	Level Heavens	Snipe
3	Ga-no-gi'-e		Turtle
4	Sä-geh'-jo-wä	Great forehead	Hawk
5	Sä-de-a-no'-wus	Assistant	Bear
6	Nis-hä-ne-a'-nent	Falling day	Snipe
7	Gä-no-go-e-dä'-we	Hair burned off	Snipe
8	Do-ne-ho-gä'-weh	Open door	Wolf

Source: Morgan 1851/1962, 64–65.

* Teyothorehkonh or "doubly cold," according to Hale 1895, p. 53.

The ideal chief was imagined to be brave, patient, long-suffering, thick-skinned, generous, fearless in pursuing justice, and a good public speaker (Thwaites 1681–83/1899 [Thwaites vol. 62], 273; Williams 1994, 101n103). Until his ceremonial investiture, a person held no extraordinary authority. Each sachem was ritually "raised up" and invested with a traditional name at the council, attended by all the sachems. Even then, they "led rather than commanded" (Fenton 1986, 22–23). They were expected to advise, deliberate, and protect and consult their followers. Consensus and unanimity, if possible, were the goals. The chiefs, too, then, were warned against failing to do their duty and instructed in the order of the councils.[20] Generic native terms for chiefs reflect their status, for example *rakow eh* (also *royaehr, rahsennowa eh, rotiyaehr* in Mohawk) and *hagowa eh, hotiyaenshoh,* or *hahsennowaeh* in Seneca or literally "He is a great one," "His name is great," all of which mean "He is a chief" (Fenton 1986, 27). Fenton further notes that "the persons to whom are ascribed the rank of *rotiya ehr* (Mohawk), *hotiya enshoh* (Seneca) comprise an honored group, bordering on an elite, for whom there is linguistic precedent and ethnological description going back to the seventeenth century, as witness *gaiander* [Bruyas 1862, 58 as cited by Fenton 1986, 28], 'a considerable man or woman'; and Lafitau's account of the elite (1724, 474–75; 1974, 294). At the turn of the eighteenth century the term Agoinanders meant the 'ancients, councilors, ancestors'" (Fenton 1986, 28).

In a society where warfare against external foes had been endemic, the founders hoped that the League, in addition to providing for mutual defense, would provide a system to regulate feuds and end revenge killings that followed Hammurabi's eye-for-an-eye stratagem. Once peace was achieved, unity allowed the Ho-De'-No-Sau-Nee to expand from New England to the Mississippi River and from the northern shores of the Great Lakes to the Tennessee River and the hills of Carolina. The aim was to coalesce under a "system of relationships, that, by its natural expansion, an Indian empire would be developed, of sufficient magnitude to control surrounding nations, and thus secure an exemption from perpetual warfare" (Morgan 1851/1962, 58). By extending and perpetuating relations of kinship, reciprocity, and goodwill between members of the League and promoting the creation of relationships of law and peace between differing people, these traditions enabled "the Iroquois to 'link arms together' and thereby establish and maintain one of the most powerful tribal confederacies of the Encounter era" (Williams 1994, 995–96, 1018, 1032).

Naming and Positional Inheritance

Reminiscent of the confusion of the early European explorers and traders who encountered the Kazembes and the matrilineal lineages of Central Africa, the first several missionaries found it hard to understand and describe the natives they so anxiously strove to convert to Catholicism in North America. Certain native groups only reluctantly revealed their names, because they believed that the churchmen wrote them down in baptismal records only to afterward tear

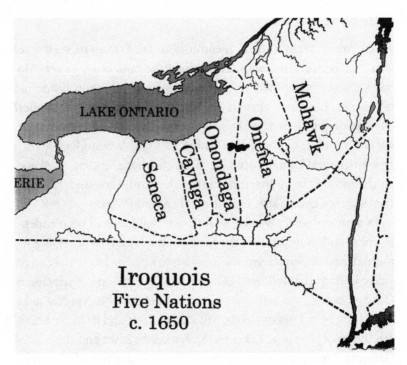

Map 2. The Five Nations, 1650. Courtesy Wikimedia commons.

out a written name, causing the individual's death (Le Jeune 1640/1898 [Thwaites vol. 19], 129). Some natives also thought that the churchmen wrote them down and sent them to France where they procured "their deaths by magic" (Le Jeune 1657/1899 [Thwaites vol. 43], 309–11). Eventually, missionaries and traders learned that natives shared no family names or what today are known as surnames (Lalemant 1642/1898 [Thwaites vol. 23], 165). But individual first names were shared, sequentially. Each lineage had its own repertoire of names (Vimont 1642/1898 [Thwaites vol. 22], 287; Morgan 1851/1901, 2:216, 238), some peculiar to men and others suitable for women. Upon the death of an individual, the name, essential for ceremonial and ritual activities, was returned to the clan for future bestowal. Clan mothers, the repositories of this knowledge, suggested names for designation to chosen candidates from those not in current use. These women not only conferred names but also could censure appointees and remove individuals, even chiefs, from office (Fenton 1986, 28; Evaneshko 1974, 103–4, 110;

Morgan 1851/1901, 2:216, 238). Ideally, names were unique, belonging
to one individual at a time (Shimony 1994, 212). Naming certified that
the person was a functioning member of society.

Common names were usually derived from natural things, for example, from animals, fish, and the seasons. One Jesuit relation translates a sampling of names as follows: Arimouchtigwan or the dog's
head; Dechinkinagadich or a small buckler; Oumithikens or the thorn
(Vimont 1642/1898 [Thwaites vol. 22], 287).[21] Chiefs' names and their
meanings, when known, appear in table 3. They often reflected the activities of the original name-holder (Cooke 1952, 428), such as hunter,
tiller of the soil, corn planter, runner, warrior, medicine man, storyteller, and name-bearer.[22] For example, Ho-Däs'-Hä-Teh of the Turtle
Tribe of the Oneidas means, according to Morgan, "a man bearing a
burden." Ho-Wus'-Hä-Da-O of the Wolf Tribe of the Oneida nation
meant "a man steaming himself" (1851/1962, 64). Some chief names
had more import, relating to a duty as peace-preserver or war chief.
Thus, the name of a Cayuga chief, Hadwennine, meant "His words
are moving" (Hale 1895, 51); Sä-Go-Ye-Wät'-Hä meant "keeper awake"
because of the eloquence of his orations in addressing others (Morgan 1851/1962, 90). Hodatchehte meant "the Quiver Bearer," the leading Oneida chief (Fenton 1986, 36).

But, as in South Central Africa, these names were unstable and
changed from time to time. Names were divided by different periods
and pursuits in life: one class for infancy and childhood, another for
adulthood, another for religious advisers or "keepers of the faith" (Ho-
Nun-De-Unt or Ho-Nun-De'-Ont) (Morgan 1851/1962, 184), and another for chiefs or sachems (Morgan, 1851/1962, 89n1; Morgan 1851/1901,
2:237–38). Each clan, as noted above, had its own clan names, which
were kept distinct and which no other clan was allowed to use. The
Jesuit missionary Paul Le Jeune relates in 1639 that the natives often
changed their names (1639/1898 [Thwaites vol. 16], 201–3). A name
was given to them at their birth, called the birth name or baby name
(Morgan 1851/1962, 89; Morgan 1851/1901, 1:85). They changed it in ad-
olescence and manhood, and took another in their old age. When
a boy shed his baby name (for example, O-Wi-Go or floating canoe;

Ga-Ha-No or hanging flower (Morgan 1851/1901, 2:238)) for one suitable for adulthood, he was then considered able to join a war party and speak in council (Morgan 1851/1901, 2:237–38). Natives also took different names when they escaped from danger, choosing one that they thought would be of "better augury" than the one they had (Vimont 1642/1898 [Thwaites vol. 22], 287).

Sometimes native sorcerers or soothsayers instigated these changes, suggesting that a sick man change his name, thinking that death or the spirit that tried to attack the patient would no longer know him under a new one. Jesuit and leader of the missions of New France Hierosme Lalemant wrote in 1639: "indeed, if any one [sic] is very sick, and does not recover from this sickness, he will sometimes give up his old name, as if it brought him ill-luck, to take another of better omen" (1639/1898 [Thwaites vol. 17], 203).[23] Thus, natives believed that some names were luckier than others (Vimont 1642/1898 [Thwaites vol. 22], 289). Even a dream was sufficient to make a man take a new name.

As in sub-Saharan Africa, ideally no important name was ever lost. Ian Cunnison's conceptualization of "positional inheritance" applied to this North American case to the extent that the substitute or name-taker reincarnated the dead person (Fenton 1986, 24).[24] Le Jeune (1634/1897 [Thwaites vol. 6]) reports that the natives call this succession of one to the other Achitescatoueth, meaning that they pass reciprocally to each other's place (163). In fact, when a family member died, it was assumed that the spirit could not rest until someone had been chosen to replace the person (R. L. Hall 1997, 32). Hence the relatives assembled quickly to consult as to which among them should take the name of the deceased. Especially for women and girls and boys, the most appropriate designated person was of the same age and gender as the deceased. The same affection shown to the lost children was shown to the resuscitated youngsters who took their names. The names shed were then assigned to other relatives.

In families, the person who took on a new name to replace a missing person also assumed the duties, qualities, and status connected with it. The individual who became head of a household, for example, took the name of his predecessor (Lalemant 1642/1898 [Thwaites vol. 23], 165–67). Le Jeune wrote: "And lo, the dead is raised to life, and the grief of the relatives is all past" (1639/1898 [Thwaites vol. 16], 201). In the case of murdered Joseph Chihwatenhwa, his elder brother Teondechorren took his name "in the hope we had that the virtue of his late brother, as well as his name, might be made to live again in his person" (Le Jeune 1640–41/1898 [Thwaites vol. 20], 147–51). The family officially bestowed the name during a banquet for a large assembly, presenting a gift to the new name-holder for the acceptance of the name. The gift bound the name-holder to take on the status, position, and responsibilities of the deceased. A man who replaced a family's head of household, therefore, was called "father" by its members (Vimont 1642/1898 [Thwaites vol. 22], 289). In this way his predecessor was resuscitated through him (Bressani 1653/1899a [Thwaites vol. 38], 265).[25]

Similar ceremonies marked the death of a brave man who had been slain by his enemies. If he had a porcelain collar or something else of value, it was offered to the new name-holder. Acceptance, as in the case above, bound the name-holder to the family. As the deceased who lived again in his person, he was expected to imitate the deceased's courage, to go to war with as many men as he could muster, to take revenge upon his enemies, and to kill some of his adversaries. To paraphrase Le Jeune: the person who took the name of a man killed in battle bound himself to avenge his death; and to assist the family of a dead man, because he who brought him back to life, and who represented him, assumed all the duties of the deceased, feeding his children as if he were their own father (1639/1898 [Thwaites vol. 16], 201–3; Vimont 1642/1898 [Thwaites vol. 22], 289).

Imitation of the deceased might extend to even renouncing drunkenness and other vices (Lamberville 1682/1899 [Thwaites vol. 62], 59–61). On the contrary, Jesuit leader of the missions of New France Hierosme Lalemant records the story of how the bestowal of a name, Oumosotiscouchie, which had been borne by several captains (chiefs) of the man's country and had been given to him in order to make them live again, "rendered him proud and insolent" (1647/1898, [Thwaites vol. 31], 261).

When a blood relative could not be found to take the name of a deceased person, the name and its legacy were remembered and kept alive through adoption. By reconstituting and extending a family and lineage, adoption strengthened the group (Hale 1883/1963, 32, 95; Morgan 1851/1962, 341). When the natives spared the life of war captives (Le Mercier 1652–53/1898 [Thwaites vol. 40], 139), they usually were doled out to families as substitutes for missing members.[26] In a 1653 account, the Jesuit François Le Mercier detailed how he was given to a family in return for a dead man "causing the departed to become alive again in my person, according to their custom." He was not alone; the same family had already adopted a captive Algonquin woman and a Huron. They treated Le Mercier well; after the adoption the family attended to his wounds and gave him a blanket, shoes, stockings, and a shirt, "and all that with so much savage kindness and so great affection, that I have not experienced more cordiality among the Savages who are friendly to us." Furthermore, in appreciation, they presented his captor with several thousand porcelain beads (1652–53/1898 [Thwaites vol. 40], 139). In another case, a chief in the 1680s adopted two women to replace his deceased sisters (Lamberville, 1682/1899 [Thwaites vol. 62], 61–63).

At the end of the seventeenth century, Pierre Millet, another missionary, wrote of his own captivity. He recounted that he was taken prisoner and prepared for martyrdom, but instead was given to Chief Gannassatiron. Gannassatiron named him Otasseté, a chief who had died long before of disease and whose name harkened back to a name of one of the first founders of the Ho-De'-No-Sau-Nee nation. He was thereupon assured of his life with the words "Satonnheton Szaksi" or "My elder brother, you are resurrected." Subsequent speeches exhorted him to uphold the interests of the nation. A few days later a feast was given in his honor, during which a new name[27] was given him "as an authentic mark that the Onneiouts had adopted me and naturalized me as an Irroquois [sic]" (1691/1900 [Thwaites vol. 64], 91–93).

The general custom provided that when received into a family to take the place of a dead kinsman, the adoptee brought the deceased back to life again by taking his name and assuming his relationships and responsibilities and even a fictitious age (Perrot c. 1700–1720/1911–12, 1:85, n. 54 citing J. N. B. Hewitt), so that the family members called him, like the dead man, "father," "brother," "son," and so on. Upon adoption, the nonkin substitute was presented with a feast of incorporation, featuring corn and meat, rejoicing, and singing to entertain the guests (Quens 1655–56/1899 [Thwaites vol. 42], 193).[28] For example, a captain living at the mission of Saint Joseph wished to bring one of his relations back to life. Giving a feast for fifty guests, he stated that he believed that everyone rose again and he had no reason to bemoan the loss of his nephew the previous year. Although his death had depressed him, life that had been taken could be restored; it was but an absence. Therefore, he resurrected his nephew by adopting another who would remind him that "my nephew is not dead" (Lalemant 1647–48/1898 [Thwaites vol. 32], 211).[29] The family expected the adoptee to live up to expectations based on the person he represented. Should the adoptee or new name-holder not display the qualities of his predecessor, as when the name-holder was a poor hunter or a coward, he would be despised and ill-treated (Perrot c. 1700–1720/1911–12, 2:38n16).

In another case of adoption, Jean de Quens, a prominent Jesuit missionary and historian, related the story of two captives who were assigned to the most honorable families to take the place of two deceased members. He then told the sad story of one of the captives that I paraphrase and shorten here: The younger and handsomer of the two was given to a great warrior of the country, named Aharihon, who was famous for his warlike exploits but as arrogant and bloodthirsty as he was brave. The adoptee was to replace one of the captain's brothers who had recently been killed. Quens noted that "the cruel Captain held his brother in such high esteem that he had already made him a sacrifice of forty men,—causing them to be burned, since he did not believe that there was any one [sic] worthy to occupy his place." He gave the young man who was to be a substitute for the deceased, however, four dogs with which to hold his feast of adoption. During the feast, Ahorihon declared the young man unworthy to atone for his brother's death, and the would-be adoptee was subsequently roasted to death (1655–56/1899 [Thwaites vol. 42], 193–95). Another Jesuit missionary, Pierre Millet, though, reports that such an act was unusual

because "the Indians having Once given a person his life, It was not
their Custom to deprive him of it" (1691/1900 [Thwaites vol. 44], 95).[30]

Interestingly, the conferring of names on European colonial leaders followed the same pattern, passing sequentially to their successors
in office. Fenton wrote:

> From Arent Van Corlaer (Curler), founder of Schenectady, the Mohawks
> derived *Corlaer*, which became the title of New York governors. Since
> these officials were appointed by the Crown, the Great King beyond
> the water became *Korah*, or with the augmentative suffix—*kowa*, "the
> great King." Later among the Seneca all Indian agents were *ko:wek*.
> After Lord Francis Howard appeared in Albany in 1684 to treat with
> the Five Nations on behalf of Virginia, whose name came through
> the Dutch interpreter as "Hower," "cutlass," *Assaragowa*, "Big Knife,"
> has designated governors of the Commonwealth. . . . Governors of
> New France were *Onontio*, "great mountain," so-called from [Charles
> Huault de] Montmagny, first governor of New France, 1636–1648. (Fen-
> ton 1986, 29–30; Morgan 1851/1901, 2:240)[31]

Thereafter, the Ho-De'-No-Sau-Nee called all of New France's governors "Onontio." Likewise, each governor of Pennsylvania was referred to as Onas or "a pen" (Acrelius 1874); presidents of the United
States bore the name given first to Washington: Hanadagá:yas (also
Hanodaganears, Hanadahguyus) or Conotocarius (also Conotocau-
rius and Caunotaucarius).

But, significantly, natives shared the custom of not uttering the deceased's name between the time that a person died and the time his
name was acquired by another (Le Jeune 1634/1897 [Thwaites vol. 7],
125, 127; 1637/1898 [Thwaites vol. 11], 105). Charles A. Cooke, in an interesting article on the subject, expanded on this, writing: "To mention one's own name or that of a deceased person, was like sacrilege,
and to keep anyone from committing such irreverence, several names
besides the main one were given to the people in high standing. For
instance, a famous Huron chief and warrior in the days of Governor
[Louis de Buade, Comte de] Frontenac [in office 1672–82 and 1689–98],
in 1680, was known as Adario, Kondiaronk, Andienk, and the Rat, with

six names attached to his person" (1952, 427). If someone had to speak of a dead person, it was with circumlocution and prefaced by a word or phrase by which the unpleasant recollection of his death might be softened (Jouvency 1610–13/1896 [Thwaites vol. 1], 267). Or, the deceased was referred to by a new name. Pierre Biard explained in his "Relation" of 1611 that, for instance, the Sagamore (chief) Schoudon, being dead, was called instead "the Father" [Père]. Membertou, a tribal chief, the oldest leader of the nation, onetime native priest of the Souriquois in Acadia, and "highly renowned in warlike virtues, [was referred to] by a name agreeing with his reputation, meaning, in their language, 'the Great chief'" (Biard 1612/1896 [Thwaites vol. 2], 227; 1611–16/1897 [Thwaites vol. 3,] 91, 131, 133; Anonymous 1613–14/1896 [Thwaites vol. 2], 223, 225, 229 (for the quote); Lescarbot 1612/1896 [Thwaites vol. 2], 135).[32] In the Condolence Council (described in detail below), the deceased was not named but referred to as the "vacant . . . seat of husk matting"; the "one in whom thou didst trust for words of wisdom and comfort"; "person"; and "him in whom he fondly trusted" (Hewitt 1944, 70–71, 75). Additional details come from the 1653 account of Italian Jesuit Gioseppe Bressani, who resided in New France from 1642 to 1645. Because the use of the unqualified name of a dead person was considered an insult, the word "deceased" was added to it; or he was referred to as the "deceased" or "he who has forsaken us." And, Bressani continued,

> on this account, when any one [*sic*] has died in some village, the Captains [chiefs] promptly announce the fact in a loud voice through the street, so that he may no more be named without "the late"; and if any one have the same name as the dead, in the same village,—he changes it for some time, in order not to irritate the wound, still fresh, of the afflicted relatives. But if the name of the deceased were famous, it is never lost, but it is assumed again by the head of the family at some solemn banquet; and this person is said to have brought him to life again. This was infallibly observed in all the names of Captains, who thus never die. (Bressani 1653/1899b [Thwaites vol. 39], 31–33)

Consequently, the dead are not heard of in ordinary conversation, but "only when it is desired (as to say) to take up or to restore the deceased to life by having another assume his name" (Le Jeune 1637/1898 [Thwaites vol. 11], 105). In taking a deceased's name, the new name-holder pledged to "preserve his memory . . . [and] imitate him 'whom we cause to live again'" (Vimont, 1642–43/1898 [Thwaites vol. 22], 49–51).[33]

Names, as alluded to above, had reputations and content, established over decades, in that they harkened back to olden times and evoked memories of men of courage, prowess, responsibility, spiritual strength, and wisdom (Le Petit 1730/1900 [Thwaites vol. 68]; Richter 1983, 531).[34] They imparted status (Morgan 1851/1962, 67, 70), which varied over time. In the mid-nineteenth century, Morgan (1851/1962) reported that the sachem To-Do-Dä'-Ho of the Onondagas, was regarded as the most noble. The Ho-De'-No-Sau-Nee showed respect and deference to this title, which stemmed from the stories of the individual who first held the name at the founding—a potent ruler and known for his military feats (63). Morgan stated that to the mid-nineteenth century when he wrote his account, the name of To-Do-Dä'-Ho was the "personification of heroism, of forecast, and of dignity of character; and this title has ever been regarded as more illustrious than any other, in the catalogue of Iroquois nobility" (68).[35] To this class of chiefs he attributed special recognition as celebrated orators, wise men, and military leaders. He wrote: "In the list of those chiefs who have earned a place upon the historic page, as well as in the 'unwritten remembrance' of their tribe and race, might be enumerated many who have left behind them a reputation, which will not soon fade from the minds of men" (101).[36]

William Fenton wrote of the names that descended in the maternal family and became attached to an office that acquired special qualities. As mentioned above, many of the titles are descriptive of activities in which the original holder was found engaged when the League was formed. The titles come with "lore telling what the founders were up to when discovered by Deganawi'dah and Hiawatha" (1950, 58). For instance, the Cayuga Council name was Sotinonnawentona, meaning "the great Pipe People." Oral tradition recorded that the chief who in the first council represented the Cayugas smoked an unusual pipe, which attracted the notice of the "name-givers" (Hale 1883/1963, 77–79).

Furthermore, the titles of chiefs became synonymous with their following, just as Kazembe (the person's name and title) became one with his followers. Horatio Hale, in a chapter on "Historical Traditions," explained: "Each of the other nations [besides the Onondaga that he previously discussed] had also its peculiar name in the Council, distinct from the mere local designation by which it was commonly called. Thus the Caniengas had for their 'Council name' the term Tehadirihoken. This is the plural form of the name of their leading chief, Tekarihoken." In his notes on the Canienga Book, he wrote:

> According to the Indian custom, the speaker regards himself as representing the whole party for whom he speaks, and he addresses the leader of the other party as the representative and embodiment of all who come with him. Throughout the speeches "I" and "thou" are used in the well understood sense of "we" and "ye." In like manner, tribes and nations are, as it were, personified. A chief, speaking for Onondagas, will say I (that is, my nation) am angry; thou (the Delaware people) hast done wrong. (1883/1963, 146)

Such usages are reminiscent of the "royal we" (Krupat 2010; Kinietz 1965, 54). Perhaps for this reason, the chief was referred to as the "tongue of the country" (Le Mercier 1653–54/1899 [Thwaites vol. 41], 113).

The clan is addressed in the singular number, as one person: Sathaghyonnighson refers to "thou who art of the Wolf clan"[37] (Hale 1883/1963, 147). Among the Hurons, before 1636, worthy chiefs were called Enondecha, "the same name by which they call the Country, Nation, district,—as if a good Chief and the Country were one and the same thing" (Brébeuf 1636/1897 [Thwaites vol. 10], 231–33).[38] They held "first rank . . . in the special affairs of the Villages as well as of the whole Country, [and] are the most highly esteemed and intellectually preëminent" (Brébeuf 1636/1897 [Thwaites vol. 10], 231–33). Elsewhere, the same correspondent writes that "when they speak of a Nation, they often name only the principal Captain,—thus speaking of the Montagnets, they will say, 'Atsirond says': this is the name of one of their Captains" (Brébeuf 1636/1897 [Thwaites vol. 10], 257–59). Or, when speaking of the nation of the Bear, they will say "The Bear has said, has done so and so; the Bear is cunning, is bad; the hands of the Bear are dangerous" (Brébeuf 1636/1897 [Thwaites vol. 10], 257). Robert A. Williams, Jr. seconded these descriptions, noting that the name of a chief was the same as his village (1994, 1007).

There were numerous occasions and ways to instruct, demonstrate, and remind followers of the content of an important name or mention what had been done for the good of the village or the whole country (Brébeuf 1636/1897 [Thwaites vol. 10], 233–35). Eloquent speeches proclaimed the merits of a name. Among other nations, during the memorial service, each relation addressed the deceased with a tribute, recounting all his deeds as well as those of his forefathers, that is, all the memorable deeds associated with the individuals who had taken the title (Le Petit 1730/1900 [Thwaites vol. 68], 149; Louis Armand 1703/1970, 2:472).[39] Songs acclaimed the dead and related the heroism of the warpath (Biard 1612/1896 [Thwaites vol. 2], 15–17, 93). Thwaites mentions the Dance of War at which the Song of War told of each warrior's heroism. Each fighter sang his own version of the campaign, emphasizing his exploits and courage and those of his ancestors (Louis Armand 1703/1970, 2:424, 501; Le Petit 1730/1900 [Thwaites vol. 68], 149).[40] Linguist and ethnographer John Napoleon Britton Hewitt's (1944) relation of the Condolence Council (detailed next) shows that the ceremonial chants mentioned the forefathers ("also grandsires") who prepared the path and established or installed the League, the ancestors, and the beginning of the Commonwealth (70–77). Williams notes that "the 'barbarian's' songs, dances, and stories echoed a sacred Iroquois tradition of law and peace long predating the Encounter era" (1994, 996–97). More specifically, the Delaware people preserved a genesis myth, a migration legend, and a genealogy of chiefs in symbols for remembering the text of a chant that were burned or carved into wood and painted red (Fenton, 1950, 2). Some praise names, like "great man-slayer," allowed a listener who understood the language to learn of a person's exploits just by hearing his sobriquet (Le Petit 1730/1900 [Thwaites vol. 68], 149).[41] Finally, the gifts that a chief liberally dispensed, and the abundance of the feasts he sponsored, indicated his generosity and hospitality and enhanced his name's reputation and that of his forebears and lineage (Roth 2002; Mauss 1925/1967).

The Condolence Ceremony or Council

As among the Kazembes, the main reason to change names was to occupy a higher status by resuscitating a dead individual. Given the missionary and administrative reports that are the most abundant sources on these North American native peoples in the colonial era, the best-documented name changes and succession accounts are to the rank of sachem. Such an occasion was highly ritualized.

The performance of the ritual, called the Condolence Ceremony or Council, transformed the evil wizard in the origin stories into a good chief. It became part of peace negotiations because it helped soothe and comfort other nations who might have a grievance against the Ho-De'-No-Sau-Nee and helped overcome the sorrow for a deceased family member who had died of disease, violence, or accident. Condolence, in short, ended revenge warfare ("mourning war") that plagued the Ho-De'-No-Sau-Nee and their neighbors and soothed the sorrow over a deceased chief or a family member, thus preserving community and the state. Because the council could be staged only after the crops were harvested in late fall or in the winter for fear that the ceremony associated with death would contaminate the growing crops, it was staged as long as a year or more after the actual death of a chief (Perrot c. 1700–1720/1911–12, 1:84; R. L. Hall 1997, 35).[42] The condolence rite assured the constant commemoration of former times through the bestowal of the well-known historical names of the chiefs upon the living, who became the personification and embodiment of the historical heroes whom the name represented. As Hewitt, himself of partial Tuscarora descent, noted, among the Ho-De'-No-Sau-Nee "an office never dies; only its bearer dies. The name is one; the bearers are many" (1944, 66; Fenton 1949, 153). Because the Condolence Council followed the burial of the deceased, sometimes by several years or longer, it was indeed a "memorial service" where an investiture was the central spectacle, rather than a funeral (Hewitt 1944, 66). Failure to perform the renaming rite within a respectable interval or without observing the forms and customs of the ancestors meant risking "the ruin of the country," portending tragedy (Lalemant 1639/1898 [Thwaites vol. 17], 161, 242–43n7).[43]

Because of the central importance of these names and their transfers to the topic of this study, the inheritance of these titles and the ceremonies surrounding them will be related in a number of stages, commencing before the ceremony with the death of the present holder of the sachemship as context of the actual rite's performance.[44] The accidental or wartime death or mortal illness of a chief began the ritual plans and preparations for his resurrection. Upon the sickness of a chief, for example, his relatives removed his symbol of power, his antler headdress.[45] Hale cited from the "Book of Rites": "As soon as he is dead, even then the horns shall be taken off. For if invested with horns he should be borne into the grave, oh, my grandsires, they said, we should perhaps all perish if invested with horns he is conveyed to the grave" (1883/1963, 125). Thereafter, family members adorned his body with fine clothes and ornaments and wrapped him in a blanket. They combed his hair with grease mixed with red paint, painted his face with vermilion, and surrounded him with necklaces and beads. His weapons were laid at his side. Women and girls wept and mourned and sang doleful songs, which mentioned their relationship with the deceased. Male relatives did not weep but sang a sad song. Neighbors, according to the French commandant in the northwest Nicholas Perrot, gave presents to the family to alleviate the grief and "wipe away the tears" of the chief's relatives (c. 1700–1720/1911–12, 1:79–82). The wampum string representing the chiefly name was returned to the matron to be conferred on the subsequent holder (Snyderman 1954, 480). Official messengers carried purple strings of wampum, sometimes attached to a notched stick,[46] to notify other clans of his passing.[47]

Then, before the Condolence Council, a family assembly, under the control of the oldest and chief matron ("clan mother" [Tooker 1970, 95] or "deaconess of the title name" [J. A. Gibson et al. 1912/1992, 677] or "chief maker" [Fenton 1975, 141] or chief's sister) of the deceased chief's kindred, a mother if she survived him, convened to select a successor who had the same virtues and characteristics as the deceased to the

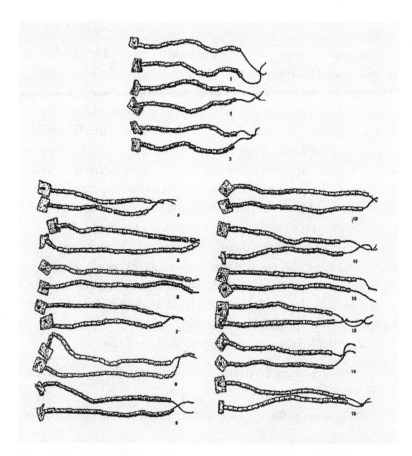

Fig. 9. Wampum strings for wiping tears. The drawings are of models restrung by J. N. B. Hewitt, with beads and information he collected about 1926–29. Published in Elisabeth Tooker, "The League of the Iroquois: Its History, Politics, and Ritual," in *Handbook of North American Indians*, ed. William C. Sturtevant, vol. 15, *Northeast*, ed. Bruce G. Trigger, Fig. 12, p. 439. Copyright Smithsonian Institution, Washington DC, 1978. Used by permission.

extent that such an individual could be found. Williams notes that the clan women "owned the chief's name and title" (1994, 1000). The one selected was normally not a son, but "properly their nephews [on his sister's side] and grandsons" of the same tribe and clan (Brébeuf 1636/1897 [Thwaites vol. 10], 233; Le Jeune 1640–41/1898 [Thwaites vol. 20], 215; Tooker 1970, 93).[48] The ideal candidate would have a great number of allies and connections, be a skilled hunter and brave warrior, be a talented manager, and be patient, generous and hospitable (Biard 1616/1897 [Thwaites vol. 3], 101; Richter 1983, 530; Brébeuf 1636/1897 [Thwaites vol. 10],181; Williams 1994, 1010). For example, Le Mercier (1668–69/1899 [Thwaites vol. 52]) wrote that women chose Nejaska-ouat, a Tadoussac war captain, to take Tekouerimat's (also Teycorimat) name before the Condolence Council began (223–24, 227).[49] The chosen individual could refuse the name: "Sometimes because they have not aptitude in speaking, or sufficient discretion or patience, sometimes because they like a quiet life; for these positions are servitudes more than anything else" (Brébeuf 1636/1897 [Thwaites vol. 10], 233). Once the selection was approved by a clan and nation, an appointed place of meeting chosen, and summons of purple beads sent out for the resuscitation of the new chief who would "lift up the horns" of the deceased predecessor, others (the condolers) came to grieve, while a great feast was cooked (Converse 1895, 347).

Fenton divided the council proper into five rituals:

1. Journeying on the Trail, sometimes called the Eulogy or Roll Call of the Founders of the League

2. Welcome at the Wood's Edge (the Deyuhuyonkwarakda ceremony)

3. Re-quickening

4. Six Songs of Farewell

5. Over the Great Forest (1883/1963, xxiii–xxiv; see also Fenton 1946; Hewitt 1944; Speck 1949)

The performance of the highly choreographed and scripted council held after the death of a chief consoled for loss, but more importantly reclaimed the name, and, in so doing, retrieved and recaptured the past, reviving it and reembodying it in the present to project it into the future. It thus presented the past as living history. The requickening component became a means to pass on power or mystic potency from one individual to another, thus perpetuating the legitimate governing apparatus of the Confederation. In the process, the ceremony reiterated the historical content of the name of the chief (Vecsey 1986, 82–94), validated his authority, and restored the governing circle of sachems. Once a name was bestowed on a successor, it could not be changed unless the chief was deposed ("dehorned") or died.[50]

The mourning ritual,[51] called "On the Journey" (after the chant that was sung as the condolers approach the mourners), "Journeying on the Trail," the Eulogy, or "the Roll Call of the Chiefs or Founders of the League" (Gibson et al. 1912/1992, xxxiii, xxxvi; Hewitt 1944, 69; Fenton 1988, 193–94), began with the "clear-minded" journey to meet the mourning hosts, and the condolers being conducted or "led by the hand"[52] to a fire at the border of the town that might also be the edge of the forest. There the hosts, happy that the condolers had escaped the dangers of the forest,[53] chanted a song that "enumerates the hereditary titles, indicating the way in which the titles are arranged into groups according to the moiety, tribal, and committee affiliations that structure relationships among the chiefs in the confederacy Council." Hewitt reminds readers that the words of the chants as well as the rituals of condolence and installation contained mystic power (or *orenda*),[54] which preserved the natives' political integrity and welfare (Hewitt 1944, 66). At the fire, the hosting mourners lighted a pipe and passed it around, while welcoming the visitors with speeches that recognized the pain and sorrow that had brought the condolers, and recalled the ancestors' charge to perform a Condolence Council when a chief died (J. A. Gibson et al. 1912/1992, xxxvi, xxxviii; Hale 1883/1963, 49; Snyderman 1961, 571; Pomedli 1995, 320; Hewitt 1944; Williams 1994, 998).

A distinguished orator of the mourning nations conducted the ceremony. The lamentations followed a prescribed routine. Each topic of condolence was indicated by a string of wampum, whose bead sequence helped the recall of the officiating chief. The orator then recited the words that were meant to restore normality and help integrate society. The restorative episode was accomplished by reciting three of fifteen "burdens"[55] or matters, each of which was accompanied by a wampum string. The three burdens or matters delivered at the fire dealt with the eyes, ears, and throat. In the process, to paraphrase Hale (1883, 60), the orator wiped away the mourners' tears so they could see clearly, opened their ears so they could hear readily, and removed

from their throats the obstruction with which their grief was chok-
ing them, so that they could ease their burdened minds by speaking
freely to their friends.

The ritual is a reciprocal one, wrote J. A. Gibson et al.: "The condolers [also known as the 'clear-minded'] perform it for the mourners and
the mourners do the same for the condolers. Such reciprocity underscores the fact that the loss of a chief is suffered by society as a whole
and not solely by the moiety of the deceased chief" (1912/1992, xl).[56]

The requickening ritual prescribed that guides lead the visiting condolers to the mourners' lodge of assembly or longhouse, with a principal speaker or singer holding a mnemonic cane[57] (see fig. 10) inscribed
with symbols, recalling the hereditary names of and events associated with their ancient chiefs (Beauchamp 1895b, 315; J. A. Gibson et al.
1912/1992, xxxvi, 684; Hewitt 1944, 69).[58] The symbols in figure 10 are
the same as those found on the cane discussed by Fenton (Shimony
1994, 103). W. M. Beauchamp mentions a chant before the approach-
ing party is led into the council house, noting: "For one hundred and
fifty years we have explicit mention of this song, by white men who
heard it, as containing the names of the renowned ancestors of the
later Iroquois. It is little more than a mere repetition of the names of
the chiefs who formed the confederacy, with general words of praise
and mourning, and occasional personal peculiarities. This one helped
to form the Great League; that one did the same; they were brothers
or cousins" (1895b, 315–16).

Fenton reiterated this, writing that "they recount the titles, positions, relationship, and accomplishments of the fifty founders" (1949,
145). Once at the longhouse, the Mohawks (Caniengas [Beauchamp
1895b, 313; Williams 1994, 1004, 1009]), Onondagas, and Senecas, the
elder nations or Brothers, sat on one side, while the Oneidas and the
Cayugas and eventually the Tuscaroras (and the Tutelos, Nanticokes,
and Delawares), the Younger Brothers, occupied the other (Hewitt
1944, 68, 81). If the deceased chief belonged to the elder nations, the
condoling ceremony was performed by the younger nations, who
mourned for him as for a father or an uncle; and, vice versa, lament-
ing him as a son or a nephew. There the rest of the addresses and songs

("burdens")[59] followed, with wampum accompanying them as attesting tokens (Pomedli 1995, 324; Fenton 1949, 148). Each burden dealt with an injury to life (e.g., bloody sitting mats that could be cleaned so that the mourners would not be reminded of their loss, and, therefore, might regain their peace of mind and their cheerfulness) in a tender and affectionate tone. Its cure was by virtue of the spiritual strength or magic power believed to be inherent in the rites.[60]

Michael M. Pomedli, in a 1995 article based on Hewitt, described the sequence of the ceremony and "its distinctive name" derived from its symbolic power and its function of restoring life or requickening. Through prescribing acts and set forms or words, the dead chief is resuscitated, "raised up," and installed and in a way reincarnated in the person of the appropriately chosen clansman who will bear the same official name and live in place of the dead lawgiver (325; Hewitt 1944, 66; J. A. Gibson et al. 1912/1992, 683; Morgan 1851/1962, 63–64).The custom of requickening the living in the name of the dead filled empty niches in the social system and restored society to working order (Fenton 1975, 143).The term "requickening" also applied to the power to heal the sorely wounded body and soothe the grief-stricken mind of a sorrowing cousin-phratry of tribes. Meanwhile, the name-taking candidate was dressed in fine and rich clothes with a collar of porcelain beads around his neck. A calumet (pipe) and tobacco were presented to him (Vimont 1644–45/1898 [Thwaites vol. 26], 157; Hewitt 1944, 68–69).[61]

A sequence of songs then bade farewell to the dead chief and called on the founding chiefs to inform all that after careful consideration the survivors were ready to replace the deceased leader (J. A. Gibson et al. 1912/1992, xlv-xlvi). The songs alluded to the charter of the Confederation, the relationships among the chiefs in the Confederation Council, and the rules that pertained to the continuity of their political institutions. In the performances, the founding ancestors were directly addressed more frequently than any other category of persons (J. A. Gibson et al. 1912/1992, xlvi). The host then announced, according to Barthelemy Vimont, a French Jesuit missionary, that "we are here to resuscitate a dead man, and to bring a great Captain back to

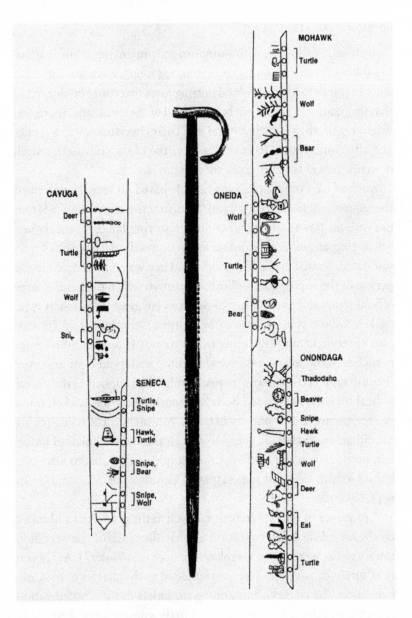

Fig. 10. Symbols on a condolence cane. The Andrew Spragg Condolence Cane. Cranbrook Institute of Science and Elisabeth Tooker, "The League of the Iroquois: Its History, Politics, and Ritual," in *Handbook of North American Indians*, ed. William C. Sturtevant, vol. 15, *Northeast*, ed. Bruce G. Trigger, Fig. 5, p. 427. © Smithsonian Institution, Washington DC, 1978. Used by permission.

life" (1643–44/1898 [Thwaites vol. 26], 157; J. A. Gibson et al. 1912/1992, 693–96). One version reads as follows:

> They will raise him up in front of the chiefs, who will call him by the name of the dead chief when they stand up the other one. . . . Now show us our new colleague! . . . Thereupon, they will call him, the appointed one, they will stand him up there in front of them, and the speaker will say "Now you two, look this way; in front of you is the one they have appointed—they and the deaconess of the titles of their clan—where a seat has become vacant, where their former chief sat. Moreover, as to this one standing in front of you, they crowned him with antlers, and he is the one they will rename with the title of the deceased chief."

The host then mentioned the deceased, and all his posterity; and related the place and manner of his death. The address ended with the words: "I have finished; now point me the man" or to paraphrase, "Now show me the warrior who is to be the new chief" (Hale 1883/1963, 61).

At this point the mourners, led by the matron, presented their choice of a successor (Fenton 1949, 149). The candidate who was to take the place and name of the deceased then stepped forward. Two chiefs grasped his arms and marched him to and fro in the council house while proclaiming his new name and office and chanting the duties to which he was then called. The audience assented at each pause. Then, for example, in one council, the speaker turned toward him who was to succeed, raised his voice, and said:

> There he is, he who is clothed with that fine robe. It is no longer he whom you lately saw, and whose name was Nehap. He has given his name to another savage. His name is Etouait (that was the name of the deceased). Look upon him as the true Captain of this tribe. It is he whom you must obey; it is he to whom you must listen, and whom you must honor. (Vimont 1643–44/1898 [Thwaites vol. 26], 157; Hale 1883/1963, 61; J. A. Gibson et al. 1912/1992, xlix, 693–95 [on "raising up"])

Thus the new leader ritually dies and is reborn into a new category, with a new name and new clothing. He becomes a different person with corresponding new responsibilities.

Finally, the condolers confirmed the choice with, according to Hale, instructions to the chief (J. A. Gibson et al. 1912/1992, xlix). John Arthur Gibson—a Seneca chief[62] who took the name Kanyadariyo, was an acknowledged native authority on Ho-De'-No-Sau-Nee tradition, and was invited to recite whenever chiefs were installed and given the names of the founders of the Confederation—published this "Charge to the chief" (Hale 1895, 51). He counseled the new chief to develop a skin "seven inches thick, which means that your mind will be strong and it will not let pass through, a pointed object meant to puncture you when you work for the Good Message, the Power, the Peace, and the Great Law" (J. A. Gibson et al.1912/1992, 698). He instructed him to protect his family and the various nations, to be evenhanded with all of the people (699), to think of others before thinking of himself, and to be, above all, devoted to the ongoing survival of the Confederation (Fenton 1949, 149). The speaker bade the people obey their new chief, and he reminded the other chiefs to be of one mind with the new one who had stood up, cooperating in his work of the Great Law (J. A. Gibson et al. 1912/1992, 698–701). The actual act consisted of the chiefs of the condoling moiety receiving the wampum string associated with the new chief's title, and by taking hold of the string as it made the rounds, each chief indicated his approval of the candidate. This, wrote Gibson, was the part where the chiefs might ask the candidate questions about his qualifications.

When the chief was seated, the *karenna*, a chant, of the Condoling Council was sung.[63] Each line came to mind with a string of wampum. The first saluted the Peace of the League and the blessings they enjoyed; the second greeted the kindred of the deceased; the third addressed warriors or men; the fourth saluted women; the fifth invoked the laws that the forefathers had established; and the sixth invited the audience to hear the wisdom of the forefathers (Hale 1883/1963, 61–64). The chiefs of Hale's day believed that the chant was composed by Dekenawidah or Hiawatha; it preceded the repetition of the ancient laws of the Confederation. The speakers mentioned the wisdom of their forefathers (their grandsires) and remembered the founders. It was, in short, an expression of reverence for the laws, for the dead, and for their history (Hale 1883/1963, 64).

The officiating orator then recited the rules that the people lived by. The first law prescribed that when a chief died, his office would not perish with him; his antlers would be taken off and transferred to his successor. The notion that "'the chief dies but the office survives'—the regular transmission of rank, title, and authority, by a method partly hereditary and partly elective—was the principle on which the life and strength of the Iroquois constitution depended" (Hale 1883/1963, 67–68). The second law proscribed wars as a result of murder (68–69). The third sanctioned the lavish mortuary customs and the feast of the dead to honor the person who had passed (70–72).

After the declaration of the laws of the League, the speaker recited all the names of the chiefs of the League to whom the united nations were indebted for their peace, followed by lamentation. In a closing litany he chanted a commemoration of the fifty chiefs who had composed the first council and whose names had remained as the official titles of their successors[64] (Hale 1883/1963, 75, 79–80). In short, it reminded those present to revere the laws and to remember the dead (Hale 1883/1963, ch. 5). At this point also,

> the wampum belts, which comprise the historical records of the federation, were produced and the officiating chief proceeded to explain them, one by one, to the assemblage. This is called "reading the archives." In this way, knowledge of the events signified by the wampum was fastened, by repeated iteration, in the minds of the listeners. Those who doubt whether events which occurred four centuries ago can be remembered as clearly and minutely as they are now recited will probably have their doubts removed when they consider the necessary operation of this custom. The orator's narrative is repeated in the presence of many auditors who have often heard it before, and who would be prompt to remark and to correct any departure from the well-known history. (61–62; Converse 1895, 343)[65]

The host then continued the discourse, briefly addressing the principal men of the various assembled lineages and showing them the presents that were intended for them. He named the captains one after the other, saying (in the case of the chief Etouait): "So and so, that

collar of porcelain beads will tell your tribe that there is a Captain in
Tadoussac, and that Etouait has come back to life." To another he said
that "this present, intended for you, will proclaim in your country the
fact that we have a Chief, and that death has not utterly destroyed the
name of Etouait" (Vimont 1643–44/1898 [Thwaites vol. 26],159). Then
another steward presented the gifts, which signified and marked the
occasion for future recall. The generosity of the gifts was meant to
awe the receivers and indicate that the chief was a good provider and
a hospitable host, thus enhancing the reputation of the chief and his
kindred (Roth 2002; Mauss 1925/1967).

Then the speaker stated: "Let us rejoice; our Captain's first act is
to invite us all to a feast." They concluded with songs and said a few
words lauding the chief who had been brought back to life, saying,
"Let us take courage; this brave man will save the country," or that
"his liberality will banish poverty" and cause his followers to live long
lives, or that this brave captain would teach them to overcome their
enemies (Vimont 1643–44/1898 [Thwaites vol. 26], 159). Only then did
the new chief address the gathering, hoping to emulate the qualities
of bravery and wisdom of Etouait (the deceased) and finally opening
the feast (Vimont 1643–44/1898 [Thwaites vol. 26], 161).

Afterward, the new chief gave presents to some of the leading men
of the tribe and some poor widows as a sign of his beneficence and
hospitality (Vimont 1643–44/1898 [Thwaites vol. 26], 163). Le Jeune's
"Relation" of 1636/1897 indicated that resuscitation was not complete
until "he who has passed away has been raised from the dead,—that
is, when his name has been given to another, and presents have been
offered to his relatives,—then it is said that the body is 'cached,' or
rather, that the dead is resuscitated" (1636/1897 [Thwaites vol.10], 277).
The ceremony marked the memory of such illustrious, valorous, and
esteemed men, which lived again in others and thus memorialized
the name and its legacy, simultaneously instructing the audience. The
ceremony involved standing persons

> placing their hands low down, feign[ing] to raise him from the
> ground,—meaning by this that they draw out of the tomb that eminent

deceased personage, and bring him back to life in the person of this other man. The latter stands up, and, after loud acclamations from the people, he receives the gifts offered by those who were present, who repeat their congratulations with many feasts, and thenceforth regard him as if he were the deceased person whom he represents. Thus, the memory of good persons, and of worthy and valorous captains, never dies among them. (R. L. Hall 1997, 35, citing Sagard 1632/1865, 209–10)

Paul Ragueneau wrote in 1646 that on such ceremonial occasions as the Condolence Council, "They are accustomed . . . to relate the stories which they have learned regarding their ancestors, even those most remote,—so that the young people, who are present and hear them, may preserve the memory thereof, and relate them in their turn, when they shall have become old. They do this in order thus to transmit to posterity the history and the annals of the country,— striving, by this means, to supply the lack of writing and of books, which they have not" (1645–46/1898 [Thwaites vol. 30], 61).[66] The totality of the council marked the newly named chief's acceptance into the Great Council of the League.

Morgan provided an example. Upon the demise of the Seneca sachem, who held the name Gä-Ne-O-Di'-Yo, a successor was "raised up" from the Turtle Tribe, in which the sachemship was hereditary, and after the ceremony of investiture the person was known among the Ho-De'-No-Sau-Nee only under the name of Gä-Ne-O-Di'-Yo. These fifty titles, excepting two, had been held by as many sachems, in succession, as generations had passed since the formation of the League (Morgan 1851/1962, 63–66).

Thus, all these chiefly names had become hereditary titles that had been borne by a line of individuals (Beauchamp 1895b, 313). To illustrate, in the mid-seventeenth century Joseph Oumosotiocouchie, or La Grenouille (the frog), embodied a name that had already been held by several captains of his nation and "had been given to him in order to make them live again" (Lalemant 1647/1898 [Thwaites vol. 31], 261). A few years from then in the late 1670s, the noted chief of the Onandagas, Teganissoren, took the name of his deceased grandfather,

Niregouentaron (Thwaites 1681–83/1899 [Thwaites vol. 62], 273). Another case is that of the name Atironta, the name of the first Huron captain who met the French. The subsequent holder of the name in 1640–41 still held his "charge and power" (Lalemant 1640/1898 [Thwaites vol. 20], 35). The chief named Otasseté, alive at the end of the seventeenth century, occupied the name of one of the first founders of the Ho-De'-No-Sau-Nee nation (Millet 1691/1900 [Thwaites vol. 44], 91).[67] Other names that continued to be taken were Thadodaho (an Onondaga chief), held from founding until at least 1745, and Dega'enyon, a Cayuga sachem, with references from c. 1691 to 1794 (Fenton 1986, 36–37).

Sequential Name-Taking

In sum, the naming conventions of preliterate people played a major role in retelling, maintaining, and perpetuating their origin stories. In the native North American case reviewed in this chapter, in ascending up the ranks of society by taking higher-ranking deceased individuals' names, the living participated in recreating the founding lore of their families, lineages, tribes, and nations, and, ultimately, in the case of the Ho-De'-No-Sau-Nee, in personifying a chief, thus repopulating and reinventing the Confederation. This direct personal link, generation after generation, to their origins refortified the power and recaptured the legitimacy of their governing institutions, and, to the extent that there was fissuring and ethnogenesis as the population recovered from its demographic collapse after European contact, established perpetual kinship ties that further reinforced and fortified unity. Sequential name-taking impersonated the founders and reincarnated the past in the present, giving rise to a living history that participants could see and no one could deny. Similar to African customs where oral king lists were repeated every time a lineage nominated a new incumbent to a title (J. C. Miller 1979, 85), the Condolence Council allowed the living to represent the first council: all fifty named chiefs were named and present. They were reminded of their rights and duties and the laws were reviewed. The ceremony, wrote Fenton, "rehearses and reinforces the code of the ancients" (1986, 25). In fact, the scenario presented the dead as if alive in the present and able and willing to lead into the future.

| Chapter Four

The Making of Andean Ancestral Traditions

Thousands of miles away and across an ocean from the Central African Kazembes, and a similar distance south of the North American Ho-De'-No-Sau-Nee, Andean peoples used positional inheritance to recollect their heroic past and focus their thoughts on their ancestors. That forms the context of a long confrontation between two Spaniards and their successors over the right to enjoy the labor and tribute of a group of fishermen on the coast of what is today Peru. The Iberian practice of indirect rule, where the Spanish relied on native lords to organize labor drafts and collect the tribute goods, meant that, with less quotidian contact in some zones, colonial authorities and, to a lesser extent, the first European settlers did not recognize nor understand positional inheritance for over three decades from initial contact. Such ethnographic ignorance, born of poor communication with native people who spoke a multitude of languages other than Spanish, Portuguese, or French, which might have been more easily understood by the Castilians, led to the tense courtroom confrontations over the jurisdiction over a group of fisherfolk. The evidentiary titles to native labor (*encomienda* grants) did not clear up the confusion. But scores of witnesses—many of them natives or local overseers who had worked among them for years—eventually revealed in their testimonies the indigenous custom of taking a different name when one ascended to a new status. This proved the key to dispelling the misunderstandings and solving the legal conundrum.

In this chapter, I will first review the court case over the fishermen under the control of a native lord, called Jayanque, and, in the 1560s, answering to his baptized successors, all called Don Francisco. I will then discuss the evidence that the Inca rulers also practiced positional succession.

Jayanque and the Don Franciscos

An indication that positional inheritance and perpetual kinship were operative in the Andes comes from the coastal *curacazgo* (chiefdomship) of Jayanque (now Jayanca) in the sixteenth century. Jayanque ruled as a paramount chief, most of whose farming subjects lived scattered about a river valley situated between the Spanish colonial cities of Piura and Trujillo. Another two hundred or so families lived in the highlands immediately inland from the main group. Some of these may have been engaged in mining silver and panning for or bartering for gold. Another smaller group of fisherfolk lived on the seacoast. The large number of the paramount lord's followers (at least four thousand families in 1540) made the polity prosperous and the *curaca* (chief or paramount lord) a major personage (Gama 1540/1974, 227).

Following the 1532 Spanish invasion, Francisco Pizarro granted the native population to meritorious Spaniards who had served the king in trust or encomienda, where the natives worked for the trustee (the encomendero) in return for protection and religious instruction. In 1534, don Diego de Almagro, Pizarro's captain, gave the Spaniard Rui Barba the people under the paramount lord Jayanque (later Jayanca). Two years later, as shown in tables 4 and 5, Pizarro further divided the natives between Francisco Lobo (who received the curaca and four *principales* [lesser lords, defined further below]) and Miguel Saucedo (who received the *segunda persona* [the second-in-command] and six principales), giving rise to the encomienda of Pácora. The halving of the population gave rise to long-lasting disputes between encomenderos Lobo and Saucedo and their successors over the jurisdiction over some of the principales and their people (most importantly over the fishermen under the stewardship of a native lord called Minimis-al), irrigation rights, tribute, and labor (Powers 1998; ANP/DI, l. 1, c. 7, 1566; DI, l. 3. c. 19, 1574; l. 31, c. 622, 1597; BNP/AI42, 1574; A371, 1594; A379, 1596; ART/CoO, l. 154, exp. 223, 15-III-1585; CoPedimento, l. 280, exp. 3634, 20-VIII-1592; ANB/EC 1588, no. 5; EC 1589, c. 1, e. 1; BMH/AII6, 1594).

Table 4. Encomenderos of Jayanca

Date	Encomendero(s)	Grant of	Notes	Source
1534	Capitan Rui Barba	Diego de Almagro	He gave his encomienda up	AGI/J418, 114, 119, 126v
April 2, 1536	Francisco Lobo*	Francisco Pizarro	Died c. 1553	AGI/J418, 62v, 237–37v, 337v
1553	Francisco Lobo	La Gasca	Confirmed	AGI/J418, 114v, 124, 447v
	Doña Isabel Palomino		Daughter of Lobo	AGI/J418, 50, 52v
c. 1555	Alonso Carrasco** y Doña Isabel Palomino	Marquéz de Cañete		AGI/J418, 2, 308v–9, 354v; Gama 1540/1975, 260

* Nuñez Vela gave the encomienda to Juan Delgadillo "because Lobo was a follower of Juan Pizarro." Later he was pardoned and the encomienda was returned to Lobo.

** Alonso Carrasco was probably in charge as early as 1544.

Table 5. Encomenderos of Pácora

Date	Encomendero	Grant of	Notes	Sources
1534	Juan de Porras	Pizarro/ Almagro	Pizarro took the encomienda from Porras or Porras gave it up	AGI/J418, 1573, 119, 126v, 142
April 2, 1536	Miguel de Saucedo	Marquéz Pizarro	He gave the natives up because they were so few or because they would not serve	AGI/J418, 1573,2v, 53, 61v–62, 114v, 177, 202v, 205
1537 (?), <1540	Diego Gutíerrez	Pizarro		AGI/J418, 1573, 122, 133, 165, 173, 202v
July 11, 1540	Doña María Gutíerrez			AGI/J418, 1573, 2, 115, 130–30v
	Doña María Gutíerrez, Luis del Canto			AGI/J418, 1573, 2v, 115, 184
May 15, 1566	Alonzo Pizarro de la Rua	Licenciado Lope García de Castro		AGI/J418, 1573, 2v, 13, 17–18; AGI/ J457, 993
May 24, 1566			Possession	AGI/J418, 1573, 26v–27, 115v
February 28, 1570			Confirmed	AGI/J418, 1573, 133v–34, 201v; Gama 1540/1975, 260

Records of these disputes show that the people of the valley and cu-racazgo of Jayanca were ruled by a ranked hierarchy of leaders from the times of the Incas or Cuzcos, as they were initially known, and more specifically from the age of Guayna Capac, the last native em-peror to have ruled the Andean peoples who occupied present-day southern Colombia south to Chile and inland to Bolivia and north-western Argentina before the Spanish invasion (map 3). Five levels of rulers are identified in the long court cases between the encomende-ros, which contain information and testimony from as early as 1539–73. The native administrative levels include:

The curaca, *cacique principal*, or *señor* (paramount lord or chief)

The *segunda persona* (literally, second-in-command) or *conoseque* (a Mochica-language term for "lord" [*seque, çique*] of a thousand [*cono*] households)

The *principales* (lesser lords, sometimes used generically as a catch-all category for any noble leader below the previous two)

The *mandones* (lesser lords, below the status of the principales)

The *mandoncillos* (literally, little overseers, below the mandones in rank) (AGI/J418, 1573, 212v, 217–18, 221v, 258, 311v, 313v, 314v, 320–21, 331, 333, 334, 375, 465v)

Cieza de León describes the person of the curaca principal, Jay-anque in 1539, in the 1540s:

> Los señores naturales destos valles [writing as he traveled through the Valley of Jayanca] fueron estimados y acatados por sus súbditos: to-dauía lo son los que han quedado: y andan acompañados y muy seru-idos de mugeres y criados. Y tienen sus porteros y guardas. (AGI/J418, 1573, 270v, 459; Cieza de León 1548–50/1984, xxv, 205).

> The natural lords of these valleys were respected and venerated by their subjects: those who remain still are treated in this way: and they go along accompanied and well served by women and servants. And they have their own porters and guards.

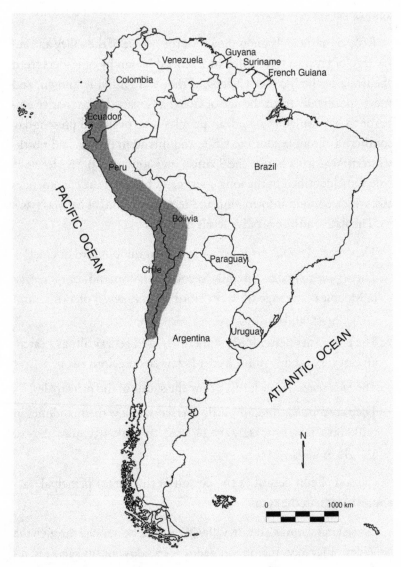

Map 3. The Inca Empire. Cartography by Dianah O. Siles.

Melchior de Morin, a forty-five-year-old local merchant who had lived in the area since c.1550, testified in 1570 that the curaca principal was the "direct descendant" (*por linia rreta*) of the founder of the polity. If the same organizing principles obtained among the Jayancas as among the populations of the central sierra and elsewhere, a direct bloodline (not necessarily through the male line) from the apical ancestor was considered one mark of a legitimate ruler. Natives differentiated between principales and mandones, saying that the former gave orders "sin ser subjeto a otro prençipal ninguno" (without being subject to any other principal) while the latter were subjects of other principales. Mandoncillos "mandan a los yndios comunes" (command the common Indians) and were themselves subject to the mandones and principales.[1]

Before 1532 all the approximately thirty principales (the word is certainly used in a generic sense here) served the curaca principal. Gaspar de Morin, born c. 1523 in the villa of Puente de Luna in Portugal and an inhabitant of the city of Trujillo, testified in the city of Piura in 1563 that he had managed the affairs (*haciendas*) of Diego Gutierrez, the encomendero of the repartimiento of Pácora, for five or six years in the early 1550s. He recalled

> que oyo des[ir] al caçique de tucume y al de pacora e a otros y[ndi]os e prençipales que en t[ien]po del ynga [<1532] e hasta que se hizo el d[ic] ho rrepartim[ien]to por el d[ic]ho marques fran[cis]co picarro [1536] que todos los yn[di]os e prençipales encomendados en el d[ic]ho diego gutierrez[2] auia sido subjetos al caçique de jayanca. (AGI/J418, 1573, 314v, 316, 320–21v, 333)

> that he heard the chiefs of Tucume and Pacora and other [common] Indians and principales say that in the time of the Incas [<1532] and until the distribution (repartimiento) [of encomiendas] was made by said Marquez Francisco Picarro [in 1536], all the Indians and principales entrusted to Diego Gutierrez had been subjects of the chieftain (cacique) of Jayanca.

They served the curaca by tilling a piece of ground for him or, in the case of the fishermen, supplying him, his family, and retinue with seafood. This latter information was seconded by the testimony of the encomendero Francisco Lobo who, in 1541, remarked that the lord of the fishermen, known as Minimisal, served the cacique principal of the people of Jayanca, sustaining him with many types of ocean fare. The farmers, such as those of the *parcialidad* or lineage of Neptur, tilled a piece of land for the curaca. This act proved, according to the Spanish witness Alonso de Fuentes, that Neptur was the curaca's subject.

En todos los prençipalazgos daua en aquel t[iem]po vna suerte de tierra al caçique prençipal e que el d[ic]ho neptur tenya senalado vn pedaço de tierra al caçique de jayanca como a su senor e q[ue] este testigo de presente auisto que en la parçialidad del d[ic]ho neptur el d[ic]ho don fran[cis]co caçique de jayanca posehe vn pedaço de tierra que haze senbrar por lo qual crehe e tiene por çierto este testigo que el d[ic]ho naptur [*sic*] hera subjeto al caçique prençipal de jayanca como el d[ic]ho caçique lo a d[ic]ho a este testigo. (AGI/J418, 1573, 229v, 311v–12, 313v, 334)

All the principalities at that time gave a plot of land to the paramount chief and the said Neptur had indicated a piece of land for the paramount chief of Jayanca as his lord, and that this present witness has seen that in the parcialidad of said Neptur the said Don Francisco cacique of Jayanca possesses a piece of land that he has sown for which [reason] this witness believes and accepts as certain that the said Naptur [*sic*] was subject to the paramount lord of Jayanca as the paramount cacique has told this witness.

Reading and reconstructing the sequence of events from the protracted court cases over water rights and the jurisdiction over the fishermen, Lord Minimisal, and his people is difficult. The testimony clearly indicates that natives, both commoners and lords, on the North Coast and elsewhere, took on more than one name at a time during a lifetime and some of these names signified positions and were not unique to one individual.

Felipe Guaman Poma de Ayala, a bilingual (*ladino*), educated native, recalled how Andeans and their ancestors

se hizieron grandes capitanes y ualerosos prinzepes de puro uallente[.] dizen q[ue] ellos se tornauan en la batalla leones y tigres y sorras y buitres gabilanes y gatos de monte. y anci sus desendientes hasta oy se llaman.poma. otorongo. ator. condor. anca. usco.. y biento acapana. paxaro uayanay. colebra machac uay serpiente amaro. y aci se llamaron

deotros animales sus nombre[s] y armas q[ue] trayya sus antepasados
los ganaron en la batalla q[ue] ellos tubieron[.] el mas estimado nombre de s[eñ]or fue poma. guaman. anca. condor. acapana. guayanay.
curi. cullque como parese hasta oy.

became great captains and valiant princes from pure courage[.] They
say that they became during a battle lions and tigers and foxes and vul-
tures, hawks, and mountain cats. And so their descendants until today call themselves Lion, Jaguar, Fox, Condor, Hawk, Mountain Lion,
and Wind *Acapana* [a cloud formation, especially at dusk, or origin
of a desired thing, omen, prediction, or announcement], Bird Parrot,
Snake, *Machacuay* [?], Serpent Snake, and so they called themselves by
other animal names and the arms they carried were those that their
ancestors won in battles that they fought[.] The most esteemed name
of a gentleman was Lion, Hawk, Hawk, Condor, Cloud Formation
[*Acapana*], Parrot, Gold, Silver as is still used today. (Guaman Poma
de Ayala, 1613/1936, 65)

Betanzos (1551–57/1987) reminds us that men who vanquished an enemy could take his name (113). Gentile writes of Uturungo Achache,
a name he took after killing a *yaguareté* (*pantera onça*), the largest fe-
line of the jungle and a purported ancestor of native groups who lived
there (Betanzos 1551–57/1987, 155).

Furthermore, the practice of changing names in life continued.
Don Diego, a self-denominated and self-promoting "cacique" (in actu-
ality a principal) of the parcialidad of Sontubilico, was also known by
the name of Xeco in 1570. Elizabeth Hart (1983) found lords with more
than one name among the native leaders of the curacazgo of Saña. In
1542 one principal was known as Ponoa and by another name, Ach-
achea, or, occasionally, Principal Ponoachachea.[3] In another case, a
lord of Jayanca appeared as don Pedro Chipporef in one citation and
don Pedro Falquen in another. Hart supposed that in this case one
name was a personal one and the other the designation of the parcialidad under his control. Elsewhere, a native of Mansiche named
Alonso Guacrasiman was also called Chinga[u]nam. A few years later and farther inland, don Alonso Caruatongo also used the name

Chuplingon as the cacique principal of the "province"⁴ of Cajamarca (also Cajamalca). Yet another example comes from a notarial document from 1579 in which Diego Limo, in jail at the time, identified himself to authorities also as don Diego Allaucan (ANP/Notariales, Protocolo de Alonso de la Cueva and Blas Hernandez, no. 29, 170–71v). Documents from the mid-seventeenth century still identified natives who admitted to or were identified as having two names. For example, Domingo Nuna Calla was known "por mal nombre sayco" (by his [literally] bad name [or nickname] Sayco).⁵ Furthermore, in certain ceremonial contexts, the authorities not only took the name of the founding ancestor but also embodied his animating force (*kamaq*) and spirit (Medinaceli and Arze 1996, 305). In so doing "se convierte en 'otro'" (he becomes another) and is rendered a sacred being (Rivière 1995b, 13, 15), the essence of positional inheritance.

The principal Mynynimysal, the main object of the litigation between the encomenderos Alonso Carrasco and Luis Canto in 1563, had a second name: "As another name he is known as *enequisquelel*" ("Por otro nombre se llama enequisquelel") (also written as *ynequisiqueal*, *ene qui si quil* [in 1557], *ynyquisiquil*, *enyquiciquil*, and *en niqui si quel*). Witnesses explained that men discarded the name or names of their youth when they succeeded to the named position of a predecessor. Alonso de Fuentes, a partisan of Alonso Carrasco, declared in 1563:

> a oydo dezir este testigo del d[ic]ho tienpo a esta parte al caçique prençipal del d[ic]ho rrepartimiento de Jayanca que llaman don fran[cis]co que el prençipal q[ue] mandaua la parçialidad de mynimysal en t[iem] po que tomo la posesion el d[ic]ho fran[cis]co lobo [April 2, 1536] se llamaua yniquisiquil e que la parçialidad e tierras⁶ donde el d[ic]ho yniquisiquil hera señor se llama mynimisal e por este nombre . . . se llama y nonbre aquel señor de y[ndi]os[,] que en este t[ien]po . . . este testigo tiene notiçia del d[ic]ho rrepartimi[ent]o e uisto por uista de ojos que tres señores que a conoçido en el d[ic]ho prençipalasgo de mynymissal que an subchedido por muerte vnos a otros se d[ec]ia que heredan el d[ic]ho senorio les llaman minimisal avnque tengan nombres propios como don hernando que se llamauan los dos dellos.

This witness has heard that from that time until now, from the paramount cacique of the said repartimiento of Jayanca whom people call don Francisco, that the principal who oversaw the principality of Mynimysal at the time that said don Francisco Lobo took possession of it [on April 2, 1536] was called Yniquisiquil and the parcialidad and lands where the said Yniquisiquil was lord of what was called Mynimisal and by this name . . . this witness knows said repartimiento and has seen with his own eyes that three lords that he has known of the said jurisdiction of Mynymissal who have each succeeded at the death of the previous one said that they had inherited the said jurisdiction of Minimisal even though they have their own names such as don Hernando, which was the name of two of them. (AGI/J418, 1573, 270v, 459; Cieza de León, 1548–50/1984, xxv, 205)

Fuentes continued that don Francisco curaca principal (who was probably the second) told him in 1556, speaking of the principal Mynymysal, "los senores que les mandan se llaman cada vno su nombre propio . . . nequesiquil hera el nombre propio del prinçipal que mandaua en el t[ien]po pasado aquella parçialidad de mynymysal e que el d[ic]ho Enyquisiquil biuio mucho t[ien]po en el d[ic]ho señorio" (The lords who rule each have their own name . . . Nequesiquil was the given name of the principal who ruled in the past that parcialidad of Minimisal and the said Enyquisiquil lived for a long time in that jurisdiction) (AGI/J418, 1573, 311v–12, 313v).

Gaspar de Morin, as Gutierrez's manager for five years in the early 1550s, had lived among the Jayancas, Pácoras, and Túcumes. He testified in 1563, explaining:

El d[ic]ho nonbre de nynymysal es nonbre del senorio e tierra[7] e prençipalazgo de aquella parcialidad que se nonbra asy e qualquier persona que subchede en aquel senorio aunque tenga nonbre propio le llaman del nonbre del señorio e que el nonbre de nequesiquil es nonbre de la persona que se mando[,] E que este t[estig]o oyo dec[i]r al caçique de jayanca e al de pacora que el d[ic]ho nequesiquil fue prençipal de la d[ic]ha parçialidad de nyminysal en t[iem]po que d[ic]ho marques [Pizarro] [1536] rrepartio la tierra.

The said name of Nynymysal is the name of the jurisdiction and lands of that principality [and] it is so named, and whoever succeeds in that jurisdiction, even though he has a given name, they call him by the name of the jurisdiction and the name Nequesiquil is the name of the person who ruled, and this witness has heard from the caciques of the Jayancas and Pacoras that said Nequesiquil was the principal of the said parcialidad of Nyminysal at the time that the said Marques [Pizarro] [1536] distributed the population. (AGI/J418, 1573, 322)

Gaspar Chiquina, a native subject of the principal Minimisal, reiterated this, testifying that

el d[ic]ho enequisyquil enenysal hera subjeto al caçique prençipal del d[ic]ho Valle de Jayanca tributandole e pagandole parte de los tributos que le cabian para dar a su encomendero confforme a la tassa[;] . . . por ser ffallesçido el d[ic]ho Enequesiquil su subchesor es subjeto al d[ic]ho caçique prençipal del d[ic]ho Valle de Jayanca, e que la cavsa por que el d[ic]ho prençipal se llamaua por dos nonbres hera e ffue porque el nonbre propio suyo hera e se llamaua enequesiquil y el nonbre del señorio se llama nynymysal e ansi el que al presente es prençipal por fin del d[ic]ho enequesiquil de mas de su propio nonbre se llamaua nynimysal por ser el apellido del señorio e atenydo notiçia de y[ndi]os viejos que los que antes auian sido antechesores del d[ic]ho enequesiquil de mas de su propio nonbre se llamauan y tomauan por sobre nonbre el apellido del señorio que es mynymysal.

Enequisyquil Enenysal was subject to the paramount lord of the Jayanca Valley, he paid him part of the tribute he had to give his encomendero, according to the tribute list . . . at the death of said Enequisyquil his successor became subject to the paramount cacique of the Valley of Jayanca, and the reason why the said principal was called by two names was because his first name was Enequisiquil and the name of the jurisdiction was Nynimysal and thus the person who is principal at present because of the death of said Enequesiquil, in addition to his given name he was also called Nynimysal being the last name of the jurisdiction, and he has heard from the elders that those who had been predecessors of said Enequisiquil, in addition to their first name they also took the surname of the jurisdiction Nynimysal as their last name. (AGI/J418, 1573, 326v–27).

Another clansman, Cuquil, born into the lineage of Mynymysal, stated that

fue prençipal de este testigo enequesiquil el qual fue prençipal de la parcialidad de nynynysal donde es natural este testigo y en toda la parcialidad no auia en su t[iem]po otro prençipal[;] mynymysal es nonbre de la parçialidad y enequesiquil fue nonbre de la persona que mando la d[ic]ha parçialidad de mynymysal[;] el qual Enequesi quil sabe este testigo por que lo vio que en el t[iem]po que los españoles entraron en la tierra [1532] hera prençipal de la d[ic]ha parçialidad de mynymysal y le mandaua[;] . . . enequesiquil . . . fue prençipal de la parçialidad de mynymysal . . . que ffue subjeto al caçique prençipal de Jayanca asi en t[ien]po de los yngas [<1532] como despues e que el dicho prençipal mynymysal tiene todos los prinçipales de Jayanca e que en todo el t[ien]po que este testigo sabe acordar sienpre hasta hagora auisto que este testigo e todos los demas y[ndi]os de la parçialidad de mynymsal an sido y son subjetos al d[ic]ho caçique principal de xayanca.

Enequisiquil was the principal lord of this witness, he was also the principal lord of the lineage of Nynymysal in which this witness originated and during his lifetime there was none other; Mynimysal is the name of the lineage and Enequisyquil was the name of the person in charge of said lineage of Mynimysal; this witness knows because he saw that when the Spaniards entered these lands in 1532 he was in charge of the said lineage of Mynymysal; . . . Enequisyquil . . . was the principal of the lineage of Mynymysal . . . that was subject to the paramount lord of Jayanca during the time of the Incas [< 1532] and after the arrival of the Spaniards, and at all times that this witness can remember he has always seen that this witness and the rest of the Indians of the lineage of Mynymsal have been and are subjects of the said paramount lord of Xayanca.

Thus the names used by lords that were the subject of the dispute between Francisco Lobo (Jayanca) and Diego Gutierrez (and later Alonso

Carrasco) were not the personal name of an individual native but
the designation of a jurisdiction over a lineage or group of lineages.[8]

Another informant, Apten,[9] a native of the neighboring fishing lineage under the principal named Mocochomí,[10] reiterated this, saying

> conosçio al prençipal que mandaua la parçialidad de minymisal al
> t[iem]po que entraron los espanoles [1532] en la tierra que se llamaua
> yniquilyquil e que el d[ic]ho nonbre de ynequecequil Era el nonbre
> que el d[ic]ho prinçipal tubo desde niño E que minymisal es el non-
> bre de la parçealidad e prençipalasgo e no de la perssona.

> he knew the lord called Yniquelyquil who ruled the lineage of Minymis-
> al at the time that the Spaniards arrived in the land [1532], and the said
> name of Yniquelyquil was the name that the said lord had since child-
> hood and Minymisal is the name of the lineage and principality and
> not of the person.

He continued:

> el d[ic]ho prençipal enequiciquil fue prençipal de la parçialidad que
> llaman mynymysal e lo hera al t[ien]po que entraron los espanoles
> en la tierra [1532] y este testigo le conoçio ser uiejo e prençipal de la
> d[ic]ha parçialidad e que es nonbre del d[ic]ho prençipal que hera de
> mynynysal hera enequesyquil nonbre propio e por causa del senorio
> se llama minynysal e que lo mesmo llaman agora a los prençipales
> de la d[ic]ha parçialidad que avnque tengan nonbre propio los lla-
> man mynymysal.

> The aforementioned Lord Enequisiquil was lord of the lineage that
> they call Minymisal and he was during the time the Spaniards en-
> tered this land [1532], and this witness knew him as an old man and
> lord of the said lineage and that the name of the lord who was lord of
> Mynynysal was Enequesyquil his given name and because of his ju-
> risdiction he was called Minynysal and the same name is given today
> to the lords of the said lineage, even though they have a given name
> they call him Mynymysal. (AGI/J418, 1573, 330v, 332)

Another native fisherman, subject to the lord Muchumy (or Mocochomí, as per the above; today spelled Muchumí), testified in 1564 that he

> conosze al prençipal minymysal e que conoxçio a su padre que se desçia yniquisiquil[11] elqual eniquisiquil murio despues que los cristianos entraron en la tierra [>1532] que se descia mynimisal yniquisiquil por el nonbre del padre.

> knows the lord Minymysal and he also knew his father whose name was Yniquisiquil, said Eniquisiquil died after the Christians entered this land [>1532] and was named Mynimisal Yniquisiquil because that was the name of his father.

So Spaniards, natives of the curacazgo of Jayanca, including those under the principal Minimisal, and natives of another fishing lineage—that of Mochumí—all agree on the practice of taking on a new name as one moved up the hierarchy of positions, leaving personal names behind. The "name" that they took was the name of the lineage or parcialidad and *señorio* (jurisdiction).[12]

The last quote suggests that the Minimisal in power in 1564 had inherited the name from his antecedent, be he his biological father (or grandfather) or not. This successor-to-successor pattern of name inheritance held at the curaca level as well. In 1532 the curaca's personal name was Pincuisoli or a variation of it. He had become Jayanque upon succeeding to office in or before 1536. He was followed by his "son" (classificatory or biological?) who had been baptized as don Francisco de Jayanca, possibly christened with the name after the encomendero at the time, Francisco de Lobo,[13] and following the fashion of Spanish kings who were known by their first names and a number (e.g., Philip II). Should this be true, his name would have identified him with service to his Spanish encomendero and lord (*amo*). He already served in the position in 1540 and lived during the time of the encomenderos Francisco Lobo (July 11,1540 to c. 1553) and Alonso Carrasco (approximately 1553–70).[14] His successor, another baptized don

Francisco, suggests an attempt to maintain the practice by taking the
Christian name of the previous holder. He already held the position
after doña María, the daughter of Diego Gutierrez, and Luis Canto
married, certainly in 1556 and maybe as early as 1554. He was succeeded by his "son," don Juan, the third leader after Pincuisoli, who held
the position in 1570 as shown in table 6.

Table 6. References to the Curacas of Jayanca

Year	Lord	Description	Sources
1532	Jayanque or Pincuisoli		AGI/J418, 211v; 459–60
1533	Caxusoli	Already old in 1532–33	Cabello Valboa 1586/1951, 498; Zevallos Quiñones, 1989, 45–50
1538	Senqueesol		AGI/J418, 219
<1540	Don Francisco	Son of Pincuisoli	AGI/J418, 212v
1549	Don Francisco	Ladino	AGI/J418, 253v
c. 1553	Don Francisco	Second son	ART/CoR: 30-VI-1576
1556	Don Francisco		AGI/J418, 256v
1557	Don Francisco		AGI/J418, 258
1558	Don Francisco	Ladino	ART/López de Córdova 1558
1560	Don Francisco		ART/COAG: 13-II-1565
1562	Don Francisco	First Don Francisco	
<1563	Don Francisco*		ART/Mata, 1569
1564–65	Don Francisco Caxusoli		Angulo 1920, 296
1566	Don Francisco Myncha	Second Don Francisco	AGI/J461, 1324, 1523–25
1566	Don Francisco	Died	AGI/J459, 2443v

1568	Don Francisco Puiconsoli Farrochumbi, *el mozo*		Zevallos Quiñones, 1989, 45–50
1570	Don Juan Caxosolo	Cacique	AGI/J460, 485; J418, 219
	or Caxosoli	Governor	AGI/J460, 480v; J461, 1398
<1572	Don Francisco Puycunsoli		AGI/J457, 991v; ANP/ Res, l. 3, c. 7, 1582, 60
1573	Don Francisco Puicunsoli	Ladino	AGI/J458, 1290v
1580	Don Francisco Poyconsoli		Brüning, 1922–25, III, 65
1581	Don Francisco Poiconsoli		Zevallos Quiñones 1974, 115
<1591	Don Juan Caxasoli Conoseque	Governor	Zevallos Quiñones 1989, 45–50
1596	Don Francisco		ART/CoO: 18-XI-1596
1616–20	Don Pedro Coscochumbi		Brüning 1922–25/1989, 4:22, 50, 65–68
1643–54	Don Gerónimo Rodríguez Puiconsoli		Brüning, 1922–25/1989, 4:22, 50, 65–68
1688	Don Gerónimo Rodríguez Puiconsoli		Brüning, 1922–25/1989, 4:22, 50, 65–68

*One witness said he had met three different don Franciscos before 1563. The witness had lived in the area since at least 1556.

Additional independent records, like the inspection trip (*visita*) of Dr. Gregorio Gonzalez de Cuenca and other administrative and judicial papers, demonstrate that after don Juan's (Caxosole, Cajasoli, Capasoli, or Ponon *çeque*)[15] stint in office, one or more don Francisco Puicunsolis led the people of Jayanca to at least the year 1596. Enrique

Brüning's (1922–25/1989) research shows that the name Puiconsoli endured as the last name of the curacas of Jayanca almost to the end of the seventeenth century.

Furthermore, the *visita* records identify don Juan not as a curaca but as a governor. This is a key distinction, because at this time the Spanish used the term *governador* to identify a native interim officeholder who was recognized not to be the legitimate one. He served temporarily when the legitimate successor to the position was deemed inept—for reasons of preparation, personal characteristics, or, more likely in this case, tender age. The don Francisco who took office from don Juan was born c. 1553, making him a youngster or adolescent at the time that don Juan's name surfaces in the records as leader. In other records of the time, don Juan appears as a principal, brother, uncle, segunda persona, or conoseque (AGI/J418, 1573, 164v, 210v, 211v–12, 213, 215v, 219, 253v, 256v, 258, 306, 374; J457, f. 991v; J458, 1290v, 1804, 2020; J459, 2443v–44; J460, 480v; J461, 1398, 1432, 1526; J462, 1863; Zevallos Qunñones 1974, 115; ANP/Res, l. 3, c. 7, 1582, 60; Brüning 1922–25/1989, 147–50; Angulo 1920, 296; ART/Juan de Mata 1569; López de Córdova 1558; CoO, 18-XI-1596; COAG, 13-II-1565; CoR, 30-VI-1576).

This case study illustrates several points. First, it shows that different individuals moved into positions of leadership at the curaca and *principalazgo* levels (Jayanca and Minimisal) as the preceding incumbents died or otherwise left or were removed from office. All the legitimate successors to the curacaship used the same name after Puiconsoli—probably a survival and adaptation of the previous practice but now in Christian guise. Likewise, two of the principal Enequesiquels' successors were named don Hernando. All of these lords began using the inherited positional name as a surname, perhaps reflecting growing Spanish pressure to use last names "para que se eviten los yerros" (to avoid mistakes).[16] Second, the inheritance pattern, if it worked as in Africa, explains the varying number of "widows" who served the leading Andean lords. Each successor would have inherited his predecessor's ex-wives along with his named position. This explains why Guaman Poma de Ayala, for example, writes that the Inca married his mother.[17] Third, the relative positions of the various names and

hierarchical levels were perpetuated according to the original relationship between the names. Jayanca is always paramount. Pácora,
as a lord of a *principalazgo*, is subordinate to Jayanca; and Neptur is
usually indicated to be of less status than Pácora.[18]

The exact kinship relationship between positions is hard to ascertain
because of vague or conflicting testimonies of early witnesses. For example, witnesses identified the first don Francisco as a son of the person who held the name and position of Jayanque in 1532, and don Juan
(the conoseque[19] and principal who acted temporarily as chief during
the minority of the third don Francisco) is identified as the "son" of
the second don Francisco. Yet it cannot be determined with the information on hand if "son" is a biological or classificatory designation.
Similarly, witnesses identified the curaca of Jayanca in 1540 as both the
brother and uncle of the principal of the Pácora people. Thus, according to Carrasco in 1570, the curaca principal Jayanca as the uncle of the
leader of the Pácora "lent" the latter one or more principales in 1540 in
time to be counted by the Spanish visitor Sebastian de la Gama. Yet,
in 1563, Gaspar de Morin identified the lord of the Pácora lineage as the
brother of the curaca principal of Jayanca. The discrepancy between
brother and uncle might be (1) a mistake, or (2) a function of two different times in the history of succession within the ethnicity. If we assume that the kinship terms refer to a consanguineal relationship, at
one time the uncle might have been Jayanque and a nephew the lord
of the Pácora; at another point the two positions may have been held
by consanguineal brothers. Or, (3) one or more terms could be classificatory, referring to the historical relationship between the names as
in perpetual kinship (AGI/J418, 1573, 202v, 210v [for 1570], 320v).

It is significant that R. Alan Covey (2006, 187–89) addresses kinship relations in the context of Cuzco succession. He notes that colonial Quechua dictionaries define the term *churi*, generally accepted as
"son"; yet it also is employed between uncle and nephew, older brother and younger brother, and as a general intergenerational term between males (González Holguin 1608/1952, 91; Santo Tomás 1560/1951,
149). Zuidema also discusses the term *churi*, pointing out that all men
of high nobility were called *capac churi* or "royal sons" (2015, 445).[20]

The same positional inheritance as indicated by naming practices is found elsewhere in the Andes. Karen Powers (1998) reports that don Francisco of the Latacunga peoples had changed his name to Hati upon assuming the chiefdomship. Subsequent censuses reveal that he had done nothing unusual. The lord's sons were always listed under surnames other than Hati and did not assume the name until they inherited the chiefdomship. Powers states that Galo Ramón Valarezo (1987) uncovered a similar practice for the Puentos, the native rulers of the Cayambe, in his book *Resistencia Andina: Cayambe, 1500–1800*. The case of the Chimu (a large and powerful ethnic group living south of the Jayances on the coast) is complicated by changing jurisdictions and Spanish meddling in the process of chief selection, but a list of leaders shows that the surname Chayguac(a) survived from the 1530s to 1781. A fortuitous and chance find in the notarial records of a North Coast native notary named Francisco Humac Minoyulli—who, after serving years with Marcos Velasquez, became a Lima notary in his own right—provides information on the central Andes. His records indicate that Chauca rimah or Chinca cuica (also *auca*)[21] was the name of the paramount lord of the lineage of Lurin Chilca (holding jurisdiction over peoples living near the villa of Cañete in the colonial era) at the time of first contact with the Spanish. His son, don Pedro de Chauca, the first Christian paramount lord of the lineage who served as early as 1560, was confirmed by Viceroy Francisco de Toledo in 1579. His successors preserved Chauca as a surname into the nineteenth century (ANP/Protocolos, l. 733, 1780–81, 479–504). Finally, Sabine Hyland (2016, 177) suggests that the name Sivi Paucar continued to be used among the Chancas between 1539 and (at least) 1694.[22]

In the south, Cari was one of the rulers of the Lupaqas in Chuquito. The noted chronicler Garcilaso de la Vega (1609–12/1985) states that the name Cari was the same as that of the ancestors from the very beginning. Their successors wanted to keep the memory through the name, inheriting it one from another. Thus it appears that the rulers of the Lupaqa accepted the name of the apical ancestor and, in so doing, kept the memory of his deeds alive (148–49).[23]

Many Andean peoples likened their first ancestor to a god and took its name. Pablo José de Arriaga, a Spanish Jesuit missionary identified with the extirpation of idolatry, writes that "todos los nombres antiguos de los pueblos son los de la Huaca principal" (all the old names of the populations are those of their principal god) and

> cada parcialidad, o Ayllo tiene su Huaca principal, y otras menos principales . . . , y de ellas suelen tomar el nombre muchos de aquel Ayllo. Algunas de estas las tienen como a guardas, y abogados de sus pueblos, que sobre el nombre propio llaman *Marcaapárac* o *Marcachárac*.

> each lineage, or ayllu, has a main god, and others lesser gods . . . , and from them many of the *ayllu* members usually take its name. Some of these consider them protectors and advocates of their populations, and besides the given name they call them Marcaapárac or Marcachárac. (Arriaga 1621/1968, 215)[24]

In sixteenth-century Quechua parlance, Marcaapárac or Marcachárac meant a rich lord, where "rich" identified an authority with a large following or, alternatively, he who "pone un hito o crea [founded] un pueblo [population] o un lugar" (he who erects a milestone or founds a lineage or a place).[25] In the sixteenth century, both the words *llacta* and *marca* referred to a people or lineage and not a place or region (Ramírez 2006a).[26] Arriaga (1621/1698, 44) writes that Andeans worship their names and *apellidos* (surnames, ancestral names), no doubt referring to the revered and sacred connotation of what or whom the names represented. Such ideas may have come from Molina (1574/1916) who, c. 1574, recorded that "en memoria de el primero que de alli salio, ponian idolos dandoles el nombre a cada guaca que ellos entendian auia tenido aquel de quien se jataua proçeder" (in memory of the first, they made idols giving each god the name of their founder). Note that one of the many names of the chief of the Sañas was Ponon çeque, which, as noted previously, translates as "Stone Idol" or "Stone Leader" where *ponon* is "stone" and *çeque* is "leader" or "idol." In many of the lineage origin stories the founding ancestor becomes a stone or mountain to guard his people and their resources.[27] Pedro

de Villagómez (1649/1919) reiterates this, writing in the 1640s that "todos los principales tienen los nombres de algunas de sus huacas y suel-
en hacer grandes fiestas cuando le ponen este nombre, que llaman
bautizarle otra vez, o ponerle nombre" (all the lords have the names
of some of their gods and they customarily have big festivals when
they give these names to them; they call this "Baptize him again" or
"Give him a name").[28] Fray Antonio de la Calancha (1638/1974–81), a
resident of the North Coast at one point in his life, reports that the
name Chicama, today the name of a valley north of Chan Chan and
Trujillo, was the corruption of Chicamac, which translates as "creator
of many things." He writes:

> Algunos quieren que el llamarse Chicamac, que significa el valle su
> vezino, fue por averse llamado su Dios Chicamac, que significa el cria-
> dor de muchas cosas, dando el nombre al valle en que vivían del Idolo
> supremo que adoravan, imitando a Pachacamac, y a Rímac, que tur-
> vieron el nombre de sus Idolos, llamandose Lima este valle, i Pacha-
> camac aquel asiento.

> Some believe that being called Chicamac, which designates the neigh-
> boring valley, was because their god was named Chicamac, which
> means "the creator of many things," giving the name of the supreme
> god that they venerated to the valley in which they lived, imitating
> Pachacamac, and Rimac, that had the name of their idols, calling the
> latter valley Lima and the former place Pachacamac.[29]

Finally, Calancha (1638/1974–81) translates the name Pacatnamu, the
Chimu captain whom the Incas appointed ruler of the Pacasmayos,
and today the name of an important archaeological site, as "Common Father" or "Father of Everyone," the epitome of an apical ancestor (3:1093; 4:1227, 1229; Molina 1575/1916, 6–7; Villagómez 1649/1919,
169; Arriaga 1621/1920, 22, 184).[30]

The practice of taking the name of an apical ancestor may highlight
and explain a contradiction between the accounts of the chroniclers
Betanzos and Sarmiento de Gamboa on the identity of "Uscovilca,"
the leader of the Chancas who audaciously demanded that the Incas

recognize his suzerainty as son of the Sun. Betanzos portrays Uscovilca as a living person, while Sarmiento de Gamboa (like Albornoz
1967) states emphatically that Uscovilca had been one of the founding fathers of the Chancas and that by the time of the war against the
Incas he was dead and embalmed. But because he had been so ruth-
less and courageous in his lifetime, his followers carried his statue
"with them in the wars and plundering. For that reason, although
they took with them other warriors, always they attributed the deeds
to the image of Uscouilca (Sarmiento 1572/1942, 97)." Therefore, it appears that Sarmiento de Gamboa portrays the struggle as between
the living forces of the ancestor god of the Chancas, Uscolvilca, and
the Incas and their allies while Betanzos fuses the name of the apical ancestor with the leader who was then using the name as holder
of the position. In Pierre Duviols's analysis of this conflict, he points
out that, according to Father Cristóbal de Albornoz, a Spanish secular priest known for his campaign against indigenous religion, Uscovilca was the *guaca* (sacred object or place) of the Ananchancas (Upper
Chancas) and Ancovilca was the guaca of the Hurinchancas (Lower
Chancas). Therefore, he concludes that "los jefes chancas que inter-
vienen en la famosa guerra eran en realidad sus dioses étnicos" (the
Chanca lords who were involved in the famous war were really their
[embodied] ethnic gods). Uscovilca, he continues, "era 'una piedra',
lo que sugiere que era un héroe divinizado, antiguo fundador de un
ayllu o de un grupo de ayllus, tal vez sacerdote mayor, y que según la
tradición mítica se había convertido en piedra y en dios tutelar de la
hanansaya" (was a stone, which suggests that he was a divinized hero,
ancient founder of an ayllu or of a group of ayllus, maybe even a head
priest, and, according to mythical tradition, he had become a stone
and guardian god of the *hanansaya* [upper half]) (Sarmiento 1572/1965,
231; 1572/1942, 97; Betanzos 1551–57/1987, 22–28, 49–50; 1551–57/1996, 93;
Duviols 1997a, especially 271, 289–90; 1997b, 328).

Such names with their sacred connotations and local representations gave a people an identity and taught them what was appropriate
behavior: how to deal with different situations, much as the fairy tales
analyzed by Robert Darnton (1984) did for European peasants. Such

names became a basis for identity for the Chancas, the peoples of the North Coast and the Central Sierra, and elsewhere. Alberto Pinillos Rodríguez, a local historian of the North Coast, states that "se llegó a identificar a los ayllus con el nombre de sus huacas" (it got to the point of identifying the ayllus with the name of their gods), where the guaca referred to the ancestor or guardian spirit (*apu*) of the group (1977, 12). The university-trained Licenciado Rodrigo Hernández Príncipe reports that the Recuay in 1622 used "el apellido de sus propias huacas" (the last name of their own gods) as a *sobrenombre* (nickname or surname) (1621–22/1923, 26). Both Karen Spalding (1984), who wrote the classic work on Huarochirí peoples who lived east of Lima, and Mary Doyle (1988), a scholar of idolatries, accept the fact that the kin group carried the name of the *huacas* (although Spalding reverses the relationship by saying that the huacas carried the name of the kin group) (67). Doyle suspects that the names of all the people in a given ayllu could be identified with particular guacas, *malquis* (ancestors), and the revered of that ayllu (137).

In fact, Sergio Barraza Lescano in a study of a native Peruvian dance called *del huacón* reports that natives, when the mummies and stone idols that represented their founding ancestors were destroyed by zealous extirpators of idolatry, replaced them with masks. He finds archaeological evidence of this phenomenon as early as 900 BCE. The masks, which were venerated, are also mentioned in colonial documents as early as 1590.

> En la concepción indígena, el uso de estas mascaras confería a sus portadores el camac del ancestro del cual habían sido obtenidos, otorgaba su fuerza vital y su anima que permitía asegurar la procreación y multiplicación.

> In the indigenous reckoning, the use of the masks conferred on their bearers the camac [also *kamaq*] of their ancestor from which they had obtained them, granting them [the masked dancer(s)] their vital force and animating spirit [camac] that permitted their procreation and multiplication. (n.d., 4)[31]

In effect, the human dancer imbibed the essence of the ancestor and assumed his identity while wearing the mask, usually at rituals that united the past and the present and were held at the beginning and end of the agricultural season.

Other authors equate the names of lineages with their curacas or leaders, as was common among the Central Africans (of chapter 2) and the Ho-De'-No-Sau-Nee (of chapter 3). The prolific historian Waldemar Espinoza Soriano writes that "los grupos humanos integrados en ayllus, pachacas, huarangas, sayas y reinos eran designados según el nombre de sus curacas [who took the name of their huacas and jurisdictions], no obstante que cada agrupación tenía su toponimia individual" (The human groups integrated in ayllus [lineages], *pachacas* [lineages of hundreds], *huarangas* [lineages of thousands], *sayas* [halves], and kingdoms were designated according to the name of their curacas [who took the names of their gods and jurisdictions], although each group had its individual toponym) (1986, 70).

Likewise, the anthropologist Alejandro Diez Hurtado (1997, 164) notes that the Mec Non and the Ñari Wallac of the Valley of Catacaos took the name of their paramount lord. As noted above, whole groups took the name of their curaca as a last name when required to do so by Christian conversion and the strengthening of the colonial state, which wanted a means to identify individuals for tax and other purposes. This happened among the peoples of the two moieties in the northern Valley of Catacaos and among the Sasaca (of Bolivia) in 1614. What is not acknowledged, perhaps because of an insufficient depth of historical memory, is that the curacas often took the name of the jurisdiction that was the name of the founding ancestor, prototype, and hero (Diez Hurtado 1997, 15, 164; 1988, 56 on Catacaos; Medinaceli 1995, 325, 330, 335 on Bolivia; Torero 1993, 222 on the Huari).

In the Andean case, as time went on these names became more and more confused with toponyms. If a name originated with the founding ancestor and became synonymous with the curaca and the population actively maintaining his memory and observing his cult, it later became a title synonymous with a lord's jurisdiction over his scattered people and finally with the rotating lands his followers occupied and used. After the *reducciones* (the concentration of scattered native households into Spanish-style settlements) of the 1560s and 1570s, the name identified a nucleated town. Villamarín (1975, 174) confirms that among the Chibchas of Colombia, the caciques' names were also the names of their jurisidctions. Hart (1983) postulates a correspondence between the names of principales and those of lands and lineages (parcialidades). She found that the name of the lineage was the same as the agricultural lands that the group worked, suggesting that the name identified and celebrated referred to the first person who created the people, worked the lands, or imported a major crop. In 1550 native witnesses affirmed that the caciques and their lands had the same name. Veninamo, a native of the Moche Valley, testifed that "algunos caciques ay que se llaman el nombre de sus tierras e otros del nombre de sus padres" (there are some lords who take the name of their lands and others who take the name of their fathers), which comes to the same thing as the Spanish who used the founder's jurisdiction over people as a basis for districts and territories (162, 204, citing AGI/J398 on Chichi). Elsewhere the cacique of Cajamarca said that "todos los yndios yungas tienen por costunbre llamarse del nombre de sus tierras especial[mente] los caciques e principales dellos" (all the lowland [yungas] Indians and especially the lords and nobles are customarily named after their lands/populations). Don Juan Puemape is an example; he used the name of his people, Puemape (and later their town [reducción] in the Jequetepeque Valley in 1566), as a surname (AGI/J458, 1941 on Puemape). An earlier example is the cacique Chichiana of the Moche Valley, whose town or people were listed as Chichi. In the south, historian Rafael Varón Gabai (1997, 197, 265) cites an encomienda grant entrusting twenty-eight persons subject to the cacique Porco, whose name also identified the mines where they worked. María Isabel Silva (1984, 8) states that indigenous pueblos or towns were named after their cacique, as were the Jayancas, Pácoras, Túcumes, and Paipayas (Sica 2008, 329, 331). This was true after the Spanish arrived and created the reducciones, but according to the Minimisal dispute records, caciques took the name of the jurisdiction that appears to have been, in some cases, the name of their founding ancestor, hero, and god.[32]

There are several problems with such equations. Many of the previous citations appear devoid of a diachronic sequence and the recognition of change over time characteristic of a multicultural situation. Thus Veninamo, without a sufficient historical memory, may not have recognized the sequence: ancestor hero —> lineage name —> curaca's name —> demographic jurisdiction's name —> toponyms or settlement's name.[33] Second, the lands that a people used were not fixed before the establishment of the Spanish-style reducciones. They were *sapçi*, common to all. Working a tract gave a farmer tenure for as long as he used it. Fertility and climatic exigencies, however, mandated rotation of fields, even on the irrigated coast.[34] As a result, agricultural peoples moved periodically to new sites (Ramírez 2016, especially 39, 55; 2018). Third, the word "tierras" must not be unconditionally and always equated with lands. Often it referred to the people of a defined group or the jurisdiction over a category of individuals and not the lands they seasonally occupied. Eventually and usually years later, the lineage names became the basis for ethnic mapping (ethnocartography), where the names were affixed to discrete territories by a state that presumed or desired to hold authority over the inhabitants therein (Worby 1994; Rowe 1946, map 3; P. Sahlins 1989).

The Incas

The Incas or the Cuzcos, as they were alternatively called, also practiced positional inheritance. Individuals took several different names during a lifetime, each signifying a changed identity and social function. As with the Ho-De'-No-Sau-Nee, babies received one name in infancy according to the attributes of the child. Often, according to Arriaga, these names were those of an ancestor (*malqui*) or a huaca (sacred shrine or object) (Arriaga 1621/1968, 215; Gentile 1999, 175–77; Cabello Valboa 1586/1951, 294; Cieza de León 1548–50/1984, 200, 207–8; Medinaceli 1995, 164–70, 333–34, 339; 2003, 27, 164–70, 210; Hernández Príncipe 1621–22/1923, 26; Cobo 1653/1956–64, 2:246–47; Garcilaso de la Vega 1609–12/1966, 1:204, 207, 210–11; 1609–12/2007, 295–97, 425–26).[35] Some chroniclers specify that children aged two to five received a second name; boys took another at puberty. A male could also use a new name when he accomplished some noteworthy deed. A military captain, for example, could take the name of the people he subjugated as a nickname, epithet, or surname (*sobrenombre*).

In a few instances chroniclers like Betanzos and Cieza de León specifically detail the inheritance of names within a family. The latter, an early and generally well-regarded observer, notes that some natives are careful to retain the names of their fathers and grandfathers (1548–50/1984, 231). Betanzos also reports that fathers and sons had the same names. In addition, he provides some examples, noting that, after the death of his brother Yamque Yupanque, Topa Inca Yupanque granted an audience to his fourteen-year-old surviving son whom he ordered to be named Yamque Yupanque, the same as his father. The emperor then gave him all of his father's possessions. Yamque Yupanqui (son) crowned Guayna Capac. Likewise, the same chronicler states that Viracocha Inca planned to leave his position and his own name to his son Urco (1551–57/1987, 166–67; 1551–57/1996, 22, 33, 117, 154, 160).[36]

The king-elect had an additional occasion to take a new name. When he succeeded to the emperorship, he left behind his personal name, which, like the names of Egyptian pharaohs or the Hebrew god, was considered too sacred to be commonly verbalized. Garcilaso de la Vega emphasizes "the majesty of his name [referring to Manco Capac], so great and so high that among them it was considered so sacred and divine that no one dared utter it, except with the greatest veneration, then only to name the king" (1602/1960–63, 2:37; 1609–12/1966, 1:59). Cieza de León confirms this, stating that "in public no one dared name his [Huáscar's] name" (1548–50/1987, 146).[37]

Instead, followers frequently addressed the emperor by a variety of praise names or titles meant to suggest the shared characteristics of the holder and a predecessor. Stories told how the person of Topa Inca Yupanqui talked to the guacas (which also talked, according to Curatola Petrocchi 2016) and knew of the coming of the Spanish (whom he called Viracochas, after the Andean creator god). Therefore, attendants called him "Viracocha Ynca" or the "omnipotent (or all powerful) Inca" (Zuidema 1983, 53). Huáscar's childhood name was Topa Cusi Gualpa Indi Illapa[38] (Sarmiento de Gamboa 1572/1942, 166; 1572/1999,

169). Atahualpa, after receiving the insignia of office and the title as "the Cuzco," received the name Caccha Pachacuti Inca Yupangue Inca, literally Idol of Battles (*caccha*); and the name World Changer or Reformer (Pachacuti). The name Inca Yupanque commemorated his great grandfather, and, according to Cerrón-Palomino, meant "digno de estima, invalorable" (worthy of esteem, invaluable) or "Señor Venerando" (Venerated Lord) (1998, 435; 2019, 180). "Inca" was synonymous with "king." Betanzos states that "in giving him this name they are saying that he imitated the idol in warfare" (1551–57/1987, 205). Inca Yupangue also responded to Pachacuti Inca (Collapiña 1542/1974, 38). Blas Valera stated that such titles or appellations, should the person possess the qualities and powers inherent in the words, made persons forget first names: "in such a way that in all parts they forgot the first names to call him by these" (1596/1945, 113). Zuidema (1983, 51–53; 2015, especially 446, 450, 464–65) postulates that the names of the kings, except Manco Capac and Guayna Capac, served more as titles and indicators of hierarchical positions than as proper names, an opinion shared by José Imbelloni (1946, 32). These supplemented the use of "el Cuzco" (Vargas Ugarte 1551–54, 1, 327; Betanzos 1551–57/1996, 74, 107, 174, 189, 205; 1551–57/1987, 83, 113, 190; Garcilaso de la Vega, 1602/1960–63, 2:37–40; 1609–12/1966, 1:393; 1609–12/1941–45, 2:229; 1609–12/2007, 425–26; Lastres 1947, 8; Cieza de León 1548–50/1987, 146; Guaman Poma de Ayala 1613/1980, 262 [264]).[39]

"Cuzco" was another name or title that was inheritable from one man to another in the same position (Imbelloni 1946, 32).[40] Evidence exists that the appellation Cuzco was the name or label of the *señorío* (lordship, jurisdiction, position) and that each of the last three rulers before the Spanish invasion took the name upon succession to the leadership position of the empire. Before the mid-1530s, "the Cuzco" is mentioned as the supreme Andean leader without much elaboration by authors such as Captain Cristóbal de Mena (Molina) (who was the first to bring news of the capture of Atahualpa to Panama in August 1533) (1531–33/1938); Francisco de Xerez (Francisco Pizarro's secretary in Cajamarca); Pedro Sancho de la Hoz (another of Pizarro's secretaries) (1534/1938, 117, 136–37, 167, 174, 176–77); Licenciado Gaspar de

Espinosa (a judge of the Real Audiencia [Supreme Court] of the city of Santo Domingo [on the Island of Hispañola] and Alcalde Mayor [magistrate] under Pedrarias Davila of Tierra Firme) (1532/1921, 12–13; 1533/1921/1921–26, 19–20); and Hernando Pizarro (Francisco Pizarro's brother and emissary to the Spanish crown) (1533/1964, 47–65). They refer to Guayna Capac as the *"Cuzco viejo"* (old Cuzco) and to his son, Huáscar, as the *"Cuzco joven"* (young Cuzco). At the death of the latter, Atahualpa, Huáscar's half brother, assumed the title. Xerez, for example, reported that Atahualpa, as son of the *Cuzco viejo*, took the title upon succession: "and as successor to the dominion he is called Cuzco like his father" (1534/1917, 42). That the title of Cuzco was sufficient identity, especially among the ethnic peoples who were not of the ruling ethnicity, is suggested by the fact that the lords of Jayanca did not immediately recognize the name Guayna Capac in 1540 (Gama 1540/1974, 226).[41]

The practice of perpetuating the title of Cuzco was all-important because it referred to the center—the biological center of a megalineage of "one birth" and "under one law" that the emperors were in the process of creating. Each king progressed throughout the Andes to reinforce personal ties and kinship that bound the empire together. As each king and his court traveled from one administrative-religious center to another (e.g., Incahuasi, Huánuco, and Tomebamba), his stops became identified as another city (figuratively) of the Cuzco. Guaman Poma de Ayala (1613/1936, 185 [187], 407 [409]) writes of many Cuzcos. At these way stations, his person stood as the administrative, political, and religious center of a peripatetic court and, ultimately, of all the peoples of the realm. He was the font of in/justice; the origin of important economic concessions and gifts; and the direct link to the deities believed to be responsible for all life and the good (and bad) around them (Guaman Poma de Ayala, 1613/1980, 185 [187]).

For that reason, the sons of the sons of the sun, as their claim went, and their supporters fought at times over succession to the position. The chroniclers note that the incoming successful Cuzco, after listening to the songs and life stories of the former holders of the title so as to understand the standard by which he was measured, eliminated rivals (Yaya 2012, 46; Salomon 1999, especially 24–26, 58, 61, 64). Upon assuming power, Guayna Capac immediately ordered the killing of his potentially competing siblings; Pachacuti killed his brother Inca Urco. This practice was commonplace. Both Titu Cusi and Guaman Poma de Ayala report that Atahualpa had Huáscar and all of his sons and forty-three of his brothers, the sons of Guayna Capac, executed. That may have been part of the reason that Cristóbal Mena reports that Atahualpa's half brothers were afraid of him. Such a massacre not only destroyed the person's body but obliterated his name, many of his kin, his memory; in short, his immortality.[42]

On the eve of the Spanish invasion, the Cuzco oversaw a hierarchy of positions.[43] The chronicles do not describe the structure in terms of names but, rather, of decimal rank. This terminology may have been a function of evolving from a chiefdomship, like the Chancas, Lupaqas, or Jayancas, into a megalineage with imperial designs and powers. The Inca decimal hierarchy and designations may have been appropriated after contact with the Chimu, who already used a decimally based hierarchy of positions to indicate rank. Among the Jayancas, the segunda persona was alternatively known as conoseque—the Mochica-language term, as mentioned in passing above, for a lord of a thousand native families (see also Zuidema 1983 and 2015 on ranks and identity). The Incas may have copied this as an attempt to systematize the expanding imperial organization with descriptive titles indicating status and relative strength, much as founders' names had done among the people of smaller ethnicities. From an imperial viewpoint, this would have been advantageous because the use of such terms would have divorced local allegiances over time from their ancestors.

Zuidema (1985, 1990) calls attention to this fixed hierarchy of positions, each of which was occupied successively by different persons— the essence of positional inheritance without actually using the phrase. The data suggest that persons taking certain names of predecessors exhibited the qualities, characteristics, and traits of the persons who originally held the name. Furthermore, the new "king" defined the positions of his own blood kin from his own central point of view after assuming his new superior position. "Even if a newly elected king,"

Table 7. Inca decimal rankings

Officials in the decimal hierarchy

Title of official	Size of jurisdiction (heads of households)
Hunu kuraka	10,000
Pichka-waranqa kuraka	5,000
Waranqa kuraka	1,000
Pichka-pachaca kuraka	500
Pachaca kuraca	100
Pichka-chunka kamayuq	50
Chunka kamayuq	10

Zuidema notes, "was a younger son of the former king, his older brothers would still be redefined by him as son, grandson, nephew and so on. . . . A living brother could be called . . . great-great-grandson, because of his low status and not because of a real generational distance" (1985, 7; 1990, 460, 496; Duviols 1997b; Medinaceli 2003, 168–70; Salomon 1999, 54).

The Incas, like each Andean ethnic group, had a variety of memory aids. As mentioned in chapter 1, people without writing kept the past alive by repeating stories and recalling memories. Some of these were standardized in song narratives and reenacted in commemorative ceremonies.[44] In the Andes, both songs and dances were integral to native worship of their ancestors. Garcilaso de la Vega recalls that the Incas performed comedies and tragedies that used memories of the past for didactic purposes in the present. The fact that ethnic groups mummified the dead and carefully preserved their founding ancestors made their bodies or the masks and images that represented them the personification of the past. As noted in chapter 1, they also kept quipus (as defined above, a system of colored and knotted strings) to help them record data and most probably other, more qualitative information as well. Other memories were elicited by the topography in which they found themselves, by symbols on drinking and sacrificial vessels, by the form and decoration of architecture, and by the weavings on their carrying cloths and vestments (Ramírez 2005, ch. 5; 2014b; Garcilaso de la Vega 1602/1960-63, 31, 79; Abercrombie 1998, 130; Urton and Quilter 2002; Urton 2006; Urton and Brezine 2013; Niles 1999; O'Phelan Godoy 1993, 10; Salomon and Urioste 1991, ch. 9, section 117, 40; Betanzos 1551–57/1996, 153, 166; Duviols 1997a, 274; 1986, 52, 54, 61, 63, 93, 145; MacCormack 2001, 430; Chang-Rodríguez 1980, 89; Perissat 2000, 625 [on native theater]).

All of these devices supposed a group responsible for the preservation of the collectively constructed story; hence the importance of the number of a person's descendants and followers. Like the Kazembe peoples of Africa, the Andean definition of "rich" or "wealthy" was a person who had many adherents. To be poor was to be an orphan, an exile, or alone, a sole survivor. Bits and pieces of information culled from the chronicles and other manuscript sources suggest that an important period in the trajectory of a potential king's life was his time spent on military campaigns. His prowess was judged, not for his ability to conquer territory, as argued by Geoffrey Conrad and Arthur Demarest (1984), but for his success in winning over (through diplomacy or war) ethnic groups, whose members would serve him and his lineage during his lifetime and after his death (Anónimo 1571/1995, 149; Titu Cusi Yupangui 1570/1916, 128; Ramírez 2005, 98). He also used bride exchange, presenting sisters and daughters to subordinate lords and taking their females as secondary wives, not only to meld the various ethnic groups into what was becoming an integrated and homogeneous whole but also to become, literally, the father, uncle (mother's brother), and grandfather, or some combination of those, of any of their offspring who might eventually inherit the jurisdiction. Only by amassing a personal following could an Andean king hope to provide for a lineage that would be charged with perpetuating the memory of his name after he died. Followers would work to support his descendants, who assumed the responsibility for preserving his mummy, reciting the poems, and singing the epic accounts of his name's triumphs and accomplishments every chance they got (Betanzos 1551–57/1996, 134–36, 139).[45]

But not all rulers founded a lineage.[46] As mentioned earlier, one of the most drastic punishments of a do-nothing or ignoble king or an opponent was to kill all of his relatives, thus destroying and obliterating his name from living memory, from the recalled and hallowed past (Romero Meza 2014, 4). As noted, Atahualpa ordered the wives and relatives of Huáscar killed. Guayna Capac did the same to his brothers, perhaps to prevent rivalries from growing and endangering his own rule.[47] Thus, not every Andean ruler's memory lasted; such expungement reduced the number of celebrated names that were honored.

Furthermore, not every leader accomplished deeds worthy of telling; an unknown number were weak or did little. Cieza de León points out that

> if there were, among their kings, one who had been remiss, cowardly, given to vices, and who preferred to enjoy himself rather than encrease [sic] the power of his empire, it was ordered that little or nothing should be said about him, and they took such good care to do so, that if anything was said it was so as not to forget his name and succession; but for the rest they were silent. This does not apply to the narrative poems of others who were good and valiant. (cited by Rowe 1945, 267)

This was true of the legendary Sinchi Roca, traditionally the second chronicler-mentioned king, who "added nothing to what his father had subjugated," and the third, Lloqui Yupanqui, who "did nothing worthy of remembrance." Both of their names, when mentioned at all, were inventoried without much elaboration in the Spanish chroniclers' accounts. Charles Gibson considers Inca Urco, son of Viracocha Inca, the eighth ruler on the standard chroniclers' short lists, one of these also, whose name was doomed to widespread social amnesia (Sarmiento de Gamboa 1572/1965, 64–65, 191; 1572/1999, 63, 65; Gibson 1948/1969, 57).[48]

Even if a respected, generous, and noteworthy ruler contributed to the renown of a name, its perpetuation was subject to a successor's whims and inclinations because the living ruler controlled the memory of the past. Three or four old men were designated to remember all the events that happened and to compose narrative poems about them so that it would be possible to recall them in the future. The present ruler, however, also had the power to edit or suppress the recitation and diffusion of the poems and songs and the knowledge of the exemplary past that they held; he could decline to authorize their performance on important ritual occasions, such as initiations. Sabine MacCormack shows how accounts of the past favorable to Atahualpa attribute the founding of the empire to Inca Pachacuti, while those favorable to Huáscar attribute it to Inca Viracocha. She concludes, "This divergence in perceptions of the past by followers of Atahuallpa and of Guascar indicates that the Çapa Inca's power was manifest not only in religious and ritual, military and economic terms, but also in the interpretation of the past and in its relevance to the present" (2001, 431). Authorizing the performance of ancient songs gave life to previous name-holders' actions and fortified and perpetuated the name and its underlying collective biography. Thus, a living ruler selectively influenced, controlled, or could make history retrospectively to potentially enhance his own power.[49]

Finally, because individual emperors were known as Cuzcos, and the use of their personal names was restricted, it would not necessarily have been always apparent to those outside the inner circle that one individual had replaced another. The comportment of the king may also have worked to hide from certain subjects the successive individuals who became "the Cuzco." The king dressed in ethnic attire with appropriate wigs and hairdos to ape those of the group he visited on his long journeys. On other occasions his features were covered in gold to the extent that seeing him in the Andean sun would "wound the eyes" (Cabello Valboa 1586/1951, 458; Ramírez 2005, 76). On less formal occasions, he sat still behind a curtain and replied to questions through spokespersons, like the mummies of his predecessors (Yaya 2015, 648). Few, other than trusted personal servants and kin, gained face-to-face audiences. Rare was the outsider to the emperor's court who would have recognized the individual. Most observed the Cuzco from afar, either prostrate on the ground or standing crowded together, saluting him with their hands and lips as he passed atop his stool and litter. Finally, because of the danger of revolt during the periods of interregnum, the ruling elites deemed it prudent to keep

Fig. 11. Inca on a litter. Guaman Poma, c. 1613/1936, folio 333.

the election of the new Cuzco secret. Thus the individual identity of any one incumbent may not have been recognized or remembered, especially by the peoples in distant locations. Such factors undoubtedly affected the historical data that the chroniclers heard and were able to collect (Betanzos 1551–57/1987, 141–48).[50]

The Spanish Colonial Transformation

The practice of inheriting names went largely unrecognized by the Spanish. The few who heard and understood the stories told in Quechua, Aymara, and other native languages of diverse individuals with the same name and sometimes multiple names found the narratives baffling. Cieza de León, long considered among the most reliable observers, admits that there were matters he did not fully understand. He is unashamedly selective, rejecting certain native informants' information. He states that "algunos yndios quisieron dezir que el un Ynga avía de ser de uno destos linajes y otro del otro, mas no lo tengo por çierto, ni lo creo" (some Indians want to say the one Inca should be from one of these lineages and another from another, but I do not believe it) (1548–50/1985, 97). Juan de Betanzos, the first Spaniard to organize his data into a sequence of imperial rulers in his mid-sixteenth-century history, writing about twenty years after first contacts and after he mastered the Quechua language and married into the native imperial elite, had time to inquire and gather more of the information related in oral traditions by, presumably, well-informed native elders, but not by unbiased actors and observers. Betanzos voices his frustrations at the difficulties posed during his own pioneering efforts. He tells of the variety of information he found in his inquiries and the differences between the conquistador and native narratives of events:

> This I believe because at that time the conquistadors paid less attention to fact finding than to subduing and acquiring the land and also because they were unaccustomed to dealing with the Indians; they did not know how to make inquiries and ask questions because they lacked an understanding of the language. Moreover, the Indians were

afraid to give them a full account. . . . If anyone should wish to argue that in the contents of this book there is anything superfluous or
left out that I forgot to include, the reason would be statements by
the common Indians, who customarily say whatever they imagine or
dream. Or it might be that it seemed so to such detractors when they
gathered information, that the Indians meant what the detractors state
now. Thus, the detractors did not understand these things fully nor
even the interpreters. In the past no one knew how to inquire and ask
what they wanted to find out and be well informed. (1551–57/1996, 3–4)

Betanzos consequently discounts the information of other Spaniards
and dismisses the tales of low-status commoner informants, preferring to highlight the stories he heard from the surviving southern
imperial elite, especially those of his wife's bloodline.

The fact that he judged the natives as "pagan" also influenced his
account; he thought that much of what the natives said was, therefore,
unworthy of confidence. In writing about their religion and gods, he
states, "Since they had no writing, were blind to knowledge, and almost without understanding, they differ in this in every way. . . . Generally, in all the land and in each of its provinces, the devil has them
confused. Everywhere that the devil showed up, he told them a thousand lies and delusions. Thus he had them deceived and blind" (44;
see also 262).

Finally, Betanzos's own cultural paradigm limited the framework
and structure of his remarks. He undoubtedly heard multiple stories
from many sources. Unable perhaps to understand culturally that
each lineage championed its own leaders (at least until incorporated
into the expanding empire), he selected and reordered his information to make it more comprehensibe to his Spanish readers; hence the
decision to present his information on the emperors as a sequence.

Garcilaso de la Vega, a mestizo and native Quechua speaker, reiterates the problems of cross-cultural communication while promising
to "include everything necessary for a full account of the beginning,
middle, and end of the Inca monarchy" while not "stray[ing] from the
true facts either by underestimating the ill or exaggerating the good

they did" (1609–12/1966, 1:51). Like Betanzos, he focuses on native errors stemming from their conditions as infidels and the method of collecting information:

> Paganism is a sea of errors, and I shall not write new and unheard of things, but will recount the same things the Spanish historians have written of these parts and their kings. . . . I shall merely act as a commentator to reveal and amplify much of what they have begun to say, but have left unfinished for lack of [a] full account. Much will be added that is missing in their histories but really happened, and some things will be omitted as superfluous because the Spaniards were misinformed, either because they did not know how to ask for information with a clear idea of the different periods and ages and divisions of provinces and tribes, or because they misunderstood the Indians who gave them it, or because they misunderstood one another on account of the difficulty of the language. The Spaniard who thinks he knows the language best is ignorant of nine-tenths of it, because of the many meanings of each word and the different pronunciation that a word has for various meanings. . . . (1:51)[51]

The method used by our Spanish historians was to ask the Indians in Spanish what they wanted to know. *Their contacts either had no clear knowledge of the old days or had bad memories and told them wrong, or gave incomplete accounts mingling the truth with poetic inventions and fabulous stories.* Worst of all, each side had only a very defective and incomplete knowledge of the other's language as a basis for asking and answering questions. This arose from the great difficulty presented by the Indian language and the little instruction the Indians then had in Spanish, so that the Indian understood the Spaniard's questions badly and the Spaniard understood the Indian's replies even worse. Very often either party understood the opposite of what was said; otherwise something similar but not the exact meaning, and it was only rarely that the true sense was conveyed. In this state of great confusion, *the priest or layman asking for information took at his will and pleasure whatever seemed closest to and most like what he wanted to know and what he thought his Indian had said. Thus interpreting things according to*

the whim of their imagination, they wrote down as true things the Indians
never dreamed of. (1:81–82) (emphasis added)[52]

In writing this, Garcilaso de la Vega admits that his bases of information are earlier European accounts; he is revising, commenting, and
expanding on other Spanish historians' views. He also is sifting their
information, judging what is right and wrong to better conform to
European cultural paradigms and imaginings. In pointing out the
failures of communication and interpretation of their predecessors
and peers, both Betanzos and Garcilaso de la Vega underscore their
own authority and, no doubt, engage to a greater or lesser extent in
bias confirmation.[53]

Each chronicler also had personal and public agendas. Betanzos not
so subtly sympathizes with Atahualpa and his lineage, not surprisingly given his matrimonial ties to this segment of the southern native
elite. Sarmiento de Gamboa wrote to specifically and explicitly dis-
credit the Cuzcos as tyrants. Garcilaso de la Vega wanted to sanitize
the Cuzcos and their civilization so as to impress the Spanish, among
whom he lived after leaving the Andes in early adulthood. Such sentiments also skewed their stories.

As a result, the early Spanish records are full of inconsistencies on
myriad points of Inca dynastic traditions. A review of the various six-
teenth- and seventeenth-century chronicles shows that there is no consensus among their authors on the number and names of the kings
who ruled the Andes in pre-Hispanic times. As summarized in table
8, the number of rulers' names in these sources ranges from as few as
four to over one hundred.[54] Betanzos's roster of kings, ending with
Atahualpa, became the standard[55] (see table 9 for his roster). Though
they differ in number, all chroniclers subscribe to the same linear,
chronological, and individual-centered structure. Other observers—
such as Pedro Sarmiento de Gamboa, writing at the behest of Viceroy Francisco de Toledo; Garcilaso de la Vega, reporting from Spain
in the seventeenth century in his old age; and the learned native Felipe Guaman Poma de Ayala, who also brought forth his account in
the early seventeenth century—reverse the order of the fourth and

fifth kings but otherwise follow Betanzos's lead. Polo de Ondegardo (1559/1916) also mentions a ruler (Rarku Waman or Tarco Human) who is unnamed in most of the other early accounts (10; Covey 2006, 174).

Table 8. Numbers of Inca rulers

Chronicler	Number of kings
Acosta	17
Anello Oliva	13
Anónimo de 1552	5
Anónimo del XVII	10
Betanzos	13
Cabello Valboa	13
Cieza de León	14
Cobo	13
Cordova y Salinas	8
Davila Briceno	12
Estete	4
Garcilaso	14
Guaman Poma de Ayala	12
Herrera	14
Las Casas	13
Molina, el Cuzqueno	6
Montesinos	c. 105
Murú	12
Ondegardo	12
Quipucamayocs	12
Santa Clara	13
Santa Cruz	13
Santillán	11
Sarmiento	12
Valera	7
Vásquez de Espinoza	14

Source: Alberto Bueno, "Los incas solo fueron cuatro," *Actas del Congreso Nacional de Investigación Histórica*, November 11–16, 1984, ed. Humberto Rodríguez Pastor, Tomo 3, Lima, CONCYTEC, 1991, p. 113.

Table 9. Chroniclers' rosters of kings

Comparison of Inca king lists

Betanzos's list (1551)	Sarmiento's list (1572)	Garcilaso's list (1615)	Guaman Poma's list (c. 1613)	Cabello Valboa's list (1586)
Manco Capac	Manco Capac	Manco Capac	Manco Capac	Mango Capac
Sinchi Roca	Sinchi Roca	Sinchi Roca	Sinchi Roca	Sinchi Roca
Lloque Yupanqui	Lloque Yupanqui	Lloque Yupanqui	Lloquie Yupanqui	Lluque Yunpanqui
Capac Yupanqui	Mayta Capac	Mayta Capac	Mayta Capac	Mayta Capac
Mayta Capac	Capac Yupanqui	Capac Yupanqui	Capac Yupanqui	Capac Yupanqui
Inca Roca	Inca Roca	Inca Roca	Inca Roca	Inca Roca
Yaguar Guaca	Yaguar Guaca or	Yaguar Guaca	Yaguar Guaca	Yaguar Guaca
Inca Yupanqui	Inca Yupangui			
Viracocha Inca	Viracocha Inca	Viracocha Inca	Viracocha Inca	Viracocha Inca
Pachacuti Inca	Pachacuti Inca	Pachacuti Inca	Pachacuti Inca	Pachacuti Inca
Yupanqui	Yupanqui	Yupanqui	Yupanqui	Yupanqui
Topa Inca Yupanqui	Topa Inca Yupanqui	Topa Inca Yupanqui	Topa Inca Yupanqui	Topa Ynca Yupanqui
Guayna Capac	Guayna Capac	Guayna Capac	Guayna Capac	Guayna Capac
Huáscar	Huáscar	Huáscar	Huáscar	Huáscar
Atahualpa	Atahualpa	Atahualpa		Atahualpa

Betanzos's sequence of kings, copied in whole or in part by subsequent chroniclers, became the "standard short list." Other chroniclers provide some dates and lengths of reigns from which it can be concluded that they were not only improbable but, undoubtedly, impossible.[56] Despite the fact that the Andeans did not reckon time in years as defined by the Christian calendar, Sarmiento de Gamboa (1572/1999) asserts that the Incas ruled from 565 CE to 1533 for a total of 968 years, as shown in table 10. The length of individual administrations is from 9 to 111 years with an average of over 75 years for the known reigns of ten of twelve kings. Cabello Valboa's (1586/1951) reckoning begins in c. 945 with an average of about 45 years per known reign as shown in table 11.[57] These can be contrasted with the average of three decades that each Habsburg king held power in Spain and with the figure that the average life expectancy of a white male at birth in 1900 in the United States was only 47. John H. Rowe, who studied these lists for dating pottery and the material record of various pre-Hispanic cultures, favors Cabello Valboa's list and dates but dismisses all dates before those for Viracocha as not "plausible," "exceedingly unreliable guesswork," or "shadowy" (1945, 277, 282; 1946, 203).[58] Zuidema (1990, 490, 496, 503) remarks that the Cuzco dynasty, as recounted orally from Pachacuti Inca back in time, had no historical value and its later history was compressed into two generations, like the practice of the ethnic lineages under the Kazembes.

Table 10. Length of king reigns, according to Sarmiento (1572/1999)

King	Year of birth	Start of reign	Date of death	Length of reign	Source
Manco Capac	521	c. 565	665	100	pp. 60–62
Sinchi Roca	548	656	675	19	p. 63
Lloque Yupanqui	654	675	786	111	p. 65
Mayta Capac	778	?	890	?	p. 69
Capac Yupanqui	876	891	980	89	p. 70
Inca Roca	985	?	1088	?	p. 72
Yahuar Guaca	<1069	>1088	c. 1184	96	p. 81

King	Year of birth	Start of reign	Date of death	Length of reign	Source
Viracocha	<1166	c. 1184	1285	101	p. 86
Pachacuti	1066	1088	1191	103	p. 139
Topa Inca Yupanqui	1173	1191	1258	67	pp. 153–54
Guayna Capac	1444	1464	1524	60	p. 169
Huáscar	1493	1524	1533	9	p. 189

Table 11. Length of king reigns, according to Cabello Valboa (1586/1951)

King	Start of reign	End of reign	Length of reign	Source
Manco Capac	c. 945	1006	61	pp. 264, 270
Sinchi Roca	1006	1083	77	pp. 275, 280
Lloque Yupanqui	1083	1161	78	p. 286
Mayta Capac	1161	1226	65	p. 289
Capac Yupanqui	1226	1306	80	p. 291
Inca Roca	1306	1356	50	p. 294
Yaguar Guaca	1356	1386	30	p. 493
Viracocha Inca	1386	1438	50	p. 301
Pachacuti Inca Yupanqui	1438	1473	35	p. 493
Topa Inca Yupanqui	1473	1493	20	p. 354
Guayna Capac	1493	1525	32	p. 294
Huáscar	1525	1532	7	
Atahualpa	1532	1533	1	

A welcome article by Covey (2006) supports these conclusions. He compares the chronicles' lists with the archaeological record (especially after 1200 CE) and finds that the names of a dozen or so kings memorialized by the Spanish chronicles are inconsistent with the material evidence. He states that "accounts of Inka ancestral origins are not historically reliable . . . the Pachakutiq myth cannot explain the available evidence adequately . . . and AD 1438 should not be used to [*sic*] as a starting date for the Inka polity and its history" (172–73, 193). This is additional evidence for genealogical foreshortening and the construction of composites.[59]

Such findings have important implications for Andean history. First, they suggest that the dynastic lists of the Incas have been compressed and foreshortened.[60] Perhaps what the chroniclers heard and collected were stories about important names that represented heroic, collective characters from the past that not necessarily succeeded one after the other. To quote and paraphrase the archaeologist Michael Moseley, who wrote on the Chimor Empire, which was conquered by the Cuzcos c. 1470, a name in the dynastic tradition (in this case Nancenpinco) represented a "merging of royal identities with the appropriation of prior political accomplishments." Such names would thus have represented archetypes, subject to selective retention or rejection, some older than others. Such a manipulation is thought to have been the case, judging by archaeological remains. He concludes that

> if the royal successions are truncated in the oral traditions, then those individuals surviving in name may be composite characters who appropriated by design, or by the vagaries of the oral transmission of history, the qualities, accomplishments, and reputations of earlier monarchs. This problem of merging of royal identities is probably more acute for the earlier rulers in a succession, those closest to the putative founders of a dynastic line, than for the more recent sovereigns who, in some cases, ruled within memory of people able to give testimony to the Spanish chroniclers. (Moseley, n.d., 26, 29–30; 1990, 33–34, 36–37)[61]

Second, such conclusions require a reconsideration of the most notorious chronicler who departed from the standard short list. The seventeenth-century Jesuit author Fernando de Montesinos's book, *Memorias antiguas historiales y políticos del Perú* (c. 1644), includes the names of over a hundred Andean rulers. Montesinos's lengthy list— heretofore almost universally discredited, considered of scant impor- tance, and neglected or suppressed for centuries, victim of a tacit censorship preventing its circulation—is the subject of Juha Hiltunen's research (1995, 1998). He believes that this list cannot be so easily dis- missed, concluding that the chronicle is "a far more reliable histor- ical account of [the] Peruvian past than has hitherto been thought" (1998, 9). Hiltunen names Inca Yupanqui Pachacuti as the major ar- chitect of Inca historiography, a position not in conflict with some chroniclers' accounts. He credits him with manipulating the official story to fit imperial propaganda needs.[62]

Hyland's (2003) research on the biography of the mestizo Jesuit Blas Valera highlights the overlap between the works of Montesinos and her subject, furthering a serious reconsideration of his informa- tion. Both Valera and Montesinos shared references to a long list of Andean kings that appears to reflect the native traditions of the Qui- to region. According to Hyland, the list may have originated with a "copious" history of the Incas that Francisco de Chaves gave to Luis Valera, Blas's father. The elder Valera eventually gave it to his friend Diego de Olivares, who shared its contents with associates. Mean- while Blas Valera's knowledge of the Andes deepened while he stud- ied liberal arts and theology in Trujillo (Peru) and there spent hours listening to native oral traditions. Later he served as the spiritual ad- viser for the Nombre de Jesús confraternity in Cuzco. In this capacity he held discussions with Andean nobles, during which he may have developed his views, considered radical by his peers, on native and Christian religions. In 1580 Valera was in Potosí, where he met the Mer- cedarian fray Melchior Hernández, who had composed texts on na- tive religious history and another analysis of Quechua prayers. Back in Quito in the mid-1590s, Valera may have met Bishop López de Só- lis, who was known for sympathizing with and defending the natives.

Here Hyland's analysis dovetails with the impressive research of Ser- gio Barraza Lescano (2003). Bishop López de Solis owned a manuscript written by a mestizo of Quito, Diego Lobato de Sosa (b. 1538–41, d. >1604), the son of a founder of Quito, Captain Juan Lobato de Sosa who had come to America in the company of Sebastian de Benalcázar and a principal wife of Atahualpa, Isabel Yarucpalla. Diego Lobato de Sosa, a Quechua-speaking ordained priest in the 1560s, wrote a history of the Incas c. 1583. He probably gathered his information in the north, farther from the Cuzco elite and perhaps less influenced by the Spanish.

Although direct contacts between Chaves, Olivares, Lobato de Sosa, and Valera cannot be documented at this time, it was there in the northern city that Valera composed his *Relación de las costumbres antiguas de los naturales del Pirú*. In it he refers to at least nine Andean rulers named Pachacuti.[63] He also compiled a vocabulary, which was used by the Italian Jesuit Giovanni Anello Oliva in writing his chronicle c. 1630–31. Anello Oliva cites Valera's *Vocabulario* to support his thesis that there were many Peruvian kings. Anello Oliva explicitly mentions Capac Raymi Amauta, the thirty-ninth king of Peru; Capac Yupanqui Amauta, the forty-fifth; Cuis Manco, the sixty-fourth;[64] and Capac Lluqui Yupanqui, the ninety-fifth; along with "other kings distinct from those that I have recounted in the genealogy [of the Cuzcos]." The works of all these authors with their repetition of the names (such as Yupanqui, Manco, and Lluqui) could be evidence of positional inheritance and a cyclical worldview (Anello Oliva 1630–31/1998, 95–96; Zuidema 1990, 489; Megged 2005, especially 186; Szemiñski 2013, 398).[65]

In fact, the reasons for these many and sundry inconsistencies may be traced to the fact that the Cuzco elite who served as the informants for early accounts may not themselves have had a deep knowledge of succession at the imperial level as claimed by Garcilaso de la Vega (above), but only of those who originated among their immediate kin group. Moreover, after about 1533 they had prolonged and constant contact with the Spanish and were the first to adapt their thinking and testimony to the new, foreign, and dominant paradigm. In this process historical traditions and collective memories may have been lost; the members of the Cuzco elite really had no choice (Duviols

1979, 78; Lorandi 1995, 86). They either had to go into exile and join the rebel Inca government in Vilcabamba or adjust, accommodate, and adapt to the new order, for their power and privileges now depended on Spanish approval. Franklin Pease (1996, 33), an acknowledged authority on the Incas, states that the introduction of a new standard for succession (i.e., heredity and primogeniture) obliged the Andeans to quickly fabricate genealogies.[66] More recently, José Carlos de la Puente Luna (2016, especially 27) details the active accommodation of members of the royal lineages to securing recognition of their noble status by using Spanish terminology and categories, and their acceptance of the general reinterpretation of Inca dyanstic history as presented by Sarmiento de Gamboa in 1572. Duviols (1979, especially 78) reiterates the point, mentioning, in an article on diarchy, that the native elites submitted to the Spanish monarchical interpretation and had no interest in explaining the Cuzco indigenous system of succession.[67]

Constant contact also certainly explains some of the erratic testimony on whether succession at the imperial level was from brother to brother (as among the Reques in 1595 [Rostworowski 1961; Romero Meza 2014, 3, 12]), son to son, or uncle to nephew (as in Colombia [Muñoz Arbeláez 2015]).[68] Zuidema (2008, 48) reports that Viceroy Francisco de Toledo ordered Sarmiento de Gamboa to impose primogeniture on the data he collected for his 1572 chronicle, a mandate that certainly skewed the chroniclers' interpretations. The king ordered male hereditary succession again in 1614 (Hyland 2016, 130).

Unlike the analysis of the naming practices of the Jayancas, which persisted at least into the seventeenth century, the evidences of positional inheritance fade quickly in the city of the Cuzco, refounded in 1534 as a Spanish administrative center. The Spanish stopped using "el Cuzco" to refer to the ruler of the native peoples, preferring to use his personal name as was the Spanish custom in referring to their own kings. This breach of native etiquette may have been a way to further denigrate an exemplary ruler and underscore that they, the Spanish, were now the lords of the Andean populace, not at all obliged to observe the Andean custom of not uttering the ruler's personal name.

This changed practice did little to help document and understand Andean history.

The names that were repeated and remembered, like the five Manco Capacs[69] and the nine Pachacutis, were those, no doubt, that were associated with prodigious accomplishments that were recalled and celebrated again and again. The individuals who held these names might be forgotten in time, but the name remained. Over the years the names came to recall great events, making the name representative of a composite or archetype—as "el Cuzco" was becoming in 1532. It would have become, like the other recurring titles and names, a label that linked the present to the renowned achievements back to the apical ancestors, the Sun and the Moon, and the power of a growing number of followers. The name became a marker that summarized all that was worthy of recall.

A Hierarchy of Sequentially Assumed Names

In sum, positional inheritance also fits the Andean data.[70] The practice continued among relatively isolated peoples, like the Jayancas, for a century or so after first contact, while the greater contact that the surviving imperial elite had with the Spanish invaders, with their imposed power structures and Iberian laws in the then refounded Spanish city of the Cuzco, quickly transformed the practice. The chroniclers did not have the undisguised familiarity with native culture that the witnesses in the Jayanca records had, many of whom were natives or Europeans who had lived among the indigenous peoples for years. In the south, the Spanish gleaned the names of past rulers from the natives' oral traditions. They translated the information both literally and culturally and placed it into a dynastic structure that Europeans could understand. Thus, close association undoubtedly influenced native thinking and the memories they selectively shared with their Spanish overlords.

| Chapter Five

Reflections on Oral Traditions as History

George Washington, Nelson Mandela, and Simon Bolivar are figures whose names are almost universally recognizable in North America, South Africa, and South America, respectively. They command attention and represent courage, fortitude, and ability. These individuals stand as cultural heroes and models worthy of emulation. In preliterate societies names also mattered, especially when they evoked memories of an imagined past peopled by heroic ancestors. They projected power; they had fame; they held meanings and, in that sense, served as historical artifacts and social types.They encoded information on religious beliefs, values, and worldviews (Akinnaso 1983, esp. 140, 145; Wieschhoff 1937). They helped people without writing to recall important deeds. Names became mnemonic devices that elicited memories, which, once selected and codified into oral traditions, recalled a group's origins. Their use explained how they received their crops and animals and came to concentrate in various locations. They gave a people identity and taught them what was appropriate behavior and how to deal with different situations, much as place names did for the Apaches and fairy tales did for European peasants (Basso 1988, 1996; Darnton 1984). Reembodied names brought selected yesterdays into the moment and projected them into the tomorrows, thus guaranteeing the continuation of society as people imagined and constructed it.

This inquiry, which centers on the question of how preliterate people remember, discusses three societies, each on a different continent and thousands of miles apart, and scattered others at different times. Such societies preserved memories and reinforced identity through the use of a naming convention, labeled "positional inheritance" by Ian Cunnison based on his 1940s ethnographic research in Central Africa. Names passed from one individual to another and their collective deeds, preserved in oral narratives, ritual, and song, built reputations that accrued not to an individual but to the name. Through repetition, a famous and even legendary name became a title, though the sequential series of individuals occupying the title and the position were forgotten. Each occupant endeavored to maintain the status inherent in the title and enhance it by showing valor and wisdom during his tenure. Nostalgia was not involved; in populating the various positions of an indigenous hierarchy, the participants were re-creating the sociopolitical structure at the time of the beginning of the group. The ritual conveying the title reminded participants and viewers alike of the stories of the group's past and invited them to relive their histories. They thus used ancestral names to support collective memories, forge identities, and evoke the past.

African explorers, travelers, missionaries, and government officials left records on the Kazembes and lineage leaders, and their succession patterns, starting in the eighteenth century. In the Luapula area, boys took adult names and sometimes ascended in status to take the name of lineage leader. They thereby learned what amounted to the biography of the name and recounted it on ritual occasions in the first person.

The second case study on the history of the Ho-De'-No-Sau-Nee name-taking is drawn mostly from missionary accounts, complemented by a few government administrators' records, from the seventeenth and eighteenth centuries. These sources, plus ethnographic studies that begin in the mid-nineteenth century, round out the picture of native North American usages, especially at the family and lineage levels. Again, individuals took successive names and statuses in their families and bloodlines. A few eventually took the name of one of the fifty hereditary chiefs of the native Confederation. In raising men up to take these names, society expected them to assume the status and responsibilities of their predecessors. During the condolence ceremony, hosts repeatedly instructed onlookers in the history of their culture and society. Participants recited the names of the chiefs and the audience could see the reembodied chiefs as imagined at the time of the Confederation's founding, a living history before their eyes.

In the Andes, judicial and administrative manuscripts and notarial records, starting in the sixteenth century, bring Andean positional inheritance into the twenty-first century, where current practices, sometimes somewhat modified, mirror those of old in some rural native communities, such as Incahuasi in northern Peru.[1] In north coastal societies, chiefs and lesser lords also took hereditary names, turned into titles, of their predecessors.

These usage reconstructions are based on admittedly fragmentary records. Yet if the details of one case study are placed alongside those of another, the details of one society's practices suggestively fill the gaps and supply the missing data to the other so that a prototype emerges. The outline of the practice—taking traditional names in the present to enliven the past—becomes clear.

Positional inheritance as practiced in these three societies shares:

A hierarchy of named positions.

The importance of perpetuating names that refer to the first person to have held or created the position. Being the first to do something important or the winner in a transcendental conflict gives one the power to name and be named. Subsequently, certain names became associated with given attributes and served to mark allegiances, identities, and relative status. Often women assigned names of predecessors to persons who displayed or had the potential to display the associated characteristics that commemorated previous name-holders. Thus the names became enshrined and synonymous with an archetype and category.

The practice of taking on more than one name during a lifetime.

The desirability of moving into vacant, senior named positions.

The perpetuation of relative positions based on kinship or quasi-fictitious kinship relationships between the original name-holders.

The retelling of the activities of individuals taking recurring, cyclically used names in two temporal dimensions—then and now. The conception of time changes for those who accept that their history is alive and relived in each succeeding generation. The past, no matter how remote, is subsumed and incorporated into the present.[2]

The names of the leaders served to identify the scattered populace subject to their jurisdiction, no matter where families lived and no matter how often they moved. Such a demographic conception of a group stands in sharp contrast to the model of ethnicity imported into Africa and the Americas by the British, French, and Spanish colonists who preferred to depict on maps "a series of mutually exclusive, nation-like ethnic entities with which individuals identified unequivocally and for all time" (Worby 1994, 375). This latter convention is the model and strategy used by John H. Rowe and many others in depicting ethnic territories on maps—which do not take into consideration scattered-site occupation (*"ocupación salpicada"*), the multilineage occupations of some towns (*"pueblos compartidos"*), and the multiple residences of one person found described in early administrative and judicial accounts (Rowe 1946, map 3; Ramírez 2005, especially ch. 6; Pärsinnen 1996, 74–77). In the Andes, some of the names of leaders, alive during the first decades after contact, survived the native-resettlement initiatives (*reducciones, congregaciones*) of the 1560s and 1570s as toponyms. Some of them exist to this day. The names Jayanca, Túcume, Íllimo, Pátapo, Pácora, Neptur, Sicán, Pacatnamu, and Xotoro became associated with places, actual settlements, and monuments, and remained stable for decades and even centuries.

Myth and History

These three case studies also contribute to the discussion of a major issue of interest to ethnohistorians and others: the controversy over myth and history. Myths, to some scholars, winnow the unintelligible masses of memories and, particularly, oral traditions into a filtered, comprehensible whole to provide answers and relevance to universal questions. In the process, actors might be elevated to heroic status and, in time, may be equated with gods and accepted as such. In societies where personal and collective memory seldom goes back more than two to four generations (O'Phelan Godoy 1993, 2; Peel 1984, 115; Henige 1974, 2), these serve as timeless examples to teach believers morality and norms, and, in so doing, link people to gods. Others disparage and dismiss myth as imagined, false, and fabricated fantasy, peopled with supernaturally powerful heroes who founded the ethnic group, provided for its lands and waters, or gifted it with basic foodstuffs (Zuidema 1992, especially 173; Maršálek 2011, 139). Often myth is characterized as synchronous and structural (as opposed to diachronous and sequential in the ordering of documentary history) (Atkinson 1975). To others, myth is ahistorical; the only "true" history is that which can be supported with records, be they carved into stone, painted on a rock, or written on parchment, leather, cloth, or paper.[3] For Heehs (1994) and positivistic historiography, myth and history are antithetical modes of explanation (1:5; Burke 1989, 103). Taking an intermediate position between these two opinions are those who posit that there may be some lived bases for the stories that the unlettered tell (Read and González 2000). But is this definitional distinction between myth and history important?[4]

Claude Lévi-Strauss, who has written on myth, characterizes oral societies as "cold" in contrast with other societies that are "hot." Lévi-Strauss's clearest explanation of his concepts appears in his published *Conversations*, edited by G. Charbonnier. There he states that cold societies are "static societies with no history," reminding readers of Eric Wolf's famous book mentioned in chapter 1. For Lévi-Strauss, cold societies remain in their initial (natural) state and are, in a sense, closed (Charbonnier 1969, 33; Lévi-Strauss 1966/1968, 90, 234–37). Members seek unanimity in decision-making because harmony is indispensable to the continuing existence of their largely egalitarian society (Charbonnier 1969, 35). The collective life of the group is cyclical, immutable, repetitious, and regular (39; Lévi-Strauss 1966/1968, 73, 82). They pass through a succession of states before returning to the starting point and beginning the rotation all over again. Levi-Strauss believed that "each of these [primitive, nonliterate, "cold"] societies considers that its essential and ultimate aim is to persevere in its existing form and carry on as it was established by its ancestors, and for the sole reason that it was so fashioned by its ancestors. . . . 'That is how we have always done it'" (Charbonnier 1969, 49–50). In other words, it is legitimate because it has endured (50). Hot societies, in contrast, are not cyclical but evolutionary and modern; they eschew unanimity and turn disequilibrium and difference into change and development (38).

Marshall Sahlins's (1981) work on Hawaii provides perspective on the issue. His iconic analysis of Hawaiian history and myth is based on his perceptive study of Captain James Cook's visits to the islands in the late eighteenth century.[5] He foreshadows the interpretations of Cook's arrival and subsequent interactions with the Hawaiians by outlining the religiopolitical beliefs of the latter. The islanders divided the ritual year into two seasons in which the gods Lono and Ku alternated (11). Lono, the god of fertility, represented peace and productive abundance. He came with the winter rains to renew growth and stayed for four lunar months, a period called Makahiki, before disappearing to invisible lands or the sky. Ku, whose earthly representation was the king or chief, was associated with human sacrifice.

Within this context, Sahlins's reconstruction of Captain Cook's actions and itinerary corresponded—not perfectly but closely enough—to the expected cultural traditions to identify him with the God Lono. Captain Cook's ships appeared offshore in 1778 (1981, 20; 1985, 74). During this first visit to the islands, he was treated as a divine appearance (1981, 17). He sailed into Hawaiian waters again on November 26, 1878, about a week from the start of the Makahiki festival. Before landing he circumnavigated the island in a clockwise direction, which the Hawaiians equated symbolically with the possession of the kingdom (1981, 19–20). This circuit began on December 2, 1778, about two weeks before Lono's annual circumnavigation was believed to begin (December 13, 1778) (1981, 20–21) and the date that Ku's temple closed and human sacrifice was suspended. Cook finally stepped ashore on January 17,

1779, at Kealakekua Bay and was called Lono by the priests as they led him to a principal temple. As he passed, bystanders prostrated themselves before him, a gesture that indicated their acceptance of him as Lono (1981, 17–18; 1985, 38). The Makahiki festivities ended about February 1, 1779, and Captain Cook sailed out of the bay three days later on February 4 (1981, 20, 22). Shortly thereafter, one of his ships needed a repair, so Cook and his crews about-faced, arriving out of season and unexpectedly during the ascendancy of Ku and the king. The latter interpreted this unexplained return as a threat to his sovereignty, and Captain Cook was ritually murdered as a dangerous rival to the chief and Ku (1981, 22; 1985, xvii). To paraphrase Sahlins, he died because he had ritually transgressed the ceremonial status that Hawaiians had accorded him (1985, xiii).[6]

Sahlins makes two points of interest to the issue. First, the Hawaiian people believed their ancestral stories (1981, 27) and interpreted Cook's appearance accordingly. Hawaiians accepted Cook's landing as an event; their ancestral spirit had returned (7). Sahlins concludes that the captain's interactions with the Hawaiians were a "stereotypic reproduction" of existing cultural categories and archetypal situations (6, 14; Peel 1984, 113).

This first point on the reality of myths is plain elsewhere in Spanish America. Aztec (Nahuatl) lore relates stories of a king and deity, Quetzalcoatl, whose name meant "Feathered Serpent." Some scholars believe "he probably once was a real ruler" who in bearing Quetzalcoatl's name also bore some of the god's power (Read and González 2000, 225). Many versions of his story exist, emphasizing his creator-side and his cultural-hero role, in which he proved "a morally upright governance model" (223). Details indicate that he dominated in central Mexico and left, going east. When he arrived at the gulf, he boarded a ship (or a raft of serpents) and sailed toward the rising sun, promising to return. Some versions add that he was light-haired and of fair complexion; others add that he marked the trees with an x as he left. The latter details may be colonial additions, but there was enough resemblance between a fair-skinned, cross-bearing Hernán Cortés, arriving by water from the east, and the ancestral stories of the Nahuatl-speaking peoples to initially consider him the reincarnated and returning god and King Quetzalcoatl. Kay Read asserts that "Quetzalcoatl's return in the form of Cortés arose not as a prediction of the Conquest but as an after-the-fact mythical explanation of it" (2000, 226).[7]

Parallel stories surround Francisco Pizarro's landing on the western coast of South America in 1531–32. The inhabitants considered Pizarro the creator god Viracocha or his messenger. Local people believed that, after finishing his work untold generations before, Viracocha had vanished across the ocean. After the Greek shipmate, Pedro de Candia, went ashore at Tumbes and shot off his arquebus, the startled natives fell to the ground or screamed; thereafter they did not question that these strangers could command "the thunder of the heavens" and were harbingers of their god (Cieza de León 1548–50/1998, 112–13). They believed him to be the son of the Sun or to have come from the sky, and they took him to their Temple of the Sun (Ramírez 2005, 101). Although the Andean emperor Atahualpa's spies quickly informed him that these strangers were mortal human beings, his doubts continued to haunt him to the day of his capture in the plaza of Cajamarca. Yet the commoners continued to call the Spaniards Viracochas into the 1560s and 1570s, testifying to their continuing beliefs in the stories they heard from their elders (Guillén Guillén 1974, especially 142; BNE/Ms. 2010, 1576; Guaman Poma de Ayala 1613/1980, 370/[372], 381/[383]; Salomon 1999, 30, 34, 36; Acosta 1590/1979, 310; Garcilaso de la Vega 1609–12/1966, 287–89; Pachacuti Yamqui Salcamayhua 1613/1879, 325; Collapiña et al. 1542/1980, 88).[8]

Sahlins's second point of interest here is that the reproduction of Hawaiian mythical structure became a lasting transformation. In other words, Sahlins used structuralism to analyze what occurred, but further shows that the categories changed in their repetition. Captain Cook's death on February 14, 1779, gave the king possession of his bones and initiated a new era of British influence (Sahlins 1981, 7; 1985, 74). In this regard Sahlins's example shows that history is not static, even when cyclical. Past and present, to paraphrase Peel, are mutually conditioning: "Where possible, present practice is governed by the model of past practice and, where change does occur, there is a tendency to rework the past so as to make it appear that the past practice has governed present practice" (1984, 113; Finley 1965, 295). In accepting change, however incremental and slow, the so-called and categorized "cold" societies move along the spectrum toward the hot pole.

This conclusion is confirmed by the Ho-De'-No-Sau-Nee condolence ceremony, which enabled attendees to reimage the mythical founding of their Confederation and the first chiefs' assumption of command. Their centuries-old chants recalling the past and their ritual symbolized the raising up of a replacement for a deceased or removed chief. Such recurring enactments of positional inheritance reiterated their history, with multiple and confirming recitations of the chiefs' names and the reminders of the Confederation's laws, both of which served as visible and oral-history lessons. But this performance and reconstitution of received ancestral tales, though cyclical, was not unchanging. It included elements of transformation because no matter how carefully the matrons chose the successor, no matter how carefully the successor learned the songs and feats of his multiple named predecessors, he brought his own skills, biases, and goals to the reincarnation (Bodenhorn and vom Bruck 2006, 5).[9] His subsequent tenure, hopefully, would live up to the reputation of the name and possibly enhance it; or it might not. Either way, the name and its reputation would be affected; it might be further "built up" or languish for inactivity. Either way, the recognized status of individual names would be affected and altered. In this manner the Ho-De'-No-Sau-Nee moved slowly away from the cold pole and into the cool zone.

Alongside the end of revenge wars for which the Confederation was originally conceived, and multiple relocations, the occasions to boastfully sing the songs that recalled the feats of namesakes with the addition of the triumphs of the incumbent diminished, sapping the vigor from communal commemorations and weakening traditions. Morgan (1851/1962, especially 64–65) reports that the meaning of some of the chief names had been forgotten already in the 1840s. Annemarie Shimony, writing about the Ho-De'-No-Sau-Nee in the 1990s, reports that, although the council of hereditary chiefs at the Six Nations

Reserve continued to hold monthly meetings and follow traditional procedures, only 31 of the 50 (62 percent) chief's names could still be translated and 19 of the 50 (38 percent) of the chief positions were vacant or the holder was unknown (1994, 99, 104–16). She notes further:

> At one time many of the names indicated status, for example the chiefs' names or the hereditary deaconship names or the Ohgi'we matron names, but today this aspect of naming is becoming more and more obsolete. Almost none of the "baby names" (which are the ordinary names assigned to the population) carry a connotation of an occupation, a status, or a privileged position; and most of the names which at one time indicated an office have been lost, or, if the name remains, the associated office is not known. Very few of the matrons, deacons, medicine-keepers, society officers, or warriors today have a name which indicates their position or was accorded to them because of the position. (213)

Only the names associated with the chiefs, she continues, "are carefully preserved" (213). Thus, the stories of the founding were no longer often repeated; in time they became almost irrelevant to many. This might not be evident in a synchronous, short-term study; the transformation becomes clear with a long-term (longue durée) analysis. The society had definitely approached the middle warm zone.

Embedded in these considerations is the temporal dimension. Many nonliterate societies did not measure time and lacked calendrical systems.[10] The Nuer, Evans-Pritchard (1939, 208–10) found, had no concept of time and consequently no developed abstract system of time-reckoning; nor did they have a numerical system of dating. "Long long ago" was never longer than fifty years. Instead they thought in terms of activities and successions of activities. Similarly, the Sakalava of Madagascar showed no idea of historical time as a specific dimension of social life (Feeley-Harnik 1978, 403). They exhibited no interest in chronologies, either relative or absolute (Finley 1965, 285).

Those societies that could calibrate the past did so in terms of king lists or genealogies. But these gauges suffer from weaknesses, distortions, and limitations. King lists were often telescoped by expunging

usurpers and those imposed by a foreign suzerain with attending periods of foreign domination and chaos (Henige 1971, 373–75; 1974, 28);
by eliminating rulers whose reigns were uneventful, disastrous, or il-
legitimate; or by the personification of an entire era by a founding
folk-hero (1974, 5–9). In contrast to such telescoping mechanisms were
means to lengthen them by listing contemporary rulers as successive
ones; extending father-to-son successions; exaggerating the length of
reigns;[11] measuring the reigns of rulers as generations; and adding fictitious names to the roll (1971, 373–83; 1974, 49). Henige cites the example
of Pictish king lists that included forty rulers attached to a list's beginning of which thirty consecutive rulers were named Brude (1971, 376).
Positional inheritance with its name repetition also compromised genealogies (1974, 21). Henige concludes that genealogies usually are shallow and their chronological value is minimal (1974, 4). Yet as many as
two hundred generations were added at the beginning of Rajput genealogies in order to please the genealogist's patron. Thus, transmitted
traditions are conflated, modified, invented, and falsified (Finley 1965,
298–99). The conversion of both lists and genealogies into Christian
years to calculate how far back they go and so determine temporal context is another difficulty. Absolute dating is difficult because it involves
assigning, often arbitrarily, an average assumed length of life or reign.[12]

In many cases time was two-dimensional: now, the present, and the
distant, unimaginably remote past, *"tiempo inmemorial"* (time before
memory) for Andeans, or "dream age" to Australian aborigines (Lévi-
Strauss 1966/1968, 237; O'Phelan Godoy 1993). Peel (1984) notes that a
living chief used the first-person-singular pronoun to describe the doings of a remote ancestor. Sahlins found that Fijians, like the Luapula,
followed this model. He noted, "A Fijian or Maori chief could quite
grammatically use 'I' in reference to the exploits of his ancestors long
dead or of his lineage long before he was born. 'I fought at such-and-
such a place, and there I died; then I moved to this village,' he could
say. 'It was here that I ate you long ago, before the white man came,
so you have no claims here'" (Sahlins's reply to Borofsky 1997, 275–76).
Eliade, as noted above, sees the phenomenon as universal among il-
literate peoples (1954, 85–86 as cited by Peel 1984, 113).

Thus, in all three societies native narratives remained flexible. In Africa, Blount (1975) (mentioned in chapter 2) recounts how lineage leaders met to try to get their stories straight. The narrative of lineage-leader successions was subject to political influence—where the most vocal and high-status authority imposed his understanding in cases of conflicting recall. Some personages and their accomplishments were deleted from the resulting official sequence, thus shortening the name genealogy and telescoping versions of former eras. Filtered versions of this official story fit the present propaganda needs of the propagators.

Implications of Close Encounters

Manipulation of succession narratives is also evident in the rosters of the Andean kings, but in the Andean case it was done first by Spanish chroniclers and only later by the natives themselves. The bilingual interpreter Juan de Betanzos collected the stories of the southern elite. He did not understand many of the stories he heard. Undoubtedly, what he heard was a collective biography of a name. He took the liberty of choosing some to populate a narrative and list; his writing later influenced many Spanish, mestizo, and Hispanized native chroniclers, including Sarmiento de Gamboa, Cabello Valboa, Garcilaso de la Vega, Guaman Poma de Ayala, and others (MacCormack 1991, especially chs. 6 and 7).[13] Such a scenario signifies that the chroniclers' accounts failed to reflect Andean mentality, imagination, and celebrated modes of recall.

The result has skewed the interpretation of native traditions and the current historiography on the Incas, especially since the Spanish failed to grasp the essence of Andean kingly narratives. As shown in chapter 4, by the 1550s Spanish writers very rapidly identified the Andean kings by a personal name as was the practice in Europe; succession ideally followed the primogeniture rule; and each king was listed as part of a European-style dynastic structure, although sequence was sometimes confused.[14] The often-cited anthropologist R. Tom Zuidema remarks that the Cuzco dynasty as recounted orally from Pachacuti Inca back in time had no historical value and its later history was compressed into two generations. Thus the founder's name was enshrined and inherited as were those of new but subordinate breakaway groups, which demanded less prestige than the first. Like an hourglass, memory was most expansive, detailed, and vivid for the first and most recent leaders; the middle was muddled. Some names were swapped; others inserted. Individuals were lost in the recounting of deeds meant to forge a collective identity.

What the Spanish, mestizo, and Hispanicized native chroniclers recorded was neither a history (as Europeans defined it) nor an accurate king list or genealogy. Their representation of the remembered past, once fixed on paper, preserved only selected ideas about the sixteenth and seventeenth centuries. These became the raw material from which contemporary observers reconstructed a story to fit their own cultural needs (Duviols 1997a; Netherly 1990; Zuidema 1982, 1990, 490, 496, 503; Ellefsen 1994; see also Salomon 1999, especially 53–55; Adorno 1982, 1986).

In the provinces change to tradition was slower, but in the seventeenth century natives contrived to mold their past to conform to Spanish norms. This is particularly evident in court cases over succession. In these cases natives tried to fit their various practices into a dynastic genealogical sequence with many gaps, conflicting information, and incongruities as a result. Karen Powers best analyzes the seventeenth- and eighteenth-century struggles over chiefly power in Riobamba, Ecuador. There the Duchiselas manipulated and misrepresented their history to preserve their hegemony. Other cases over leadership are replete with confusing testimonies, claims, and counterclaims—some referring to brother-to-brother succession, others to uncle-to-nephew, and finally, some others to father-to-son inheritance of the overlordship. Each contestant presented witnesses who attempted to say the "right" things to convince the colonial judges that their party had the right to rule, but in so doing they often hopelessly confused the facts (ANP/Derecho Indígena (DI), legajo (l.) I, cuaderno (c.) 7, 1566; DI, l. 3. c. 19, 1574; l. 31, c. 622, 1597; BNP/A142, 1574; A371, 1594; A379, 1596; ART/ CoO, l. 154, expediente (exp.) 223, 15-III-1585; CoPedimentos, l. 280, exp. 3634, 20-VIII-1592; ANB/Expedientes Coloniales 1588, no. 5; EC 1589, c. I, e. I; BMH/A116, 1594; Powers 1998; Rostworowski 1961). Over time the competitive pattern of brother-to-brother succession before the office fell to the next generation, always favoring the most apt, was replaced by father-to-son legitimacy of rule.

Alan Durston, one of the foremost scholars of Quechua literacy, found that by the mid-seventeenth century reading and writing became widespread among Peruvian indigenous elites, but "the offices and institutions of colonial indigenous self-rule in the Andes did not make use of alphabetic record keeping" to the same extent as their Mesoamerican counterparts (2007, 44). Perhaps for that reason, some seventeenth-century natives in the central Andes presented uncontested genealogies going back eight to ten generations to their purported first ancestor who settled an area or introduced an important crop. In some cases their descendants believed that these remote forefathers had descended from a god or were themselves divine. Spanish and Creole extirpators rooting out what they considered the lingering pagan practices of infidels located the preserved bodies or representations of these first founders in the mid-seventeenth century. Informants estimated that some of the mummies of these individuals were two hundred or even eight hundred years old. Either number would give such remembered heroes and their lineages improbably long reigns, suggesting that the accounts were constructed for the purpose (Ramírez 2005, ch. 4; Polia Meconi 1996, 214; 1999, 419; Zuidema 1990). Zuidema's analysis concludes that the genealogy of the *pachaca* (group of one hundred families) of Allauca displays "genealogical foreshortening." Thus, in the provinces, manipulation of collective memories is manifested in the many succession disputes in the litigation records in the international, national, and regional archives, but later than in the native-population concentrations of the south (Jurado 2014; Salamon 1999, 31, 37). Oral traditions thrived in relative isolation from European influences. But European cultural norms, once in close quarters with these traditions, took a similar toll on native naming practices.

The Illusion of Knowledge

The mention of manipulation and loss inherent in oral traditions returns the discussion to the questions of what we know and how we know it. Understanding the nature—both generation and use—of knowledge is fundamental to understanding and evaluating the knowledge itself. This topic is the broad, underpinning assumption of this analysis of native naming traditions in Africa and the Americas. Literate societies depend on documents to construct their histories. In doing so, they make their narratives relatively fixed; their sequences and lists are comparatively immutable while still being open to interpretation.

In contrast, the positional-inheritance model, the flexible native customs of the creation and preservation of memories in general, the incongruities in both insider and outsider accounts of native societies, and the experience of collecting and recording these stories after contact invite scholars to reflect on oral traditions and what they divulge.[15]

A challenge that many—if not all—students of other cultures face is how to make the exotic familiar. Language differences pose the problem of complete or partial untranslatability. Struggles to find word equivalences exacerbate the broader challenge of cultural equivalence. Ian Cunnison, like other trained contemporary ethnographers, used participant-observation methods to successfully decode the name-transmission tradition in sub-Saharan Africa. In the Andean case, untrained Spanish, mestizo, and Hispanized native writers, unlike Cunnison, faced the task of understanding various languages and of conceptualizing sometimes incomprehensible, inconceivable, and misunderstood information on succession practices for a curious but nonrelativist audience. Untrained writers listened to sometimes contradictory stories that privileged certain names that were associated with their values or prized deeds. Specific names were repeated and discussed and remembered. What the listeners did not grasp and did not know at the time, in this third example, is that a name could be assumed by multiple individual holders. Individuals died, but the collective reputation of the name and the lessons it embodied could and did persist. Over time, the name and its repute represented a composite. It became a template and an archetype, like the names of the Ho-De'-No-Sau-Nee chiefs. But the sixteenth- and seventeenth-century Spanish chroniclers had no inkling of such a system; they confessed to being befuddled. So they converted what they heard and put the information and their impressions into a form that their cultural brethren could understand. MacCormack captures the essence of the process, making her words worthy of quoting at length:

> In the very process of translating and writing down what they were told, Spaniards inevitably introduced notions of their own that had, strictly speaking, no Andean counterparts. One such notion concerned the historicity of the long-distant past. Sixteenth-century Europeans interpreted the book of Genesis and Greco-Roman myths of origins as historical narratives, not as mythic or allegorical accounts of creation and human beginnings. It was thus natural for Spaniards to view Andean myths of primeval floods and conflagrations and the origins of society as historical narratives of a similar kind. This led Cieza, Betanzos, and the other sixteenth-century historians of the Incas to extrapolate from legendary accounts they heard about Inca origins and social organization the history of a dynasty of twelve rulers, going back some five hundred years or even longer. Although historicizing Andean myths in this fashion amounted to misunderstanding them profoundly, the dynasty had its uses, because it provided the invaders with a conceptual framework within which they could understand Inca imperial expansion. (1991, 83)

This inevitably led to a measure of distortion, which significantly affected the construction of the past, especially in this case. Guaman Poma de Ayala, for instance, inserted Andean oral traditions into the Christian narrative by alluding to five eras, including the mention of Noah's Flood. He and other chroniclers recorded an abbreviated representation of the native recollections that conserved selected ideas about what the society valued and that was often contentious and continually changing. Native stories were not meant to be a history (as Europeans defined it) nor accurate genealogies of succession.

Thus the process of turning Andean oral traditions into a commonly accepted historical narrative in a colonial setting is found to be deficient and in need of recasting and decentering. Furthermore, this study shows that given, first, the circumstances of information

Fig. 12. Noah and his Ark. Guaman Poma, c. 1613/1936, folio 24.

gathering, based as they were on an imperfect, almost ahistorical system of indigenous recall, and, second, the cultural and religious filters of the Europeans who interpreted and even transformed the narratives, it is not surprising that the written record is flawed.

In the Andes, chroniclers' lists, conceived decades after first contact, became the standard over the centuries and today most scholars accept one or another list and believe that a ruler's name identifies an individual king, each with a list of noteworthy accomplishments. Yet if one accepts that each name on a list is a composite and not the identifier of a single individual ruler, then Andean history as we have known and accepted it requires a serious rethinking. Instead of saying that Pachacuti (and Thupa Inka Yupanqui [and sometimes also Capac Yupanqui]) conquered the Alca in Chumbivilca, Soras, Tomebambas, Pacaibambas, and Hatun Cañares, future historians to be more accurate will have to write that the multiple individuals who took Pachacuti's (and the others') names (according to Valera and Montesinos) conquered the Alca in Chumbivilca, Soras, Tomebambas, Pacaibambas, and Hatun Cañares (D'Altroy 2002, 66, 85; Pärsinnen 1992, 76–77).

Perspectives

Finally, this entire discussion in elucidating native conceptions of their identity sheds light on our own. The fact that the institution of positional inheritance downplayed any given incumbent except the first, the epitome and stereotype of what the consummate ruler was, shows native concern with community, lineage, and family continuity, in contrast to the European and our own cultural emphasis on individualism. The orally transmitted collective memories of a relatively recent and cyclical past were modified and put into a chronologically written account that highlighted individuals, usually the great men (for the most part) of the culture. Europeans reconfigured native history in their own image. Martínez Cereceda, a top-notch Andean anthropologist, grasps this point. After stating that chiefs (the curacas) take the name of huacas (citing Arriaga), he writes:

La noción de persona y la categoría 'yo' en sociedades que, como la andina, estaban basadas en la reciprocidad y la redistribución, es por completo diferente a la europea. En aquellas sociedades el nombre juega un papel preciso dentro de la configuración del grupo y se considera a su poseedor como partícipe de las características del prototipo a quien representa . . . el nombre de una divinidad, usado por el hombre permite a éste asumir su representación bajo la condición de un 'poseído' por ella. (Martínez Cereceda 1988, 69–70)

The notion of personhood and the category of "I" in societies that, like the Andean, were based on reciprocity and redistribution is completely different from the European. In those societies a name defines a precise role within the configuration of the group and gives the possessor as a participant the characteristics of the prototype that he represents . . . the name of a divinity used by a man permits him to assume the representation of his [the divinity's] being, as if "possessed" by him.

Such a perspective cautions us to be wary of our own cultural paradigms, assumptions, categories, and definitions that undoubtedly color our own interpretations and hinder the recovery of the native worldview. To quote Patricia Netherly, another ethnohistorian, "History as we know it is an artifact of Western culture. . . . The choices of Western historians [in constructing historical interpretation] are as culturally constrained as those of non-Western historiographers" (1990, 461).

Are myths and histories mutually exclusive? Where do myths end and histories begin? Both rely on selectivity to construct their accounts; both are interpretations; both are accepted and believed by their partisans; both are manipulated and subject to changes that reflect parrochial goals. The differences lie in the temporal dimension and the reliability of oral versus written records (neither of which are flawless). For the societies that construct them, these two forms of history are valid. An incident is an event for one; for another it isn't (Fogelson 1989; Harris 1995). In short, different cultures can have equally valid but different historicities. It bears repeating that we must make "a determined effort to try to comprehend alien forms of historical consciousness and discourse" (Fogelson 1989, 134; Wilson 1995, 7; Burke 1989, 99).[16]

Lastly, in doing the research for and writing this book, I learned why comparative histories are relatively few. I also gained valuable knowledge about myself, certain cultural perspectives, and the historian's craft.

| Appendix

The Accomplishments of the Pachacuti(s) according
to Betanzos and Montesinos

The accomplishments of Pachacuti according to Betanzos	The accomplishments of the various Pachacutis according to Montesinos
Constructed the Sun Temple	Pachacuti I: associated with stone construction and the construction of the Sun Temple
Assigned lands around the city of the Cuzco; improved lands; constructed irrigation works	
Constructed storehouses	
Canalized rivers; married women; organized the supply of food	
Established a nobility	
Established a calendar and festivals	Pachacuti III and IV: defined the calendar
Reconstructed the city of the Cuzco	
Divided the people of Cuzco into upper and lower parts	
Used songs as history	
Repaired roads; constructed bridges	Pachacuti IX: constructed roads
Established a system of runners; defeated the Soras	
Made laws; defeated the Chancas	Pachacuti I: extended Peru to Quito, except the Chachapoyas and part of the coast
	Pachacuti III: fought the Chimu
	Pachacuti VI: fought the Collaos

Pachacuti IX: defeated the
Chachapoyas, Paltas, Cañares,
Quitos, Latacungas, Sinchos,
Hampatos; fought the Chimus

Sources: Betanzos 1551–57/1996, pp. 44, 50–51, 55, 59, 65, 71, 79, 83, 86, 112; Montesinos (1644/1930), pp. 25, 28, 64, 67–68, 79, 134, 137, 140–41, 151, 155

| Notes

1. Alternative Ways of Remembering

1. Graña (2000) mentions the use of writing and written documents to reposition himself after the Spanish invasion in 1532. Megged (2005) writes analogously on the reconstitution of memories and ethnic identities in central Mexico from 1530 to 1990. See also K. B. Maxwell (1983); Street (1993); Basso (1989).

2. For reviews, discussions, and uses of the concept and the book, see Sheridan (1988); Rebasa (2005); Asad (1987); Vansina (1965, 1985); J. C. Miller (1980); Cunnison (1951b); T. D. Hall (1984); Kimmel (1984); Worsley (1984).

3. Oral tradition is defined by Henige as "those recollections of the past that are common or universally known in a given culture" (1982, 2). See also Vansina (1965).

4. Edward Shils in *Tradition* wrote: "A society to exist at all must be incessantly reenacted; its basic communications must be repeatedly re-said" (quoted in Basso 1988, 120).

5. Bards are professional storytellers, poets, and music composers, usually in service to a patron to commemorate one or more of the patron's ancestors or the patron himself.

6. On oral tradition as historical sources, see Motzafi-Halla (1994).

7. On praise singers in Niger, see Stoller (1994). Gordon (2006, 37) mentions praise singers in Central Africa for the Lunda king (Kazembe or Cazembe) without details. See also Mushikiwabo and Kramer (2006, especially 63), who mention African heroic ballads that stress bloodlines, not the individual. Another author who focuses on heroic and collective history is M. Sahlins (1983, 523–24).

8. As the northern Mexican *corridos* do today. Cerrón Palomino (1998); Ramírez (2005); Estenssoro Fuchs (2003).

9. I translated Spanish quotations into English, unless otherwise indicated.

10. On European use of ritual in colonial Mexico, see Cañeque (1996).

11. On ritual, see also Kelly and Kaplan (1990).

12. See Turner (1975) on pilgrimages (ch. 5, especially 177) and on rituals (ch. 1). More on rituals can be found in Acuto (2005).

13. Author's textile collection.

14. Horacio H. Urteaga (1919, especially p. 50) also argues that quipus and petroglyphs, among other things, are a form of symbolic writing if one defines writing as symbols, drawings, or representations that serve to evoke an idea, conserve a memory, or transmit a thought or emotion. See also Escobari de Querejazu (1982–83, especially 165–66), who quotes the hypothesis of David de Rojas y Silva (1981) that *tocapus* identified lineages by the positioning of the squares; and Tanodi de Chiapero (1994), who argues that the Incas and their antecedents developed symbolic systems of writing (in addition to the quipus and *tocapus*). She discusses painted stones (*tejas peruanas*), decorated beans (*pallares*), the Nazca lines, and hieroglyphics. Eeckhout and Danis (2004) also discuss *tocapus* as a heraldic symbol. On *queros*, see Lizárraga Ibáñez (2009); Cummins (2004). See also Cummins (2011); Zuidema (n.d., 3–5).

15. See also Zuidema (1977) on the Inca calendar.

16. José Carlos de la Puente Luna recently (2019) published an article linking quipus to time management. See also Brokaw (2002) and Curatola Petrocchi and de la Puente Luna (2013).

17. See also Jackson (2011) on Moche iconography and its meanings as a communicative system understood by several communities and Moya (1986) on the woven symbols in Ecuadorian textiles.

18. See also Curatola Petrocchi and de la Puente Luna (2013). R. Alan Covey (2006, 171) in a modern reassessment of Inca historical traditions does not find that quipus are necessarily chronologically accurate.

19. For a typology of quipus, see Urton and Brezine (2013). See also Urton (1998, 2006); Urton and Brezine (2005); Zuidema (1977, 1989).

20. Patrón (1906, especially 294–95) writes of a similar device, a baton covered with lines and symbols, that the Incas used to convey meaning.

21. Snyderman notes that the word "wampum" comes from Algonquian *wampŏmpeag* (or *wampumpeag*), meaning "white string of shell beads." The Senecas in the 1950s referred to wampum as *gŏt-gŏh-ĕh*, which included wampum in all its forms (beads, strings, and belts) (1954, 469). Tylor (1897, 252–53) states that Hiawatha's name meant "maker of the wampum belt," from *ayuñwa* or "wampum belt" and *katha* or "to make." See also Jennings et al. (1985) and Fenton (1988, ch. 16, especially 224) for discussions of wampum.

22. Snyderman (1954, 469–77) posits that wampum signified money from the European point of view and sometimes served as such. In pre-European-contact times, in contrast, it was not used as a standard medium of exchange. See also Converse (1895).

23. Although this naming system is understudied, names and naming are not. See, for example, a history of naming in Spain and Latin America by Herzog (2007); and more specific studies, such as Wright (1983–84); Herbert (1997); Suzman (1994); Foerster (2010); A. R. Ramos (1974); Beidelman (1974); Klerk and Bosch (1996); Valladares Huamanchumo (2013); Tebbenhoff (1985); Kendall (1980); Smith (1985); Blum (1997); Geertz and Geertz (1964); Grant and Zelenietz (1983).

24. Joanne Rappaport (1990, especially 67–73) describes positional inheritance, without using the phrase, in her book on the Paez historical traditions.

25. See Bateman (2002) for similarities between the Kongo naming patterns and those of Black Seminoles.

26. On multiple name-taking, see also N. Miller (1927); Grant and Zelenietz (1983, 180); Bamberger (1974, especially 365–67); Moore (2007) and others too numerous to mention here.

27. On nicknames, see also Gentile (n.d.); Holland Jr. (1995, 280); Kendall (1980, 269).

28. Jan Szeminski (2001) comes to the same conclusion.

2. "Positional Inheritance" in Africa

1. The Luapula River is a southern tributary of the Congo River. It flows northward and empties into Lake Mweru on the border of Zambia and the Democratic Republic of Congo. This is one of the most densely populated regions in rural South Central Africa.

2. Francisco José Maria de Lacerda defines Mwata as "king" (Burton 1798/1873, 102). Gamitto defines it as "sovereign" (Gamitto/Cunnison 1831–32/1960, 2:127).

3. Kazembe is a name that became in time a hereditary title, taken by a Lunda tribal king. The word was also used by Europeans as the name of the peoples he controlled (i.e., the Kazembes) and the lands on which these peoples lived (Beke/Burton 1831–32/1873, 250). I have sometimes standardized and modernized the spelling of selective native words and names to facilitate reading.

4. Crawford, a later missionary to the peoples of Central Africa, corrects Livingstone who translated the word as "general." Crawford asserts that it means "stinging bush fly" (tsetse) (Tilsley 1929, 398; Gordon 2006a, 298).

5. Other names or titles for chiefs are (Gamitto/Cunnison 1831–32/1960, 1:68, 92, 132) Mambo Kazembe, Kalso, or Unde. Travassos Valdez (1861, 2:214) mentions Mambo as "emperor" (as in Mambo Muatianf) as well as other words of address, such as "lord" or "master" or "Muatianfa" (Matiamvo) or "Miané" (specifically for "sir") (2:214, 232, 257). Note the similarity between Muatianfa and Matiamvo and Mwata Yamvo, a sequence of rulers of West Central Africa in the seventeenth and eighteenth centuries.

6. Paul Bohannan (1953) finds the same phenomenon among the Tiv of Nigeria. He notes that a lineage name is the plural form of the given name of its apical ancestor (261). This may have been the case for the Jayancas of the northern Andes until the first Christian baptism of the paramount lord (see ch. 4).

7. Vansina reaches back and discusses Mwata Yambo from the time of Muaant Yaav Naweej. "Muaant Yaav" literally means "Lord of the Viper" (1966, 80–81). Vansina notes that his personal name—Yaav—became a generic title for Lunda kingship. For an interesting article placing the title of Mwata Yambo in a lineage context, see J. C. Miller (1976, ch. 5).

8. He ruled over the peoples and lands of Chief Ngola or Angola (de Lacerda/Burton 1798/1873, 41).

9. Also known as Mukanzu or Mukanzo (Kazembe XIV/Cunnison 1948/1961, 29; Cunnison 1956c, 131, following Baptista), Muropeó, Murôpúe, Murôpóe, Muropúe, Mustiamfa, and Muátá Yanvo, Mwaant Yaav (Yav) (de Lacerda/Burton 1798/1873, 104).

10. Livingstone (1874, 1:252) wrote that the first Kazembe was attracted by the abundant fish of the Mofwe Lagoon. Also note that there are many versions of the origin story of the Kazembes. For the brief historical account offered here, I followed early writers rather than Kazembe XIV's account because I felt the latter was farther from the events and may have highlighted some aspects while minimizing or excluding less flattering ones.

11. Gamitto (Gamitto/Cunnison 1831–32/1960) describes the son as having a turbulent and sanguinary disposition (Travassos Valdez 1861, 2:257–62).

12. For a more detailed and alternative version of this history, see Vansina (1966, especially 165–74 and 227–35).

13. Cunnison (1957, 21, 26) notes that the invading Kazembe conquerors came from the patrilineal society of Muata Yamvo to the west. The people they conquered, in contrast, were matrilineal. Intermarriage gradually changed this custom among some peoples (Cunnison 1954, 22). Cunnison goes on to note that the Lunda adopted much of the kinship terminology of the matrilineal people under their control (1957, 21, 26).

14. See also Travassos Valdez (1861, 2:258–60).

15. Other versions of the history are in Baptista/Burton (1806–11/1873, 231–32); Gordon (2006b, 23), and in Cunnison (1956c), where he systematically compares travelers' reports with the Lunda version of the history written down by Kazembe XIV and his consultants (Kazembe XIV/Cunnison 1948/1961). Baptista presents important details; he names the slave of Yamvo's son, Mutanda, and Kazembe's ancestor Chinyanta (Cunnison, 1956c, 133).

16. Portuguese *pombeiros* (traveling merchants, frequently slaves or of slave descent) (Gordon 2006b, 31).

17. Villages moved, but the name and the identity of the people remained the same (Cunnison 1956a, 3–4; Livingstone 1874, 2:247).

18. Cunnison (Gamitto/Cunnison 1831–32/1960, 1:73–75) adds that the people believed that they received all good and evil from their ancestral spirits, according to their pleasure or displeasure over their behavior. Society's calamities were attributed to the lack of offerings and first fruits to these spirits. Good and evil spirits required gifts of everything that their descendants possessed; otherwise they punished them by entering their bodies until promises were made in public.

19. An important market, especially for slaves until the mid-nineteenth century (Baptista/Burton 1806–11/1873, 221, 223, 226; Vansina 1966, 145, 181, 201–2).

20. It was added, however, that the memory of Kazembe Lukwesa was respected and revered. He could cause problems for the living; his anger had to be mollified with gifts to the present Kazembe.

21. Kazembe XIV (Kazembe XIV/Cunnison 1948/1961, 117–18) mentions that his wife was the third to inherit the name Katuti Nakafwaya in 1948.

22. See also Stefaniszyn (1954).

23. See Cunnison's (1956a, 11) article on headmanship, which details these beliefs and practices.

24. Poor from the European perspective. He continued to be regarded as wealthy by his native subjects because of his large number of wives and children and followers, in general.

25. Kazembe VIII, according to Cunnison (1956c, 135).

26. Labrecque noted in 1934 concerning the Bembe, a people subject to Kazembe, that the heir enjoyed the same role as the deceased with regard to the family. He called his uncles and aunts "brothers and sisters" and his younger brothers and sisters as well as his cousins "nephews and nieces or sons and daughters" (1934, 101). This is confirmed by Brelsford (1944), who stated that for the Bemba paramountcy passed through all the sons of the eldest sister before passing on to the sons of the next sister. All the sons of the sisters of the same generation had to pass through before the line switched to the younger generation. It passed from brother to brother in a genealogical generation, and when that horizontal line was exhausted it dropped to the eldest nephew, son of the senior female in the next generation. See also Coxhead (1914) on "positional succession" of the Bemba. Some Andeans shared the practice of brother-to-brother succession (Rostworowski 1961).

27. Clay (1956, 137–38) asserts that Arnot is not reliable and that he is probably mixing up people of the same name. For examples of the name changes of

chiefs, see Kazembe XIV/Cunnison (1948/1961, 50, 69–70, 111, 117). Andrew Roberts (1967, 128) notes that there was another chief called Kazembe on the Lualapa River. This Kazembe was actually a Chief Cisenge (Vansina 1966, 166, 169). Vansina also mentions others with the same designation (167–68).

28. David M. Gordon wrote that according to Montiero and Gamitto in 1832, Kanyembo and Chinyanta "probably were the same person" (2006b, 32).

29. I refer readers to Cunnison for a detailed analysis of the differences among the different lists. Cunnison concludes that "none of the lists considered offer irreconcilable differences" (1956c, 134). But the differences, however they are explained away, illustrate, as we will see below, the cultural blindness of the observers.

30. Another complication is that among the Imbangala, a person may have one name by which he is known to Portuguese Christians and another by which he is known to the locals (J. C. Miller 1979, 70). David P. Henige (1974, 1981) expounds on the sources of discrepancies in oral traditions that include faulty genealogies; the practice of telescoping or its opposite, lengthening reigns, king lists, genealogies, or some combination of those; the omission of usurpers and periods of foreign rule; and the elimination of rulers who did not complete the installation sequence, of those whose reigns were inglorious, and of those with questionable legitimacy.

31. Vansina (1966) outlines the history of the African savanna before c. 1700, noting positional inheritance (especially 80–82).

32. See J. C. Mitchell (1956); Richards (1950); Gray (1953); Cunnison (1957).

33. Susan Gillespie (1988) wrote of a similar system operating among the Aztec kings. See also J. D. Y. Peel (1984, 111) on "stereotypic reproduction" and positional inheritance found among the Yoruba and the Polynesians studied by Marshall Sahlins (1981).

34. Women also inherited names, but because of a lack of published information on them and little mention of the women of the tribe, they cannot be included in the analysis here. See Cunnison's (1951b, 38) note on female succession and Brelsford (1944), who mentions the hereditary names of mothers (*namfumu*) of chiefs (*chitimukulu*, the oldest name and traditionally the mother of the earliest Chitimukulu) and Mukukamfumu in the 1940s. A third name is Mushimba, which was used in 1943 in a deliberate attempt to make a third name into a hereditary one. The first to take the Mushimba name died in 1928. The holder in 1943 was called Samba, a Chitimukulu classificatory granddaughter of the deceased. See also Travassos Valdez (1861, 2:220); W. H. Whiteley (1950, 15); Kazembe XIV/Cunnison (1948/1961, 7, 118, 121).

35. Both Cunnison (1956a, 3) and Macola (2002, 70) assert that the legitimate heir was the sister's son. Cunnison (1957, 23) elaborates on instances where

a successor takes the name of his uncle and, therefore, becomes of the generation of his uncle, although he is referred to as a brother. Beidelman (1974) notes the taking of multiple names that reflect kin status among the matrilineal Kaguru of eastern Tanzania.

36. This may account for confusion in early Spanish-American manuscripts where one person is identified as both uncle and son of another. Could the informants be reexamined, it may have been that one kinship term referred to the classificatory relationship between positions and the other kinship term to the biological relationship—which may have been more important to the Spanish inquirers. These contradictions may have resulted from the wrong questions being asked by colonial authorities (see ch. 4 on this point). See also Gordon (2006b, 39–44) on perpetual kinship.

37. Cunnison (1951, 42; 1956b, especially 39 and 42; 1957, 22, 29). In fact, in parts of West Africa whole lineages are conceived as one named person (see Armstrong 1954, 1052).

38. Cunnison (1951b, especially 33; 1957, 24) gives more examples of using the first-person singular to recount memories. Mainga (1966) also finds that oral traditions of the Lozi ignore the temporal element. See also Evans-Pritchard, who found that the Nuer "have no concept of time and, consequently, no developed abstract system of time-reckoning." The Nuer have "very limited means of reckoning the relative duration of periods of time intervening between events, since they have few, and not well-defined or systematized, units of time. They have no numerical system of dating and no idea of an age in terms of years" (1939, 208–11). Paul Bohannan noted that the Tiv also had no general system for measuring time; "Tiv, by and large, do not even correlate events over a period of time beyond a generation or two" (1953, especially 260–61).

39. See also J. C. Miller (1979, especially 67, 78).

40. Peel (1984) reports that among the Yoruba an incoming successor of a deceased ruler spent three months learning the duties and knowledge of his predecessor and his new position.

41. On the invention of a "more general, universal and hegemonic history" or "impersonal history" of the Kazembe Kingdom, see Gordon (2006b, 21).

42. Roberts (1967) corrects several inaccuracies of Cunnison's (1956c) attempt to establish a definitive list of Kazembes, based on documents unavailable to Cunnison.

43. Laura Bohannan's (1952) article also shows how genealogies are invented and manipulated.

44. R. T. Zuidema makes a similar argument for the Incas as discussed in chapter 4.

45. The Imbangala or Mbangala were seventeenth-century groups of Angolan warriors and marauders who founded the Kasanje Kingdom. They inhabited northwestern Angola between c. 1620 and 1912 (J. C. Miller 1979, 51).

46. Henige's (1971) article on king lists supports Miller's conclusions. See also Peel (1984, especially 117).

47. For examples of how the living recall events and the interaction between the royal genealogy and lineage history, see Cunnison (1957, 28).

48. Gordon (2006b) updates Cunnison's analysis by tracing the "invention of tradition": namely, how personal, subclan, close-relative "histories" were reconstructed into general histories of the Kazembe Kingdom by associating shrines and natural landscape features with ancestral heroes who played key roles in the Kazembe conquests and migrations. Through this process, identities came to be broadened and a "universal and hegemonic history" was born (21). It became a widely accepted and impersonal oral tradition, which was based on the compilation of several lineage histories (27). This history of the past was written down by Kazembe XIV in the mid-twentieth century and is now celebrated annually in the Mutomboko ceremony (26).

3. Ho-De'-No-Sau-Nee History

1. The natives called themselves Ho-De'-No-Sau-See or Wi:s Nihwenjiada:ge:. The French gave them the name Iroquois meaning "People of the Longhouse." I use the former, except in direct quotes.

2. Morgan (1851/1962, 61–72 and 101) distinguishes between sachems and chiefs, the former held a higher rank than the second. But other writers use the words "sachem," "chief," and "captain" as synonyms, and I will adopt the latter practice. I suspect that the equivalence developed over time as status and activities changed and may, at times, also have been due to the writer's ignorance about the finer distinctions of the native sociopolitical and religious hierarchy.

3. Also, Six Nations Confederacy (Fenton 1988, 51).

4. On the similarities between the Huron and Ho-De'-No-Sau-Nee cultures, see Tooker (1970, 90). See also the notes on adoption below. Note that Fenton (1988, 3) asserts that the Hurons, originally occupying Ontario, and the Ho-De'-No-Sau-Nee, occupying New York, may be considered one "cultural province."

5. The French, who served as early missionaries and wrote about the peoples around the Great Lakes, had no word for "clan"; they used "nation." Morgan used "tribe" as a synonym for clan. See Campisi (1982, 1997) on the changing meaning of the terms "tribe" and "nation" in reference to the Ho-De'-No-Sau-Nee; see also Barbeau (1917). The clans are named after animals that include the turtle, snipe, deer, beaver, heron, hawk, eel, bear, and wolf.

6. Fenton characterizes the Confederation as a "kinship state" (1975, 140). It was also known as the League of Peace and Power.

7. The origin story of the Senecas and the nation's history is recounted in Houghton (1922, especially 32–33).

8. Hewitt (1944, 80) groups the Mohawks, Onondagas, and Senecas into a male or father moiety (also known as the "three brothers") and the Oneidas and Cayugas into the female or mother group. On moiety division, see also Shimony (1994, 117–19).

9. I narrowed the date of his work from the year after the date of his retirement (1699) to the year before a Jesuit missionary is known to have had his manuscript. He was still alive in 1718 (Blair 1911–12, 2:256).

10. Perrot gives the date as "about" 1726 (c. 1700–1720/1911–12, 1:85). According to D. C. Scott and the Committee of Chiefs (1911, 195), it was after 1715. Richter (1983, 557) gives the date as about 1722. The Tutelos, Delawares, and others joined the League later (Hewitt 1944, 81). See also Morgan (1851/1962, 98).

11. Strachey in his *Historie* of 1612 (–1849, 47) notes that the native rulers of Virginia were known by multiple names.

12. Fenton comments on these stories that: "Like all oral documents it changes with each telling, it erodes with time, and interpolations are inserted. Nevertheless, it is regarded as gospel, although demonstrably it is composed of part myth, part historical legend, part projection of nineteenth century political structure and ceremonial observances into the prehistoric past. Much of it is couched in archaic language no longer spoken, and it is loaded with rich metaphor and symbolism that relate to an earlier cultural period" (1975, 132).

13. See Fenton's analysis of this oral tradition (1975, especially 137–40; 1988, part 1).

14. Hewitt (1944, 80) remarks that because of this paternity he was like all other great national heroes who came from heaven.

15. Vecsey (1986, especially 82–94) pushes the origins back to mythical times. Crawford and Smith (1996, 782) carry their history back to 900–1000 CE when natives migrated into the Northeast, bringing with them maize horticulture and matrilineal social organization. Hewitt (1944, 80) indicates that the League had already been formed by 1570. Hale (1883/1963, xx) dates the origins of the Senecas and Tuscaroras to 150 years before Samuel de Champlain (or the mid-fifteenth century). Archaeologists push the date back to 1400 CE (Hale 1883/1963, xxi).

16. Or Hayawatha, a name that meant "maker of wampums" (Jennings et al. 1985, 18). On Hiawatha, see also Hale (1895), who remarks that he lived four hundred years ago (from 1895) and "whose name, and the names of his companions in the first council, descended, like those of the first two Caesars, or

like the territorial names of English peers, to be titles of honour for their successors" (46–47).

17. Among the Ho-De'-No-Sau-Nee, wampum served as the "word" or "voice"; it gave confirmation of words spoken (Jennings et al. 1985, 88). For wampum's role in diplomacy, see Williams (1994, especially 1017).

18. J. N. B. Hewitt writes that the number of chiefs was not always fixed at fifty; the first "traditionally authentic" number was forty-seven to which two Seneca chiefs were added later (1917, 432). See also Fenton (1950, 69) on the totals of forty-nine versus fifty.

19. For other lists, see Fenton (1950, 59–67) and Shimony (1994, 104–17).

20. See Fenton (1975, especially 136–40); Scott and the Committee of Chiefs (1911, 198–226); and the discussion below.

21. On name changes among the Fox and Sauk, see United States agent at Fort Armstrong Thomas Forsyth (1826/1912, 2:210–12).

22. For a complete list and a discussion of names, see Cooke (1952).

23. See also Vimont (1642/1898 [Thwaites vol. 22], 287–89).

24. Anthropologist Dean Snow (2007) describes the case of the Mohawk chief known in English as Hendrick Peters, who, it turns out, was actually two Mohawk chiefs whose lifetimes overlapped. Each took the title sequentially.

25. See also the discussion of names for the natives of the Upper Mississippi Valley by Le Roy (1753/1912, 2:57–58, n. 34), which constitutes another case of positional inheritance.

26. See also Le Mercier (1637/1898 [Thwaites vol. 13]), 39. Giving prisoners to families that had suffered a loss was also a practice among the Fox, Sauk, and Pottawattamies (Le Roy 1753/1912, 2:37; Marston 1820/1912, 2:162; Forsyth 1826/1912, 2:197, 237; Blair 1911–12, 2:293).

27. Fenton (1986, 36) wrote that his new name was Hodatchehte (or Quiver Bearer), a leading Oneida sachem that was continuously taken from the time of Father Millet and held to at least 1794.

28. See also Bressani (1653/1899b [Thwaites vol. 39], 199); Hale (1883/1963, 146).

29. Perrot (c. 1700–1720/1911–12, 1:83–85) for another example.

30. A variation is mentioned by Claude Charles Le Roy, who reports that some adoptions were large-scale. The Senecas adopted the Tuscaoras as kindred and they took a place in the Ho-De'-No-Sau-Nee League (1753/1912, 2:37, n. 16; Fenton 1949, 151). Daniel K. Richter (1983, 541) states that by the mid-1660s several missionaries reported that over two-thirds of the Ho-De'-No-Sau-Nee villages were adoptees. In another mid-seventeenth-century account, Barthelemy Vimont recalls that in one instance the men of the village called Ononjoté were exterminated by the Hurons, to the point that the village asked the Agnierronons

(Ho-De'-No-Sau-Nee) for men to marry the girls and widows so that their tribe might survive. That is why the "Hiroquois call that village their Child" (1643–44/1898 [Thwaites vol. 27], 295–97). In an analogous sense, then, the Ho-De'-No-Sau-Nee had adopted a male population to reconstitute the village, establishing ties of perpetual kinship (as posited by Cunnison). Finally, Hale reports on the adoption of entire nations. In one procession a Cayuga chief (Wage or Hadwennine or "His Words Are Moving") was followed by a line of chiefs of younger nations—Cayuga, Oneida, Tuscarora, Delaware, Nanticoke, and Tutelo, "for so far has the confederacy been enlarged by later adoptions" (1895, 51). The Hurons, like the Ho-De'-No-Sau-Nee, practiced adoption, meaning that the group members intermingled. The name Huron was extended to other neighboring tribes who had a common language, although they had separate interests (Le Jeune 1639/1898 [Thwaites vol. 16], 231). Thus, in a letter to Le Jeune, Lalemant writes that the Hurons were "only an assemblage of various families and petty Nations, which are associated together for the purpose of maintaining themselves against their common enemies" (1640/1898a [Thwaites vol. 17], 195). Furthermore, his description of the "country of the Hurons" (Le Jeune 1639/1898 [Thwaites vol. 16], 225) reveals that there lived "four Nations, or rather four different collections or assemblages of grouped family stocks,—all of whom, having a community of language, of enemies, and of other interests, are hardly distinguishable except by their different progenitors, grandfathers and great-grandfathers, whose names and memories they cherish tenderly. They increase or diminish their numbers, however, by the adoption of other families, who join themselves now to some, now to others, and who also sometimes withdraw to form a band or a nation by themselves" (225–27, 231).

In the language of the country, they were called Wendat; the individual names are Attignawantan, Attigneenongnahac, Arendahronons, and Tohontaenrat. "The first two are the two most important, having received the others into their country . . . and adopted them,—the one fifty years ago, and the other thirty. These first two speak with certainty of the settlements of their Ancestors, and of the different sites of their villages, for more than two hundred years back"—even though they changed the location of their villages at least every ten years (Le Jeune 1639/1898 [Thwaites vol. 16], 227–29). Again, the fact that some split off to form their own lineages and villages suggests another example of perpetual kinship.

31. Montmagny (in office 1636–48) was the first governor who engaged in open warfare with the Ho-De'-No-Sau-Nee (Williams 1994, 1007, n. 82, and 1025).

32. Membertou was further described thus: "By the testimony of all the inhabitants of the province, this one man, in strength of mind, in knowledge of the

military art, in the great number of his followers, in power, and in the renown of a glorious name among his countrymen, and even his enemies, easily surpassed the Sagamores who had flourished during many preceding ages. This universal honor and renown he could not have attained, even among Savages utterly un-taught, except from an established reputation, the knowledge also of the excep-tional justice of his character, and his temperance" (Anonymous, 1613–14/1896 [Thwaites vol. 2], 227). On wealth as people, see Guyer and Eno Belinga (1995).

33. See also Brébeuf in Le Jeune (1636/1897 [Thwaites vol. 10], 267).

34. Le Petit (1730/1900 [in Thwaites vol. 68], 149) for information on the con-tent of names among the Natchez.

35. See Morgan (1851/1962, 101) on the reputations of certain chiefs.

36. He (on 103) offers two good examples of his point.

37. Hale's clan is Morgan's tribe.

38. Also quoted in Kinietz (1965, 54).

39. Jouvency (1610–13/1896 [Thwaites vol. 1], 263), referring to the Natchez, wrote in the early seventeenth century that after death, speakers praised the dead.

40. Hewitt (1917, 435) mentions a personal song particular to one of the first chiefs, Wathatotarho (or Adodarho or Atotarho) (the alternative names are ac-cording to Hale 1895, 57). Brébeuf notes in 1636 that the present name-holder sometimes sang the song of his predecessor (1636/1897 [Thwaites vol. 10], 281–89; Greer 2000, 65). In the 1650s and 1660s, Lalemant mentions that the Hurons sang a death song before they were killed, but he does not discuss the song's con-tent (Lalemant [c.] 1659–61/1899 [Thwaites vol. 44], 61; Lalemant 1661–62/1899 [Thwaites vol. 47], 163, 179).

41. Among the Natchez of Louisiana, particular names distinguish those who had killed a greater or lesser number of the enemy. According to Mathurin Le Petit, a Jesuit writing from New Orleans in 1730, "The old war-Chiefs dis-tribute these names according to the merit of the warriors. To deserve the title of a great man-slayer, it was necessary to have taken ten slaves or to have scalped twenty individuals. The name itself of a warrior enables one to learn of his ex-ploits" (1730/1900 [Thwaites vol. 68], 149).

42. Le Mercier wrote that the place of the famous captain Noel Tekoueri-mat, "out of honor rendered to his virtue and courage, had been left without a successor for several years. . . ." (1668–69/1899 [Thwaites vol. 52], 223). Dablon, a French Jesuit missionary, noted in another case that a captain's name was resur-rected after three years (1670–71/1899 [Thwaites vol. 55], 137). He was revered by a great many chiefs of different nations and their people because of a great vic-tory against the Ho-De'-No-Sau-Nee.

43. For a condensed description of a Condolence Council in 1803, see Kirkland (1803/1980, 380–81).

44. On the Condolence Council and rites see Hale (1883/1963), who published *The Iroquois Book of Rites* with their speeches and songs, and the descriptions by J. A. Gibson et al. (1912/1992) and Vimont (in 1643–44/1898 [Thwaites vol. 26], 155–63). Details in each description vary. For the analogous customs of the eastern woodland natives, see Thurman (1984).

45. See Fenton (1946, 118) on the antlers' or horns' significance. He reports the belief that should an ill chief die while wearing the horns of authority, "we should all perish."

46. Fenton notes that the Ho-De'-No-Sau-Nee, as late as 1950, sent out notched invitation sticks summoning delegates to councils. Some of these are described as "notched stick calendars" and "notched message sticks" (1950, 2, 6–8). Beauchamp (1895b, 314) describes purple wampum as a single string with ends brought together if the deceased was a war chief, or three strings with the ends free if he was a higher-ranking principal chief. One observer noted that by 1636, council sticks were "all the books and papers of the Country" (Brébeuf 1636/1897 [Thwaites vol. 10], 293).

47. Converse (1895, 346) reports that black beads covered with white clay conveyed the news of the death of a chief. For a full discussion of wampum, see Fenton (1988, ch. 16).

48. See also Le Petit (1730/1900 [Thwaites vol. 68]), 133, 135.

49. See also Hale (1895), 64.

50. See Fenton (1988, chs. 9–10) for another detailed description of later Condolence Councils.

51. J. A. Gibson et al. (1912/1992, xi) note the performance of this ceremony as early as 1535 when the French explorer Jacques Cartier visited the Ho-De'-No-Sau-Nee village of Hochelaga, situated on the island that is now Montreal.

52. Or "by the arm" (Williams 1994, 999).

53. Note that the sequence of events and the spelling of various words differ by author (Fenton 1946, 113; Hale 1895, 45; 1883/1963, 117).

54. Hewitt defines orenda as a potency or potentiality to achieve or affect results that is mystically held by humans, animals, as well as superhumans. He notes that the condolence ritual was "so laden with magic power, which was useful in achieving welfare and yet so uncontrollable and sinister when evoked out of season, that it was believed [by the Ho-De'-No-Sau-Nee] imperative to hold this solemn assembly only in autumn or in winter. This was because the rites were so deeply concerned with the dead and with the powers that quicken and preserve the living from the hostile activities of the Great Destroyer that

it was thought that the rites might be deadly and destructive to growing seeds and plants and maturing fruits, should their performance occur during spring or summer, the period of rebirth and growth" (1944, 66; 1902, 38), as was noted in part above. The Ho-De'-No-Sau-Nee orenda is regarded as directly related to singing and to anything used as a charm, amulet, or mascot (Hewitt 1902, 43).

55. Gibson (1912/1992, xliii) describes the burdens on xl–xliii. He also gives the name of each burden, following Hewitt. See also Fenton (1946, 119–20).

56. Jennings et al. (1985, 18–19) analyze the Condolence Council as having sixteen steps or parts.

57. On such mnemonic canes, see Fenton (1950, especially 10–38). See also Hale (1883/1963, ch. 4). Noble states that such devices helped a special lineage of females who exhibited the "known tenacity of Iroquoian memory culture" by remembering back 340 years (1985, 133). See Hewitt (1944, 68) for greater detail; he presents the text of the fifteen burdens of the requickening address (70–78). Fenton (1946, 115) describes a Condolence Council held in 1945 and the role of the cane.

58. Gibson (1912/1992), relying on Fenton (1950, 43–49), writes of the Eulogy of the Founders of the League or roll call of the founders, and the hymn or processional hymn of confederation sung to the fifty chiefs. He prints the lyrics on pages 50–52 of several versions of this hymn (see also Gibson 1912/1992, xxxvi, xxxviii).

59. Hewitt (1944) uses "matters," "articles," and several other words as synonyms of these burdens.

60. On the spiritual aspects of the council, see Hewitt (1902).

61. Versions and sequences of the council vary by describer.

62. Not to be confused with his father, John Gibson, an Onondaga chief who went by the name of Atotarho (Hale 1895, 49).

63. Hale describes it as the "National Hymn of the Iroquois" (1883/1963, 63). Hale also wrote that the entire Book of Rites "is sung. . . . It is, in fact, an ancient historical chant; and this accounts for the great accuracy with which it has been transmitted from one generation to another. They have continued to sing the words even after the meaning of some of them has become uncertain" (1895, 55).

64. Hale (1883/1963, 129–39) lists them.

65. For an example of reading the wampum in 1765, see Kirkland (1803/1980, 6).

66. The Europeans chastised the natives upon hearing their oral traditions. One retorted to native narratives: "Seeing that thou tellest only fables, which have no foundation but lies, I have more right to speak than thou. Where are the writings which give us faith in what thou sayest?" (Ragueneau 1645–46/1898 [Thwaites and vol. 30], 63).

67. See also Forsyth (1826/1912, 2:212) on not uttering names in common conversation of the Fox and Sauk; and Brébeuf (1636/1897 [Thwaites vol. 10], 267).

4. Andean Ancestral Traditions

1. AGI/J418, 1573, 151v–52, 221v, 320; Ramírez (2005, ch. 4); Saignes (1987, 139, on the "señor verdadero de linaje" [true lord of the lineage]; and 155 on Juan Colque Guarachi, "cacique principal del repartimiento de los Quillacas and Asanaques"); Zevallos Quiñones (1994, 26, on the [il]legitimacy of the succession of don Pedro Ocxaguaman to the *cacicazgo* (chieftainship) of Chimu because he was not a direct descendant of a cacique).

2. The grant of natives or encomienda that became the repartimiento of Pácora.

3. Note the similarity of the second names of Uturungo Achache and the principal of Saña, Ponoachachea.

4. The word "province" in Spain that was brought to the Americas is defined by Weeks (1947, 63–64). MacCormack (1998) discusses the term in the Roman sense (9).

5. On Sontubilico, AGI/J418, 1573, 211; Hart 1983, 163 (on Saña, citing AGI/J420, 100; and on Jayanca, citing ART/Escrituras 70); ART/CoP, l. 280, exp. 3621, 7-VIII-1587, 2 on Chinga[u]nam; on Chuplingon, ART/CoP, l. 280, exp. 3634, 20-VIII-1592, 1; on Nuna Calla, Duviols (1986, 326–27). "Mal nombre" is equated with "apodo" (nickname) by Gentile (2008, 1–2; 1996, 5, 7). I would rather translate it as "native" or "pre-Christian name."

6. In sixteenth-century manuscripts, the world *tierra* is often used to refer to a population. See Ramírez (2005, ch. 3).

7. See n. 5.

8. In 1532, the witness "era muchacho" (was a youth). Therefore, he could have been born about 1522 (AGI/J418, 1573, 207v, 328v–29v). The ethnologist Gilles Rivière (1997, section 2) found that in 1970s and 1980s Bolivia, authorities and their wives took on the name of the communal or founding ancestors when they assumed power. They were "possessed" by the spirits of their male and female founders (*mallku* or *t'alla*) (1995a, 118, 120, 122). Elsewhere Rivière provides a list of the names of the curacas of seventeenth- and eighteenth-century Carangas. Between c. 1550 and 1835, all seven authorities for which he has identities used the name Vilka (personal communication, July 13, 2004; 1995b, 5).

9. He was about six years old when the Spanish arrived, so he was probably born c. 1526. This may be late; in 1563 the witness looked old to the notary (AGI/J418, 1573, 330v).

10. His name now identifies the community of Muchumí.

11. He was "*viejo*" or old in the lifetime of the previous witness (AGI/J418, 1573, 332).

12. AGI/J418, 1573, 370–70v. The father of Minimisal of 1532 had the same name. There is evidence of telescoping here; the witness Fuentes had known three lords named Minimsal in less than about twenty years.

13. He could also have been named for Francisco Pizarro.

14. In 1563 he had been encomendero approximately eight years and married to doña Isabel for nine years. He may have taken over the administration of the encomienda at the death of her father and been confirmed encomendero thereafter (AGI/J418, 1573, 303v, 309).

15. Literally, "stone lord," "stone idol," or "leader," perhaps "strong leader." Duviols (1979, 71) notes that the names of native authorities were given to stone statues.

16. Vargas Ugarte (1951–54, 1:327); Medinaceli (1995, 335; 2003b, 10, 177) on the effect of the Concilio Limense of 1583 on indigenous naming; Scott, Tehranian, and Mathias (2002).

17. Manco Capac and possibly Inga Roca married their mothers (Mróz 1988, 67–68). Espinoza Soriano asserts that the Cajamarca lords did not marry their biological mothers (1977, 406), although they did inherit the widowed secondary wives of a father and brother (406, 428, 437).

18. AGI/J418, 1573, f. 325v for 1563 and the testimony of the division of Jayanca. Guaman Poma de Ayala (1613/1993, 93) (as cited by Hernández Astete 1998, 112).

19. *Conoseque* translates literally as "lord (*seque, çique*) of a thousand (*cono*)" (households) in the ancient Mochica language.

20. Complicating the use of kinship terms is the fact that the Andean kinship system is cyclical; the fifth generation occupies the same position as the first. In addition, Espinoza Soriano (1977, 410), writing on polygamy in Cajamarca, states that the terms for "mother," "father," and "child" could also be used to describe aunts, uncles, cousins, nephews, and nieces. He clarifies the use of *churi*, stating that men called their male children *churi* and their female children *ususi*; while women called their male and female children *guagua* (434), the latter a term still in common use today.

21. The word *auca* (from *aucca* or *auccak*) is translated as "warrior," "enemy," "rival," "rebel," "soldier," "tyrant," or "valiant" (González Holguin 1608/1952, 38).

22. Note that the interim governors took other names. Some of the certifications of baptisms and marriages of the principal personages of the lineage presented in the testimony have erroneous dates. See also on the Guaraches of the Aymara kingdom of Quillaca-Asanaque: Espinoza Soriano (1981) and Graña (2000). On the same phenomenon for the names of the lords of Pakasa, see Choque Canqui (1998, 325–40). On name repetitions among the lords of Andean

ethnic groups, see the abundant litigation over succession in Powers (1991): citing ANH/Q, Curacazgos 4, especially 287–91v; Ramón Valarezo F. (1987, 76); Murra (1968, 125); Zevallos Quiñones (1989, 1992, 1994) (on the Chimu and the north Peruvian coast); ART/CoO, l. 147, exp. 11, 15-X-1561; l. 147, exp. 22, 6-X-1562; l. 147, exp. 26, 2-VI-1563, 1–7; l. 147, exp. 27, 12-VI-1563; l. 147, exp. 29, 27-VIII-1563, 1–7; l. 149, exp. 91, 14-VII-1569; l. 161, exp. 430, 27-IX-1610; l. 207, exp. 1532, 21-IX-1689; l. 232, exp. 2071, 3-XI-1774; l. 235, exp. 2120, 28-I-1781; Asuntos de Gobierno, l. 266, exp. 3073, 16-III-1607; l. 267, exp. 3144, 18-V-1645; Juez de Residencia, l. 274, exp. 3414, 7-VI-1564; Juez de Censos, l. 277, exp. 3501, 18-II-1654; CoPedimentos, l. 281, exp. 3650, 24-V-1601; l. 285, exp. 4208, 13-III-1693; ANP/DI, l. 32, c. 636, 1692 (for the parcialidades of La Punta de la Aguja, Nonura, and Pisura reduced to the town of Sechura); and Hyland (2016, especially 130–31).

23. No one can state definitively the date of Garcilaso de la Vega's work. I have adopted the range of dates (following Spalding 2006, xviii) from the publication of part of his work and the date when he is supposed to have finished the second.

24. Urteaga translates the words as "los defensores o guardianes de la región o marca" (the defenders and protectors of the region or population) (1621/1920, 22).

25. Alfredo Alberdi, personal communication, February 27, 2004. See also Ramírez (2006a), where a discussion of the word *marca* shows that it referred to "population" until the mid-nineteenth century when it became synonyous with "district" or "territory."

26. Taylor (1987/1999) translates *marca* and *llacta* as "population," "divinity," "protecting ancestor," and "the ceremonial center protected" (30–33); Szeminski (1997a, 8).

27. One example is from the Huarochirí manuscript (Spalding 1984, 63).

28. This reference to fiestas and giving a new name seems an Andean equivalent of the Condolence Ceremony of the Ho-De'-No-Sau-Nee.

29. Note that both the Rimac and Pachacamac idols were oracles, suggesting that Chicamac may also have served that purpose. Today the valley's name is Chicama.

30. See also Husson (1995, 31); Rivière (1997, section 2; 1995a, 118, 120, 122). Rowe (1985, 201–2) notes that "father" sometimes is used as a synonym for "ancestor."

31. On possession of a living body by an ancestral spirit, see Castro-Klarén (1993, 168). Medinaceli and Arze (1996, 305) also found that the paramount lord of the Charkas had spiritual and temporal power. See also Yaya (2015, 642, 646).

32. Urban (2015, 195) also notes how names became titles in the far north, using Caius Julius Caesar as an analogy. See also Ramírez (2005, ch. 4); Hamilton (1978, 14); Medinaceli (1995, 330); Quiroga Zuluaga (2015) for Colombia.

33. Barraza Lescano (2003, especially 35) maintains that personal names or appellations come from the toponyms. I ask: Where did the latter come from? See also Rowe (1985, 204).

34. Natives considered lands *sapçi*—that which is common to all. The rule on tenure rights was based on labor. If someone worked the land, he had rights to the product; once abandoned, the land was open to use by another. For a complete discussion with examples, see Ramírez (2016, 2018).

35. The Spanish, cognizant of the practice, tried to curb the custom of taking the names of huacas or the thunder god. Doyle (1988, 137) cites a reference in the Archivo Arzobispal de Lima:

> Quando nasen los muchachos el echisero de su aillu pide ofrendas a sus padres para llebarles a sus ydolos y malquis y preguntalles que nombre le an de poner al muchacho de sus mesmos ydolos y echos los sachrificios a los ydolos dice el echisero al padre o padres del muchacho que los ydolos y malquis disen que les pongan el nombre de tal guaca o ydolo como es Llibiac Guari Bilca y otros a este tenor.

> When boys are born the sorcerer of his ayllu asks his parents for offerings to give to their idols and ancestors so as to ask them what name of their idols they want to give the boy, and once the sacrifices to the idols are made the sorcerer tells the boy's father or parents that the idols and ancestors say that they give the name of such and such god or idol, like, for example, Llibiac Guari Bilca and others of the same category.

The Concilio Limense of 1583 ordered all natives to be given Christian names and surnames "para que entre sí se diferencien" (to differentiate one from another). Males were to take the name of their father and females that of their mother. Subsequently, the Spanish prohibited such names as Curi, Manco, Missa, Chacpa, Libiac, and Santiago; natives thereafter were to take only Spanish names (Vargas Ugarte 1951–54, 1:327; Duviols 1986, 517; Herzog 2007, 25). For an example of another Andean who took multiple names, see Itier (2011, 187).

36. Medinaceli (2003b, 207–13) also documents the repetition of names within lineages.

37. Pease (1991, 128) writes that the Spanish did not know Huáscar's or Guayna Capac's given name. Pedro Pizarro (1572/1978) states that the names of Atahualpa and Guáscar "no heran sus mismos nombres de su alcuña, sino que el uno al otro se los pusieron por ygnominia" (were not the same names as their origins; instead both were given to indicate ignominy) (1978, 46). Betanzos has another view. Atahualpa's father, he asserts, gave him the name at his haircutting ceremony; later, at manhood, he received the name by which he and his lineage were

to be known (1551–57/1996, 174). Note that even the Hispanized mestizo chronicler Garcilaso de la Vega used four different names during his lifetime (Solano 1991). See also Herzog (2007) on naming in Spain and Latin America in the modern era; Sarmiento de Gamboa (1572/1988, 83, 89) for an example of a king taking another name; and Yaya (2015, 651) on praise names as replacements for personal names. See also Ramírez (2005, 20).

38. The name also appears as Tupac Cuxi Gualpa, Titu (or Tito) Cusi Hualpa Inti Illapa, and variations of the same in different editions of the work.

39. See also on other titles: Betanzos (1551–57/1996, 60); Sarmiento de Gamboa (1572/1965, 219, 227; 1572/1988, 83, 89); Quipucamayocs (1542–44/1920, 27); Yaya (2012, 81–82). Rowe (1946, 202) lists variations on the standard Inca names.

40. Women's names were also inheritable. Espinoza Soriano (1977, 424) mentions that women's names also indicate position and status (in Cajamarca). See Imbelloni (1946, 51–53, 268).

41. Medinaceli (2003a, 212) suggests that the names of ethnic lords also indicated a position or cargo.

42. Betanzos (1551–57/1987, 181–83, 189; 1551–57/1996, 52); Guaman Poma de Ayala (1613/1980, 116–17); Titu Cusi Yupangui (1570/1916, 89); Mena (1531–33/1938, 325–26); de la Calancha (1638/1974–81, 1:237); Kubler (1944, 256). Atahualpa also had the leading members of Tupa Yupanqui's *panaca* (a lineage of his royal descendants) killed along with the *quipucamayocs* who maintained the records of his reign (Yaya, 2012, 48). Conflict over succession is not limited to the imperial level of jurisdiction. Peruvian archives preserve many court cases involving ethnic struggles over who will become the next paramount lord. A nonrepresentative sampling includes: ANP/Tierras de Comunidades, l. 5, c. 41, 1802; RA-Civiles, l. 41, c. 266, 1721; Derecho Indigena, l. 27, c. 519, 1796; Derecho Indigena, l. 40, c. 832, 1780. Published transcriptions of disputes include Sala Vila (1989); Gutiérrez Flores (1590/2005). On the *panaca*, see n. 46 below.

43. That may have included *vila oma*, usually identified as the chief solar priest. The title itself can be translated as "the magician" or "wizard (*mago*) who speaks." Guillén Guillén (1991, especially 427–34).

44. From chronicler descriptions, they may have been a recitation of a collective biography of a name rather than a single person. On the role of commemorative songs, see Yaya (2015, 651–52).

45. Bride exchange was also used by ethnic lords to enlarge their following (Espinoza Soriano 1977, 406–7).

46. I use lineage and bloodline in the text to avoid labeling them *panaca*. Recent research by Itier (2011) questions the concept of a royal lineage or *panaca*

founded by some of the Inca kings. For more traditional views, see Hernández Astete (2008) and Zuidema (2002, 2004), among many others.

47. Yaya (2012, 48; 2015, 653) showcases another instance of the punishment and murders of royal rivals: that of Tupa Yupanqui. Another author further mentions that witnesses during Viceroy Francisco de Toledo's inspection presented a truncated account of dynastic succession, identifying Pachacuti as son of the founder Manco Capac (Covey 2020, 422).

48. See also Duviols (1997a, 275) on Urco.

49. MacCormack (2003); Hiltunen (1998, 4, 8) (on Pachacuti's possible manipulation of dynastic lore).

50. The 1552 text of Cristóbal de Molina "el chileno" (the Chilean) also records the confusing history of the natives and the fact that they were not well informed about their history (Molina 1552/1943, 41).

51. See Cerrón Palomino (2004, 1991) on Garcilaso de la Vega's own mixing of Quechua and Aymara terminology. See Pedro de Quiroga (1560s/2009, 361), whose "Coloquios de la verdad" is translated and annotated by Ana Vian Herrero.

52. See also Rostworowski (1997, 300); Covey (2006, 184).

53. On the perils of cultural filters and of translation, see Fabian (1995).

54. Imbelloni (1946, 66) discusses these numbers.

55. John Rowe (1946, especially 203–8) canonized this short list of king's names.

56. Other chroniclers also give average lengths of reigns. See, for example, Poma de Ayala (136 years), Gutierrez de Santa Clara (60 years), Giovanni Anello Oliva (56 years), and Garcilaso de la Vega (36 years), cited by Imbelloni (1946, 58, 248–50).

57. Yaya (2012, 39) provides additional data on the Inca dynasty of eleven kings (from Manco Capac to Guayna Capac), who reigned anywhere from 520 to 1,496 years.

58. See also Duviols (1979, 67).

59. Dennis E. Ogburn (2012) also questions the lists of kings in his reconsideration of the chronology of Inca imperial expansion. See also Szeminski (2013, 404).

60. That this is true is evident from the scattered references to Inca kings that were not included in the dynastic list constructed by Betanzos. Covey (2006, 174) mentions Tarku Waman (Tarco Guaman) who was omitted or eliminated from the Betanzos list.

61. Other notices of composites include: Urban (2015, 193); Medinaceli (2003a, 14).

62. Abercrombie (1998, 130) asserts that the Spanish goal of uncovering the past usually destroyed it. See also Zuidema (1997, 258). Rostworowski (1997, 31) speculates that some of the names given by Montesinos are for Guari rulers. Note that such a "long count" of Inca kings is also favored by Szeminski (1997a) and

Carlos Espinosa (2000). The latter argues that the long list may represent manipulation by lengthening to fit Inca lore into the five-millennium schema of "universal history" that was ascendant in Europe at the turn of the seventeenth century. It made the New World diachrony mirror the Old World and thereby fit both into one overarching salvation history.

63. Imbelloni (1946, 66–68, 73) discusses the nine Pachacutis.

64. Cuismanco was also an important lord of the Cajamarcas (Espinoza Soriano 1977, 401, 403, 426–28).

65. Note that Hiltunen points out that many of the deeds of the first ten kings on the list, whom he labels Guari, "are identical with the deeds of Inca Pachacuti" (1995, 17), suggesting that Pachacuti is a composite. See the appendix for a comparison between the activities attributed to Pachacuti by Betanzos and Montesinos's discussion of the accomplishments of nine kings named Pachacuti. It shows a clear correspondence between the two, buttressing the archtype hypothesis in a different way. On suppressed chronicles, see Chang-Rodríguez (1980, 87). For a general overview of various interpretations of Cuzco names, sequences, and the assumed lineages that they represent, see Duviols (1979); Rowe (1985); Imbelloni (1946).

66. See the detailed article by Jurado (2014) on the genealogical proofs submitted by ethnic leaders to gain privileges or legitimize their power. Many of these relied on false testimonies to prove their rights.

67. Other authors also note the "creative manipulation" of the natives, who had to distort their subjects to present them to the Spanish (Adorno 1979, especially 28–29).

68. It may have been both: "son" being classifactory and "brother" being the consanguineal description.

69. On the Manco Capacs, see Szeminski (1997a, 2001). He hypothesizes that the name represents a composite and many individuals who had taken the epithet.

70. Isabel Yaya's (2012) well-regarded book uses positional inheritance in explaining the dual structure of Inca historical recall.

5. Oral Traditions as History

1. Personal communication from Spanish anthropologist Luz Martinez, Trujillo, in the early 2000s.

2. As mentioned below, MacCormack believes that references to the distant past were the product of the Spaniards who wrote down the first traditions heard from the native elite.

3. The latter did not exist before c. 700 BCE (Finley 1965, 290; Hechs 1994).

4. On memory in general, see Megged (2005) and Connerton (1989).

5. For a critique of Sahlins, see Borofsky (1997).

6. See also Borofsky (1997).

7. Borofsky (1997, 257) points out rightly that the idea of the European as a god to native peoples is common in the history of colonialism. On Quetzalcoatl, see also Wilson (1995).

8. See also Krupat (2010, especially 533) for an example of native Americans accepting mythical narratives as true.

9. In Ijesho society, the new successor to a title spent three months learning the duties and knowledge of his new office (Peel 1984, 115).

10. Zuidema has written on the Inca calendar, but the Incas did not chronicle the years in numerical succession (1964/1966, 1982, 1989).

11. In pre-Muslim India, regnal lengths of thirty-two, thirty-nine, and forty-eight years were recorded for precolonial dynasties, whereas the average regnal length for the historic period was less than eleven years (Henige 1974, 49–50).

12. See J. C. Miller's (1972, especially 549–52) excellent article on the problem of assigning a chronology to king lists of the Imbangala of Angola.

13. MacCormack (1991) mentions which early colonial writers influenced whom. Thus, Juan Polo de Ondegardo influenced José de Acosta, Miguel Cabello de Valboa, and Martín de Murúa. Acosta influenced Antonio de Herrera and Bernabé Cobo. Bartolomé de Las Casas influenced Miguel Cabello Valboa, Jerónimo Román, and Luis Jerónimo Oré who, in turn, influenced Felipe Guaman Poma de Ayala, and so forth.

14. On the rapidity of change, see Ramirez (1996); MacCormack (1991, 84, 91, 179).

15. See Henige's (2009) article for an overview on the debate over the reliability of oral history.

16. See also Kan (2019); Rappaport (1990, 10–11).

References

Archives

AGI. Archivo General de las Indias Justicia (J)
ANB. Archivo Nacional de Bolivia (La Paz)
ANP. Archivo Nacional del Perú (Lima)
    Derecho Indígena (DI)
    Residencias
ART. Archivo Regional de Trujillo (now the Archivo de La Libertad)
    Corregimiento Ordinario (CoO)
    Corregimiento Asuntos de Gobierno (COAG)
    Corregimiento Pedimentos (CoPedimentos)
    Corregimiento Residencia (CoR)
    Juan de Mata
        Juez de Censos
        Juez de Residencia
    López de Córdova
BMH. Biblioteca del Museo Histórico (Pueblo Libre, Lima)
BNE. Biblioteca Nacional de España (Madrid)
BNP. Biblioteca Nacional del Perú

Published Works

Abercrombie, Thomas A. 1998. *Pathways of Memory and Power: Ethnography and History among an Andean People*. Madison: University of Wisconsin Press.

Acosta, Padre José de. 1590/1954. *Historia natural y moral de las Indias*. Biblioteca de autores españoles, vol. 73. Madrid: Ediciones Atlas.

———. 1590/1979. *Historia natural y moral de las Indias*. Edited by Edmundo O'Gorman. México: Fondo de Cultura Económica.

Acrelius, Israel. 1874. "The History of New Sweden." Translated by William M. Reynolds. *Memoirs of the Historical Society of Pennsylvania*, vol. 11. Philadelphia: Historical Society of Pennsylvania.

Acuto, Félix A. 2005. "The Materiality of Inka Domination: Landscape, Spectacle, Memory, and Ancestors." In *Global Archaeological Theory: Contextual Voices and Contemporary Thoughts*, edited by Pedro Pablo Funari, Andrés Zarankin, and Emily Stovel, 211–36. New York: Kluwer Academic/Plenum.

Adorno, Rolena. 1979. "Of Caciques, Coyas, and Kings: The Intricacies of Point of View." *Dispositio* 4 (10): 27–47.

———. 1981. "On Pictorial Language and the Typology of Culture in a New World Chronicle." *Semiótica* 36 (1–2): 51–106.

———. 1982. *From Oral to Written Expression: Native Andean Chronicles of the Early Colonial Period*. Syracuse NY: Maxwell School of Citizenship and Public Affairs, Syracuse University.

———. 1986. *Guamán Poma: Writing and Resistance in Colonial Peru*. Austin: University of Texas Press.

Agustinos. 1550/1992. *Relación de los agustinos de Huamachuco*. Lima: Pontificia Universidad Católica del Perú.

Akinnaso, F. Niyi. 1983. "Yoruba Traditional Names and the Transmission of Cultural Knowledge." *Names* 31 (3): 139–58.

Albornoz, Cristóal de. 1967. "Instrucción para descubrir todas las guacas del Piru y sus camayoc y haciendas." *Journal de la Société des Americanistes* 56 (1): 7–39.

Anello Oliva, Giovanni. 1630–31/1998. *Historia del reyno y provincias del Peru y vidas de los varones insignes de la Commpania de Jesus*. Lima: Pontificia Universidad Católica del Perú.

Angulo, Domingo. 1920. "Fundación y población de la Villa de Zaña." *Revista del Archivo Nacional del Perú* 1 (2): 280–99.

Anónimo. 1571/1995. *El anónimo de Yucay frente a Bartolomé de las Casas (1571)*. Edited by Isacio Pérez Fernández, OP (Ordo Praedicatorum). Cuzco: Centro de Estudios Regionales Andinos "Bartolomé de las Casas." Original in the BNE/ms. 19569, titled "Dominio de los Ingas."

Anonymous. 1613–14/1896. "Relatio Rervm Gestarum in Novo-Francica Missione, Annis 1613 and 1614." In *The Jesuit Relations and Allied Documents . . . 1610–1791*, edited by Reuben Gold Thwaites, vol. 2 (1613–14/1896): 193–286. Cleveland: Burrows Brothers, 1986.

Anonymous. "US Presidents—Hanadagá:yas." Accessed November 15, 2019. https://www.onondaganation.org/history/us-presidents-hanadagayas/.

Armstrong, Robert G. 1954. "A West African Inquest." *American Anthropologist* 56:1051–75.

Arriaga, Pablo José, S. J. 1621. *Extirpación de la idolatría del Perú: Dirigido al Rey N. S. en su Real Consejo de Indias*. Lima: Geronymo de Contreras, Impressor de libros.

————. 1621/1920. "La extirpación de la idolatría en el Perú." In *Colección de libros y documentos referentes a la historia del Perú*, edited by Horacio H. Urteaga, Second Series, vol I. Lima: Imprenta y Librería Sanmartí y Ca.

————. 1621/1968. "La extirpación de la idolatría en el Perú." In *Crónicas Peruanas de interés indígena*, edited by Francisco Esteve Barba, 191–278. Biblioteca de autores españoles 209. Madrid: Ediciones Atlas.

Asad, Talal. 1987. "Are There Histories of Peoples without Europe? A Review Article." *Comparative Studies in Society and History* 29 (3): 594–607.

Ascher, Marcia, and Robert Ascher. 1981. "El quipu como lenguaje visible." In *La tecnología en el mundo Andino*, edited by Heather Lechtman and Ana María Soldi, 407–33. México: Universidad Nacional Autónoma de México.

Atkinson, R. R. 1975. "The Traditions of the Early Kings of Buganda: Myth, History, and Structural Analysis." *History in Africa* 2:17–57.

Bamberger, Joan. 1974. "Naming and the Transmission of Status in a Central Brazilian Society." *Ethnology* 13 (4): 363–78.

Baptista, P. J. 1806–11/1873. "Journey of the Pombieros P. J. Baptista and Amaro José across Africa from Angola to Tette on the Zambeze." Translated by B. A. Beadle. In *The Lands of Cazembe*, edited by R. F. Burton, 167–244. London: John Murray.

Barbeau, C. M. 1917. "Iroquoian Clans and Phratries." *American Anthropologist*, New Series, 19 (3): 392–402.

Barnes, Monica. April 19–20, 2002. "Towards a Geography of Guaman Poma." Paper presented at the symposium "Peru in Black and White and in Color: The Unique Texts and Images in the Colonial Andean Manuscripts of Martín de Murúa and Guaman Poma de Ayala." Chicago: Newberry Library.

Barraza Lescano, Sergio. n.d. "La dinastía prehispánica de Fernando de Montesinos: Identificación de su fuente." Unpublished paper, copy in author's possession.

————. n.d. "Reminiscencias coloniales y modernas de ritos agrarios prehispánicos dedicados a los ancestros: La danza del huacón." Unpublished paper, copy in author's possession.

————. 2003. "La dinastía prehispánica de Fernando de Montesinos: Identificación de su fuente." In *Voces y quehaceres archivisticos en el Perú: Homenaje a Mario Cardenas Ayapoma*, edited by Beatriz Montoya Valenzuela and Marita Dextre Vitaliano, 27–40. Lima: Pontificia Universidad Catolica del Peru.

Basso, Keith. 1984. "'Stalking with Stories': Names, Places, and Moral Narratives among the Western Apache." In *Text, Play, and Story: The Construction and Reconstruction of Self and Society*, edited by Edward M. Bruner, 19–35. Prospect Heights IL: Waveland.

———. 1988. "Speaking with Names: Language and Landscape among the Western Apache." *Cultural Anthropology* 3 (2): 99–130.

———. 1989. "The Ethnography of Writing." In *Explorations in the Ethnography of Speaking*, edited by Richard Bauman and Joel Sherzer, 425–32. New York: Cambridge University Press.

———. 1996. *Wisdom Sits in Places: Landscape and Language among the Western Apache*. Albuquerque: University of New Mexico Press. Bateman, Rebecca B. 2002. "Naming Patterns in Black Seminole Ethnogenesis." *Ethnohistory* 49 (2): 227–57.

Beauchamp, W. M. 1895a. "Mohawk Notes." *Journal of American Folklore* 8 (30): 217–22.

———. 1895b. "An Iroquois Condolence." *Journal of American Folklore* 8 (31): 313–16.

———. 1891. "Iroquois Notes." *Journal of American Folklore* 4 (12): 39–46.

Becker, Marshall Joseph. 2008. "Small Wampum Bands Used by Native Americans in the Northeast: Functions and Recycling." *Material Culture* 40 (1): 1–17.

Beidelman, T. O. 1974. "Kaguru Names and Naming." *Journal of Anthropological Research* 30 (4): 281–93.

Beke, C. T. 1831–32/1873. "Resume of the Journey of MM. Monteiro and Gamitto." In *The Lands of Cazembe*, edited by R. F. Burton. London: John Murray.

Beschefer, Thierry. 1683/1900. "Lettre au R. P. Prouincial de la prouince de france; Quebec, October 21, 1683." In *The Jesuit Relations and Allied Documents . . . 1610–1791*, edited by Reuben Thwaites, vol. 62 (1681–83/1900): 190–268. Cleveland: Burrows Brothers, 1900.

Betanzos, Juan de. 1551–57/1987. *Suma y narración de los Incas*. Madrid: Ediciones Atlas.

———. 1551–57/1996. *Narrative of the Incas*. Austin: University of Texas Press.

Biard, Pierre. 1612/1896. "Missio Canadensis: Epistola ex Porturegali in Acadia, transmissa ad Praepositvm Generalem Societatis Jesu, Port Royal, January 31, 1612." In *The Jesuit Relations and Allied Documents . . . 1610–1791*, edited by Reuben Gold Thwaites, vol. 2 (1612–14/1896): 57–118. Cleveland: Burrow Brothers, 1896.

———. 1616/1897. "Relation de la Novvelle France, de fes Terres, Natvrel du Pais, & de fes Habitans. [Chs. i-xxv.] Paris, 1616." In *The Jesuit Relations and Allied Documents . . . 1610–1791*, edited by Reuben Gold Thwaites, vol. 3 (1611–16/1897): 21–284. Cleveland: Burrow Brothers, 1897.

Blair, Emma Helen, trans. and ed. 1911–12. *Upper Mississippi and Region of the Great Lakes*. 2 vols. Cleveland: Arthur H. Clark.

Blount, Ben G. 1975. "Agreeing to Agree on Genealogy: A Luo Sociology of Knowledge." In *Sociocultural Dimensions of Language Use*, edited by Mary Sanches and Ben G. Blount, 117–35. New York: Academic Press.

Blum, Susan D. 1997. "Naming Practices and the Power of Words in China." *Language in Society* 26 (3): 357–79.

Bohannan, Laura. 1952. "A Genealogical Charter." *Africa: Journal of the International African Institute* 22 (4): 301–15.

Bohannan, Paul. 1953. "Concepts of Time among the Tiv of Nigeria." *Southwestern Journal of Anthropology* 9 (3): 251–62.

Bodenhorn, Barbara, and Gabriele vom Bruck. 2006. "'Entangled in Histories': An Introduction to the Anthropology of Names and Naming." In *The Anthropology of Names and Naming*, edited by Barbara Bodenhorn and Gabriele vom Bruck, 1–30. Cambridge: Cambridge University Press.

Boone, Elizabeth Hill, and Walter Mignolo. 1994. *Writing without Words: Alternative Literacies in Mesoamerica and the Andes*. Durham NC: Duke University Press.

Borofsky, Robert. 1997. "Cook, Lono, Obeyesekere, and Sahlins." *Current Anthropology* 18 (2): 255–82.

Brébeuf, Jean de, 1636/1897. "Relation de ce qui s'est passé en la Novvelle France, en l'année 1636. [Part II, being Brébeuf's *Relation of the Hurons* for this year, originally published as an appendix to Le Jeune's *Relation of 1616*, and thus completing the document.] Ihonatiria, July 16, 1636." In *The Jesuit Relations and Allied Documents . . . 1610–1791*, edited by Reuben Gold Thwaites, vol. 10 (1636/1897): 5–318. Cleveland: Burrow Brothers, 1897.

Brelsford, William Vernon. 1944. *The Succession of Bemba Chiefs: A Guide for District Officers*. Lusaka, Northern Rhodesia: Government Printer (doc. 6 in EHRAF collection of Ethnography, section 1, b.) Accessed November 3, 2005. https://ehrafworldcultures.yale.edu/ehrafe/citation.do?method=citation&forward=browseAuthorsFullContext&id=fq05-006.

Bressani, Francesco Gioseppe. 1653/1899a. "Breve Relatione d' alcvne missioni de' PP. Della Compagnia di Giesù nella Nuoua Francia. [Part I, Chaps. i-iv, first installment of the document.] Macerata, Italy, July 19, 1653." In *The Jesuit Relations and Allied Documents . . . 1610–1791*, edited by Reuben Gold Thwaites, vol. 38 (1652–53/1899): 203–88. Cleveland: Burrow Brothers, 1899.

———. 1653/1899b. "Breve Relatione d'alcvne missioni de' PP. Della Compagnia di Giesù nella Nuoua Francia. [Remainder of Part I, all of Part II, and Chaps. i–v of Part III, being the second installment of the document.] Macerata, Italy, July 19, 1653." In *The Jesuit Relations and Allied Documents . . . 1610–1791*, edited by Reuben Gold Thwaites, vol. 39 (1653/1898):11–264. Cleveland: Burrow Brothers, 1899.

Brokaw, Galen. 2002. "Khipu Numeracy and Alphabetic Literacy in the Andes: Felipe Guaman Poma de Ayala's Nueva corónica y buen gobierno." *Colonial Latin American Review* 11 (2): 275–303.

Brüning, Enrique. 1922–25/1989. *Lambayeque: Estudios Monográficos*. Lima: SICAN.

Bruyas, Jacques. 1862. *Radical Words of the Mohawk Language with their Derivatives*. New York: Cramoisy.

Burke, Peter. 1989. "History as Social Memory." In *Memory: History, Culture and the Mind*, edited by Thomas Butler, 97–113. Oxford, UK: Basil Blackwell.

Burton, Richard Francis, ed. 1798/1873. *The Lands of Cazembe: Lacerda's Journey to Cazembe in 1798*. London: John Murray.

Buteux, Jacobus. 1640/1898. "Epistola ad R. P. MutiumVitelleschi, Praepositum Generalem Societatis Jesu, Romae. Tria Flumina [1640]." In *The Jesuit Relations and Allied Documents . . . 1610–1791*, edited by Reuben Gold Thwaites, vol. 17 (1639–40/1898): 232–38. Cleveland: Burrow Brothers, 1898.

Byock, Jesse L. 1984–85. "Saga Form, Oral Prehistory, and the Icelandic Social Context." *New Literary History* 16:153–73.

Cabello Valboa, Miguel de. 1586/1951. *Miscelánea antártica*. Lima: Universidad Nacional Mayor de San Marcos.

Calero, Luis Fernando. 1988. "Pasto, 1535–70: The Social and Economic Decline of Indian Communities in the Southern Colombian Andes." PhD diss., University of California at Berkeley.

Campisi, Jack. 1982. "The Iroquois and the Euro-American Concept of Tribe." *New York History* 63, (2): 165–82, 455–72.

Cañeque, Alejandro. 1996. "Theater of Power: Writing and Representing the *auto de fe* in Colonial Mexico." *The Americas* 52 (3): 321–43.

Capoche, Luis. 1585/1959. *Relación general de la villa imperial de Potosí*. Madrid: Ediciones Atlas.

Castro-Klarén, Sara. 1993. "Dancing and the Sacred in the Andes: From the Taqui-Oncoy to Rasu-Ñiti." In *New World Encounters*, edited by Stephan Greenblatt, 159–76. Berkeley: University of California Press.

Cerrón Palomino, Rodolfo. 1991. "El Inca Garcilaso o La Lealtad idiomática." *Lexis* 15 (2): 133–78.

———. 1998. "El cantar del Inca Yupanqui y la lengua secreta de los Incas." *Revista Andina* 32 (2): 417–52.

———. 2004. "Las etimologías toponímicas del Inca Garcilaso." *Revista Andina* 38 (1): 9–41.

———. 2015. "Toponimia Andina: Problemas y métodos." *Lexis* 39 (1): 183–97.

————. 2019. "La tesis del quechuismo primitivo y su efecto distorsionador en la interpretación del pasado prehispánico." In *El estudio del mundo andino*, edited by Marco Curatola, 177–86. Lima: Pontifícia Universidad Católica del Perú.

Chang-Rodríguez, Raquel. 1980. "A Forgotten Indian Chronicle: Titi Cusi Yupanqui's Relacion de la Conquista del Perú." *Latin American Indian Literatures Journal* 4:87–95.

Charbonnier, G. 1969. *Conversations with Claude Lévi-Strauss*. London: Jonathan Cape.

Charles, John. 2007. "Unreliable Confessions: *Khipus* in the Colonial Parish." *The Americas* 64 (1): 11–33.

Choque Canqui, Roberto. 1998. "El parentesco entre los caciques de Pakasa." In *Gente de carne y hueso: Las tramas de parentesco en los Andes*, compiled by Denise Y. Arnold, 325–40. La Paz, Bolivia: Instituto de Lengua y Cultura Aymara.

Cieza de León, Pedro de. 1548–50/1984. *La crónica del Perú: Primera Parte (1553)*. Lima: Pontificia Universidad Católica del Perú, Academia Nacional de la Historia.

————. 1548–50/1985. *La crónica del Perú: Segunda Parte*. Lima: Pontificia Universidad Católica del Perú, Academia Nacional de la Historia.

————. 1548–50/1987. *La crónica del Perú: Tercera Parte*. Lima: Pontificia Universidad Católica del Perú, Academia Nacional de la Historia.

————. 1548–50/1998. *The Discovery and Conquest of Peru*. Translated and edited by Alexandra Parma Cook and Noble David Cook. Durham NC: Duke University Press.

Clay, Gervas. 1956. "Comment on Cunnison." *Northern Rhodesia Journal* 3 (2): 137–38.

Cobo, Bernabé, S. J. 1653/1956–64. *Historia del Nuevo Mundo*. Biblioteca de Autores Españoles, vols. 91–92. Madrid: Ediciones Atlas.

Cohen, D. W. 1989. "The Undefining of Oral Tradition." *Ethnohistory* 36 (1): 9–18.

Collapiña, Supno y otros Quipucamayocs [literally, and other quipu keepers]. 1542/1974. *Relacion de la descendencia, gobierno y conquista de los Incas*. Lima: Ediciones de la Biblioteca Universitaria.

————. 1542/1980. *Relacion de cuatro quipucamayocs al Virrey Vaca de Castro*. Colección Pendoneros. Otavalo, Ecuador: Instituto Otavaleño de antropologia–Centro de Estudios, 58–376.

Connerton, Paul. 1989. *How Societies Remember*. Cambridge: Cambridge University Press.

Conrad, Geoffrey W., and Arthur A. Demarest. 1984. *Religion and Empire: The Dynamics of Aztec and Inca Expansionism*. Cambridge: Cambridge University Press.

Converse, Harriet Maxwell. 1895. "The Wampum-Records of the Iroquois." *The Monthly Illustrator* 4 (14): 342–47.

Cooke, Charles A. 1952. "Iroquois Personal Names: Their Classification." *Proceedings of the American Philosophical Society* 96 (4): 427–38.

Covey, R. Alan. 2006. "Chronology, Succession, and Sovereignty: The Politics of Inka Historiography and Its Modern Interpretation." *Comparative Studies of Society and History* 48 (1): 169–99.

———. 2020. *Inca Apocalypse: The Spanish Conquest and the Transformation of the Andean World*. New York: Oxford University Press.

Coxhead, John Charles Codington. 1914. *The Native Tribes of North-Eastern Rhodesia: Their Laws and Customs*. London: Royal Anthropological Institute of Great Britain and Ireland.

Crawford, Gary W., and David G. Smith. 1996. "Migration in Prehistory: Princess Point and the Northern Iroquoian Case." *American Antiquity* 61 (4): 782–90.

Cummins, Thomas B. F. 2004. *Brindis con el Inka: La abstracción andina y las imágenes coloniales de los queros*. Lima: Universidad Nacional Mayor de San Marcos.

———. 2011. "Tocapu: What Is It, What Does It Do, and Why Is It Not a Knot?" In *Their Way of Writing: Scripts, Signs, and Pictographies in Pre-Columbian America*, edited by Elizabeth Hill Boone and Gary Urton, 277–318. Washington DC: Dumbarton Oaks Research Library and Collection.

Cunnison, Ian. 1951a. "The Death and Burial of Chief Kazembe XIV." *Northern Rhodesia Journal* 1 (4): 46–51.

———. 1951b. *History on the Luapula: An Essay on the Historical Nations of a Central African Tribe. Rhodes-Livingstone Papers*, no. 21. London: Oxford University Press.

———. 1952. "The Installation of Chief Kazembe XV." *Northern Rhodesia Journal* 1 (5): 3–10.

———. 1954. "A Note on the Lunda Concept of Custom." *Rhodes-Livingstone Journal*, no. 14: 20–29.

———. 1956a. "Headmanship and the Ritual of Luapula Villages." *Africa: Journal of the International African Institute* 26 (1): 2–16.

———. 1956b. "Perpetual Kinship: A Political Institution of the Luapula Peoples." *Rhodes-Livingstone Papers*, no. 20: 28–48.

———. 1956c. "The Reigns of the Kazembes." *Northern Rhodesia Journal* 3 (2): 131–38.

———. 1957. "History and Genealogies in a Conquest State." *American Anthropologist*, New Series, 59:20–31.

———. 1959. *The Luapula Peoples of Northern Rhodesia*. Manchester: Rhodes-Livingstone Institute and Manchester University Press.

———. 1961. "Kazembe and the Portuguese 1798–1832." *Journal of African History* 2 (1): 61–76.

———. 1966. "Kazembe and the Arabs to 1870." In *The Zambesian Past: Studies in Central African History*, edited by Eric Stokes, 226–37. Manchester: Manchester University Press.

Curatola Petrocchi, Marco. 2016. "La voz de la huaca: Acerca de la naturaleza oracular y el trasfondo aural de la religión andina antigua." In *El Inca y la huaca: La región del poder y el poder de la religión en el mundo andino antiguo*, edited by Marco Curatola Petrocchi and Jan Szeminski, 259–316. Lima: Pontificia Universidad Católica del Perú.

Curatola Petrocchi, Marco, and José Carlos de la Puente Luna. 2013. *El Quipu colonial: Estudios y materiales*. Lima: Pontificia Universidad Católica del Perú.

Dablon [also D'Ablon], Claude. 1670–71/1899. "Relation de ce qui s'est passé . . . en la Nouvelle France, les années 1670 & 1671. [Second installment, concluding the document.] [Quebec, 1671.] Estienne de Carheil [Goiogouen], n.d., Louys André, n.p., n.d." In *The Jesuit Relations and Allied Documents . . . 1610–1791*, edited by Reuben Gold Thwaites, vol. 55 (1670–72/1899): 19–228. Cleveland: Burrow Brothers, 1899.

———. 1671–72/1899. "Relation de ce qui s'est passé . . . en la Nouvelle France, les années 1671 & 1672." In *The Jesuit Relations and Allied Documents . . . 1610–1791*, edited by Reuben Gold Thwaites, vol. 55 (1670–72/1899): 229–314. Cleveland: Burrow Brothers, 1899.

D'Altroy, Terrence N. 2002. *The Incas*. Malden MA: Blackwell.

Danwerth, Otto. 2013. "Performances for the Dead: Public Rituals Involving Deceased Rulers in Late Inca and Early Colonial Peru (ca. 1450–1550)." *Image-Object-Performance: Mediality and Communication in Cultural Contact Zones of Colonial Latin America and the Philippines*. Münster, Germany: Warmann VerlagGmbH, 65–91.

Darnton, Robert, 1984. *The Great Cat Massacre and Other Episodes in French Cultural History*. New York: Basic Books.

De la Calancha, Fray Antonio. 1638/1974–81. *Crónica moralizada (del orden de San Agustín en el Perú [1638])*. Edited by Ignacio Prado Pastor. 6 vols. Lima: Universidad Mayor de San Marcos.

De Lacerda, Francisco José Maria. 1798/1873. "Lacerda's Journey to Cazembe in 1798." In *The Lands of Cazembe*, edited by Captain Richard Francis Burton, 55–106. London: John Murray.

de la Puente Luna, José Carlos. 2014. "That Which Belongs to All: Khipus, Community, and Indigenous Legal Activism in the Early Colonial Andes." *The Americas* 72 (1): 1–36.

————. 2016. "Incas pecheros y caballeros hidalgos: La desintegración del orden incaico y la génesis de la nobleza incaica colonial en el Cuzco del siglo XVI." *Revista Andina* 54:9–95.

————. 2019. "Calendars in Knotted Cords: New Evidence on How Khipus Captured Time in Nineteenth-Century Cuzco and Beyond." *Ethnohistory* 66 (3): 437–64.

————. n.d. "Khipus as Legal Archives: Tribute, Justice and Strategic Translation in Early Colonial Peru." Unpublished paper, copy in author's possession.

Diez Hurtado, Alejandro. 1988. *Pueblos y caciques de Piura, Siglos XVI y XVII*. Piura, Peru: Centro de Investigación y Promoción del Campesino.

————.1997. "Caciques, cofradías, memoria y parcialidades: Un ensayo sobre el origen de la identidad cataquense." *Anthropologica* 15:151–72.

Doyle, Mary Eileen. 1988. "The Ancestor Cult and Burial Ritual in Seventeenth and Eighteenth Century Peru." PhD diss., University of California at Los Angeles.

Durston, Alan. 2007. "Native-Language Literacy in Colonial Peru: The Question of Mundane Quechua Writing Revisited." *Hispanic American Historical Review* 88 (1): 41–70.

————. 2014. "Cristobal Choquecasa and the Making of the Huarochirí Manuscript." In *Indigenous Intellectuals: Knowledge, Power, and Colonial Culture in Mexico and the Andes*, edited by Gabriela Ramos and Yanna Yannakakis, 151–69. Durham NC: Duke University Press.

Duviols, Pierre. 1979. "La dinastía de los Incas, monarquía o diarquía? Argumentos heurísticos a favor de una tesis estructuralista." *Journal de la Société des Américanistes* 66:67–83.

————. 1986. *Cultura Andina y represión: Procesos y visitas de idolatrías y hechicería. Cajatambo, Siglo XVII*. Cuzco: Centro de Estudios Rurales Andinos "Bartolomé de las Casas."

————. 1997a. "Cosmovisión y ritual solar de sucesión: La guerra de los Incas contra los Chancas. Ensayo de interpretación." In *Pensar America: Cosmovisión mesoamericana y andina*, compiled by A. Garrido Aranda, 271–93. Córdoba: Ayuntamiento de Montilla.

————. 1997b. "El Inca, rey solar responsable y garante de la fertilidad, de la armonía cósmica, social y política." *Journal of the Steward Anthropological Society* 25 (1–2): 312–46.

Edwards, Mark W. 2003. "Homer and the Oral Tradition." *Oral Tradition* 18 (1): 65–67.

Eeckhout, Peter, and Nathalie Danis. 2004. "Los tocapus reales en Guamán Poma: ¿Una heráldica incaica?" *Boletín de arqueología* 8:305–23.

Eliade, M. 1954. *The Myth of the Eternal Return, or Cosmos and History.* Bellington Series, no. 46. Princeton NJ: Princeton University Press.

Ellefsen, Bernardo. 1994. "La genealogía de los Incas." *Sequilao: Revista de historia, arte y sociedad* 3 (6): 5–15.

Escobardi de Querejazu, Laura. 1982–83. "La heráldica Incaica y los caciques Cusicanqui de Pacajes." *Arte y arqueología* 8–9:163–66.

Espinosa, Carlos. 2000. "Entre Noe, Santa Elena y Manco Capac." *Boletín del Instituto Riva-Agüero* 27:151–82.

Espinosa, Licenciado Gaspar de. 1532/1921/1921–26. "Carta á S. M. del Licenciado Espinosa acerca de las conquistas de Francisco Pizarro y desavenencias con Diego de Almagro." In *Gobernantes del Perú: Cartas y papeles del siglo XVI*, edited by Roberto Levillier, vol. 2, 11–16. Madrid: Sucesores de Rivadeneyra.

———. 1533/1921/1921–26. "Carta del Licenciado Espinosa a S.M. con las nuevas de los descubrimientos y conquistas que hacia Francisco Pizarro. . . ." In *Gobernantes del Perú: Cartas y papeles del siglo XVI*, edited by Roberto Levillier, vol. 2, 17–30. Madrid: Sucesores de Rivadeneyra.

Espinoza Soriano, Waldemar. 1981. "El reino aymara Quillaca-Asanaque." *Revista del Museo Nacional* 45:175–274.

———. 1977. "La poliginia señorial en el reino de Cuismanco." In *Historia de Cajamarca*, compiled and edited by Fernando Silva Santesteban, Waldemar Espinoza Soriano, Rogger Ravine, and Rebeca Carrión Cachot, vol. 2, 69–108. Lima: Instituto Nacional de Cultura, 1986, and in *Revista del Museo Nacional* 43:399–466.

Estenssoro Fuchs, Juan Carlos. 1992. "Los bailes de los indios y el proyecto colonial." *Revista Andina* 10 (2): 353–404.

———. 2003. *Del paganismo a la santidad.* Lima: Pontificia Universidad Católica del Perú.

Estete, Miguel de. 1534/1924. "Noticia del Perú." *Historia de los Incas y Conquista del Perú.* In *Colección de libros y documentos referentes a la historia del Perú*, edited by Horacio H. Urteaga, Second Series, vol. 8, 3–56. Lima: Imprenta y Librería Sanmartí y Ca.

Evaneshko, Veronica. 1974. "Tonawanda Seneca and Ethnic Identity: Functional and Processual Analysis." PhD diss. University of Arizona. Ann Arbor MI: University Microfilms International, doc. 59.

Evans-Pritchard, E. E. 1939. "Nuer Time-Reckoning." *Africa: Journal of the International African Institute* 12 (2): 189–216.

Fabian, Johannes. 1995. "Ethnographic Misunderstanding and the Perils of Context." *American Anthropologist* 97 (1): 41–50.

Feeley-Harnik, Gillian. 1978. "Divine Kingship and the Meaning of History among the Sakalava of Madagascar." *Man*, New Series, 13 (3): 402–17.

Fenton, William N. 1883/1963. "Horatio Hale." In *The Iroquois Book of Rites*, edited by Horatio Hale, vii–xxvii. Toronto: University of Toronto Press.

———. 1946. "An Iroquois Condolence Council for Installing Cayuga Chiefs in 1945." *Journal of the Washington Academy of Sciences* 36 (4): 110–27.

———. 1949. "Seth Newhouse's Traditional History and Constitution of the Iroquois Confederacy." *Proceedings of the American Philosophical Society* 93 (2): 141–58.

———. 1950. "The Roll Call of the Iroquois Chiefs: A Study of a Mnemonic Cane from the Six Nations Reserve." Miscellaneous Collections (vol. III, no. 15, pp. 1–73), Smithsonian Institution, Washington DC.

———. 1975. "The Lore of the Longhouse: Myth, Ritual, and Red Power." *Anthropological Quarterly* 48 (3): 131–47.

———. 1986. "Leadership in the Northeastern Woodlands of North America." *American Indian Quarterly* 10 (1): 21–45.

———. 1988. *The Great Law and the Long House: A Political History of the Iroquois Confederacy*. Norman: University of Oklahoma Press.

Finley, M. I. 1965. "Myth, Memory and History." *History and Theory* 4 (3): 281–302.

Foerster, Rolf. 2010. "Acerca de los nombres de las personas (üy) entre los mapuches: Otra vuelta de tuerca." *Revista de Antropología* 21 (1): 81–110.

Fogelson, Raymond D. 1989. "The Ethnohistory of Events and Nonevents." *Ethnohistory* 36 (2): 133–47.

Forsyth, Thomas. 1826/1912. "An Account of the Manners and Customs of the Sauk and Fox Nations of Indians Tradition (1827)." In *Upper Mississippi and Region of the Great Lakes*, translated and edited by Emma Helen Blair, vol. 2, 183–248. Cleveland: Arthur H. Clark.

Fossa, Lydia. 2000. "Two Khipu, One Narrative: Answering Urton's Questions." *Ethnohistory* 42 (2): 453–68.

Frank Exner, Little Bear. 2007. *Creating Identity: North American Indian Names and Naming*. Saarbrücken, Germany: VDM Verlag Dr. Müller.

Galloway, Patricia. 2006. "Choctaw Names and Choctaw Roles." In *Practicing Ethnohistory*. Lincoln: University of Nebraska Press, 202–22.

Gama, Sebastian de la. 1540/1974. "Visita hecha en el Valle de Jayanca [Trujillo] (1540)." *Historia y cultura* 8:215–28.

———. 1540/1975. "El Valle de Jayanca y el reino de los mochica, Siglos XV y XVI." *Bulletin de l'Institut Francais de Etudes Andines* 4 (3–4): 243–74.

Gamitto, A. C. P. 1831–32/1960. *O Muata Kazembe, King Kazembe and the Marave, Cheva, Bisa, Bemba, Lunda, and Other Peoples of Southern Africa being the*

Diary of the Portuguese Expedition to that Potentate in the Years 1831 and 1832. Translated by Ian Cunnison. Vols. 1–2 (42–43). Lisbon: Junta do Investigações do Ultramar.

Garcilaso de la Vega, Inca. 1602/1960–63. *Obras completas del Inca Garcilaso de la Vega.* 4 vols. In Carmela Saenz de Santa María, Biblioteca de Autores Españoles, vols. 132–35. Madrid: Ediciones Atlas.

———. 1609–12/1941–45. *Los comentarios reales de los Incas.* 6 vols. Lima: Librería e Imprenta Gil, S.A.

———. 1609–12/1959. *Comentarios reales de los Incas.* Lima: Universidad Nacional Mayor de San Marcos.

———. 1609–12/1966. *Royal Commentaries of the Incas and General History of Peru.* Translated by Harold V. 2 vols. Livermore. Austin: University of Texas Press.

———. 1609–12/1985. *Comentarios reales de los Incas.* 2 vols. Caracas: Biblioteca Ayacucho.

———. 1609–12/2007. *Comentarios reales de los Incas.* Lima: Universidad Inca Garcilaso de la Vega.

Geertz, Clifford, and Hildred Geertz. 1964. "Teknonymy in Bali: Parenthood, Age-Grading and Genealogical Amnesis." *Journal of the Royal Anthropological Institute of Great Britain and Ireland* 94 (2): 94–108.

Gentile, Margarita E. 1996. "Apodos de españoles en los Andes (siglos XVI–XVII)." *Sequilao* 9–10:5–10.

———. 1999. "Rutuchicuy: La ceremonia incaica de imposicion del nombre propio y su persistencia." In *Huaca muchay, religion indigena.* Buenos Aires: Instituo Nacional Superior del Profesorado de Folklore, 169–94.

———. 2008. "Apodos de indígenas y mestizos en los Andes (siglos 15–17)." *Espéculo: Revista de Estudios literarios.* Madrid: Universidad Complutense, vol. 40, año 14: 169–94 or 1–10. Accessed September 19, 2011. http://www.ucm.es/info/especulo/numero40/apodos.html.

———. n.d. "Tocapu: Unidad de sentido en el lenguaje gráfico Andino." No. 45. Accessed July 8, 2010. http:/www.ucm.es/info/especulo/numero45/tocapu.html.

Gibson, Charles. 1948/1969. *Inca Concept of Sovereignty and the Spanish Administration in Peru.* Westport CT: Greenwood.

Gibson, John Arthur, H. Woodbury, R. Henry, and A. Goldenweiser. 1912/1992. *Concerning the League: The Iroquois League Tradition.* Edited by Hanni Woodbury. Winnipeg: Algonquian and Iroquoian Linguistics.

Gillespie, Susan D. 1988. *Aztec Kings: The Construction of Rulership in Mexican History.* Tucson: University of Arizona Press.

Goldenweiser, A. A. 1914. "The Social Organization of the Indians of North America." *Journal of American Folklore* 27 (106): 411–36.

Góngora, Mario. 1980. "Sondeos en la antroponimia colonial de Santiago de Chile." In *Estudios de historia de las ideas y de historia social*. Valparaíso: Ediciones Universitarias de Valparaíso, 277–304.

González [Gonçalez] Holguin, Diego. 1608/1952. *Arte y diccionario Qquechua-Español*. Lima: Imprenta del Estado.

Goody, Jack, and Ian Watt. 1963. "The Consequences of Literacy." In *Literacy in Traditional Societies*, edited by J. Goody, 27–68. Cambridge: Cambridge University Press.

Gordon, David M. 2006a. *Nochituti's Gift: Economy, Society, and Environment in Central Africa*. Madison: University of Wisconsin Press.

———. 2006b. "History on the Luapula Retold: Landscape, Memory and Identity in the Kazembe Kingdom." *Journal of African History* 47:21–42.

Graña, Mario Julio. 2000. "Autoridad y memoria entre los killakas: Las estrategias discursivas de don Juan Colque Guarache en el sur andino (siglo 16)." *Histórica* 24 (1): 23–47.

Grant, Jill, and Martin Zelenietz. 1983. "Naming Practices in Kelenge." *Names* 31:179–90.

Gravier, Jacques. 1701/1900. "Relation ou Journal du voyage en 1700 despuis le Pays des Illinois Jusqu'a l'Embouchure du Fleuve Mississipi, Fort de Mississipi, February 16, 1701." In *The Jesuit Relations and Allied Documents . . . 1610–1791*, edited by Reuben Gold Thwaites, vol. 65 (1696–1702): 100–179. Cleveland: Burrow Brothers, 1900.

Gray, Robert F. 1953. "Positional Succession among the Wambugwe." *Africa: Journal of the International African Institute* 23 (3): 233–43.

Greer, Allan. 2000. *The Jesuit Relations: Natives and Missionaries in Seventeenth-Century North America*. New York: Macmillan.

Guaman Poma de Ayala, Felipe. 1613/1936. *Nueva corónica y buen gobierno*. Paris: Institut d'ethnologie.

———. 1613/1980. *El primer nueva corónica y buen gobierno*. Edited by J. V. Murra and Rolena Adorno. 3 vols. México DF: Siglo XXI Editores, S. A.

———. 1613/1987. *Nueva crónica y buen gobierno*. Madrid: História 16.

———. 1613/1993. *Nueva corónica y buen gobierno*. Lima: Fondo de Cultura Económica.

Guillén Guillén, Edmundo. 1974. *Versión Inca de la conquista*. Lima: Milla Batres Editorial.

———. 1991. "Dos notas históricas y un documento inédito: Mélanges en hommage à Pierre Duviols." In *Cultures et soeiétés: Andes et Méso Amérique*, compiled by Raquel Thiercelin, vol. 2, 421–39. Aix-en-provence: Université de

Provence. Gutiérrez de Santa Clara, Pedro. c. 1600/1963. *Historia de las guerras civiles del Perú*. Biblioteca de Autores Españoles 166. Madrid: Ediciones Atlas.

Gutierrez Flores, Juan. 1573/2005. *La visita de Juan Gutierrez Flores al Colesuyu y pleitos por los cacicazgos de Torata y Moquegua*. Lima: Pontificia Universidad Católica del Perú.

Guyer, Jane I., and Samuel M. Eno Belinga. 1995. "Wealth in People as Wealth in Knowledge: Accumulation and Composition in Equatorial Africa." *Journal of African History* 36 (1): 91–120.

Haeberli, Joerg. 1995. "The Brooklyn Museum Textile No. 38.121: A Mnemonic and Calendrical Device, a Huaca." *Journal of the Steward Anthropological Society* 23 (nos.1–2): 121–51.

Hale, Horatio, ed. 1883/1963. *The Iroquois Book of Rites*. Toronto: University of Toronto Press.

———. 1895. "An Iroquois Condoling Council: A Study of Aboriginal Society and Government." *Proceedings and Transactions of the Royal Society of Canada* 1 (2) (second series): 45–65.

Hall, Robert L. 1997. *An Archaeology of the Soul: North American Indian Belief and Ritual*. Urbana: University of Illinois Press.

Hall, Thomas D. 1984. "The Rise of the Modern World-System: The View from the Periphery." *Contemporary Sociology* 13 (1): 33–35.

Hamilton, Joe. 1978. "Plebe and Potentate: History and Society of Prehispanic North Central Coast Peru." Unpublished paper, copy in author's possession.

Harris, Olivia. 1995. "'The Coming of the White People': Reflections on the Mythologisation of History in Latin America." *Bulletin of Latin American Research* 14 (1): 9–24.

Hart, Elizabeth Ann. 1983. "Prehistoric Political Organization on the Peruvian North Coast." PhD diss., University of Michigan.

Heehs, Peter. 1994. "Myth, History, and Theory." *History and Theory* 33 (1): 1–19.

Henige, David P. 1971. "Oral Tradition and Chronology." *Journal of African History* 12 (3): 371–89.

———. 1974. *The Chronology of Oral Tradition*. Oxford: Clarendon.

———. 1982. *Oral Historiography*. New York: Longman.

———. 2009. "Impossible to Disprove, yet Impossible to Believe: The Unforgiving Epistemology of Deep-Time Oral Tradition." *History of Africa* 36:127–234.

Herbert, Robert K. 1997. "The Politics of Personal Naming in South Africa." *Names* 45 (1): 3–17.

Hernández Astete, Francisco. 1998. "Roles sexuales en la organización Incaica." *Histórica* 22 (1): 93–134.

———. 2008. "Las panacas y el poder en el Tahuantinsuyu." *Bulletin de l'Institut Français d'Estudes Andines* 37 (1): 29–45.

Hernández Príncipe, Licenciado Rodrigo. 1621–22/1923. "Mitologia Andina (1621–22)." *Inca: Revista trimestral de estudios antropológicos* 1:25–78.

Herzog, Tamar. 2007. "Nombres y apellidos: ¿Cómo se llamaban las personas en Castilla e Hispanoamérica durante la época moderna?" *Juhrbuchfür Geschichte Lateinamerikas* 44:1–36.

Hewitt, John Napoleon Britton. 1902. "Orenda and a Definition of Religion." *American Anthropologist* 4 (1): 33–46.

———. 1917. "Review." *American Anthropologist*, New Series, 19 (3): 429–38.

———. 1944. "The Requickening Address of the Iroquois Condolence Council." *Journal of the Washington Academy of Sciences* 34 (3): 65–85.

Hiltunen, Juha J. 1995. "Re-evaluation of Fernando Montesinos' Peruvian Kinglist." Paper presented at the 23rdAnnual Midwest Conference on Andean and Amazonian Archaeology and Ethnohistory, Chicago, February 25–26, 1995. Unpublished paper, copy in author's possession.

———. 1998. "The Reliability of the Chronicle of Fernando de Montesinos." Unpublished paper, copy in author's possession.

———. 1999. *Ancient Kings of Peru: The Reliability of the Chronicle of Fernando de Montesinos*. Helsinki: Suomen Historiallinen Seura.

Holland Jr., Theodore. 1995. "Words to Live By: Investigating Navajo Naming Practices." *Names* 43 (4): 275–93.

Houghton, Frederick. 1922. "The Traditional Origin and the Naming of the Seneca Nation." *American Anthropologist*, New Series, 24 (1): 31–43.

Howe, James. 1979. "The Effects of Writing on the Cuna Political System." *Ethnology* 18 (1): 1–16.

Husson, Jean-Philippe. 1995. "En busca de las fuentes indígenas de Waman Puma de Ayala: Las raices Incas y Yaruwillka del cronista indio." *Histórica* 19 (1): 29–71.

Hyland, Sabine P. 1998. "The Imprisonment of Blas Valera: Heresy and Inca History in Colonial Peru." *Colonial Latin American Historical Review* 7 (1): 43–58.

———. 2000. "Montesinos y los reyes de Huari." *Boletin de arqueologia* 4:641–48.

———. 2003. *The Jesuit and the Incas: The Extraordinary Life of Padre Blas Valera, S.J.* Ann Arbor: University of Michigan Press.

———. 2007. *The Quito Manuscript: An Inca History Preserved by Fernando de Montesinos*. New Haven CT: Yale University Press.

———. 2010. "Sodomy, Sin, and String Writing: The Moral Origins of Andean Khipu." *Ethnohistory* 57 (1): 165–73.

———. 2016. *The Chankas and the Priest: A Tale of Murder and Exile in Highland Peru*. University Park: Pennsylvania State University Press. Imbelloni, José.

1946. *Pachacuti IX: El Incario crítico.* Buenos Aires: Editorial Humanior, Biblioteca Humanior.

Itier, César. 2011. "Las panacas no existieron." In *Estudios sobre lenguas andinas y amazónicas: Homenaje a Rodolfo Cerrón-Palomino,* edited by W. Adelaar, P. Valenzuela Bismarck, and R. Zariquiey Biondi, 181–93. Lima: Pontificia Universidad Católica del Perú.

———. 2013. "Una institución política mal interpretada: El panaca." *Libros y Artes: Revista de la Biblioteca Nacional del Perú* 11 (62–63): 4–6.

Jackson, Margaret A. 2011. "Moche as Visual Notation: Semasiographic Elements in Moche Ceramic Imagery." In *Their Way of Writing: Scripts, Signs, and Pictographies in Pre-Columbian America,* edited by Elizabeth Hill Boone and Gary Urton, 227–50. Washington DC: Dumbarton Oaks Research Library and Collection.

Jacobs, Wilbur R. 1949. "Wampum: The Protocol of Indian Diplomacy." *William and Mary Quarterly* 6 (4): 596–604.

Jamieson, Susan M. 1981. "Economics and Ontario Iroquoian Social Organization." *Canadian Journal of Archaeology,* no. 5: 19–30.

Jennings, Francis, William N. Fenton, Mary A. Druke, and David R. Miller, eds. 1985. *The History and Culture of Iroquois Diplomacy: An Interdisciplinary Guide to the Treaties of the Six Nations and Their League.* Syracuse NY: Syracuse University Press.

Jiménez Borja, Arturo. 1946. "La danza en el antiguo Perú." *Revista del Museo Nacional,* no. 15: 122–61.

Jouvency, Joseph. 1610–13/1896. "De Regione et Moribus Canadensium seu Barbarorum Novae Franciae." In *The Jesuit Relations and Allied Documents . . . 1610–1791,* edited by Reuben Gold Thwaites, vol. 1 (1610–13/1896): 239–98. Cleveland: Burrow Brothers, 1896.

Jurado, M. Carolina. 2014. "'Descendientes de los primeros': Las probanzas de méritos y servicios y la genealogía cacical. Audiencia de Charcas, 1574–1719." *Revista de Indias* 74 (261): 387–422.

Kan, Sergei. 2019. "Raymond D. Fogelson's 'The Ethnohistory of Events and Non-events.'" *Ethnohistory* 66 (1): 171–77.

Kapches, Mima. 1990. "The Spatial Dynamics of Ontario Iroquoian Longhouses." *American Antiquity* 55 (1): 49–67.

Kazembe XIV, Mwata (or Chinyanta Nunkula) (with the help of Father E. Labrecque). 1948/1961. *Historical Traditions of the Eastern Lunda: A Translation from the Bemba by Ian Cunnison of Ifikolwe Fyandina Bantu Bandi (My Ancestors and My People).* Lusaka, Zambia: Rhodes-Livingstone Institute.

Kelly, John D., and Martha Kaplan. 1990. "History, Structure, and Ritual." *Annual Review of Anthropology* 19:119–50.

Kendall, Martha B. 1980. "Exegesis and Translation: Northern Yuman Names as Texts." *Journal of Anthropological Research* 36 (3): 261–73.

Kimmel, Michael S. 1984. "Review of *Europe and the People without History*." *American Journal of Sociology* 89 (5): 1219–21.

Kinietz, W. Vernon. 1965. *The Indians of the Western Great Lakes, 1615–1760*. Ann Arbor: University of Michigan Press.

Kirkland, Samuel. 1803/1980. *The Journals of Samuel Kirkland: Eighteenth Century Missionary to the Iroquois, Government Agent, Father of Hamilton College*. Edited by Walter Pilkington. Clinton NY: Hamilton College.

Klerk, Vivian de, and Barbara Bosch. 1996. "Naming Practices in the Eastern Cape Province of South Africa." *Names* 44 (3): 167–88.

Krazanowski, Andrezej, and Jan Szeminski. 1978. "La toponimia indígena en la Cuenca del rio Chicama (Perú)." *Estudios Latinoamericanos* 4:11–51.

Krupat, Arnold. 2010. "Patterson's Life; Black Hawk's Story; Native American Elegy." *American Literary History* 22 (3): 527–52.

Kubler, George. 1944. "A Peruvian Chief of State: Manco Inca (1515–1545)." *Hispanic American Historical Review* 24 (2): 253–76.

Labrecque, E., ed. 1934. "La religión du Noir Infidele: Coutumes matrimoniales chez les Babembe." Ilondola, Zambia: Bembe Cultural Data, part 1, 1–104.

Lafitau, Joseph-François. 1639/1898b. "Relation de ce qvi s'est passé en la Novvelle France, en l'année 1639. [Chapters ii–xi, completing Part I of the document; and Chapters i, ii of Part II, being Lalemant's Huron report.] Paul le Jeune; Sillery, September 4, 1639. Hierosme Lalemant; Ossossané, June 7, 1639." In *The Jesuit Relations and Allied Documents . . . 1610–1791*, edited by Reuben Gold Thwaites, vol. 16 (1639/1898): 7–254. Cleveland: Burrow Brothers, 1898b.

———. 1640/1898a. "Epistola ad R. P. Mutium Vitelleschi, Praepositum Generalem Societatis Jesu, Romae. Apud Hurones, April 1, 1640." In *The Jesuit Relations and Allied Documents . . . 1610–1791*, edited by Reuben Gold Thwaites, vol. 17 (1639–40/1898): 226–31. Cleveland: Burrow Brothers, 1898.

———. 1640/1898b. "Lettre a Monseigneur l'Eminentissime Cardinal Duc de Richelieu. Des Hurons en la Nouvelle-France, March 28, 1640." In *The Jesuit Relations and Allied Documents . . . 1610–1791*, edited by Reuben Gold Thwaites, vol. 17 (1639–40/1898): 218–25. Cleveland: Burrow Brothers, 1898.

———. 1640/1898c. "Relation de ce qvi s'est passé en la Novvelle France, en l'annee 1640. [Chaps. ix–x of Part II, and postscript, completing the document.] Des Hurons, May 27 and August 3, 1640." In *The Jesuit Relations and*

Allied Documents . . . 1610–1791, edited by Reuben Gold Thwaites, vol. 20 (1640–41/1898): 17–87. Cleveland: Burrow Brothers, 1898.

———. 1642/1898. "Relation de ce qvi s'est passé en la Novvelle France, en l'année 1642. [Chaps. ii–xii of Part II, completing the document.] Ste. Marie aux Hurons, June 10, 1642." In *The Jesuit Relations and Allied Documents . . . 1610–1791*, edited by Reuben Gold Thwaites, vol. 23 (1642/1818 [*sic*] 1898): 17–235. Cleveland: Burrow Brothers, 1898.

———. 1647–48/1898. "Relation de ce qvi s'est passé. . . . en la Novvelle France, en annés 1647 & 1648. [Chaps. i–viii of Part I, first installment of the document.] Quebec, October 15, 1648." In *The Jesuit Relations and Allied Documents . . . 1610–1791*, edited by Reuben Gold Thwaites, vol. 32 (1647–48/1898): 111–306. Cleveland: Burrow Brothers, 1898.

———. c. 1659–60/1899. "Relation de ce qvi s'est passé. . . . en la Novvelle France, és années mil fix cent cinquante neuf & mil fix cent foixante." [Chaps. v–viii, completing the document.] [*Hierosme Lalemant*], n.p., n.d. In *The Jesuit Relations and Allied Documents . . . 1610–1791*, edited by Reuben Gold Thwaites, vol. 46 (c. 1659–61/1899): 21–125. Cleveland: Burrow Brothers, 1899.

———. 1661–62/1899. "Relation de ce qui s'est passéla Novvelle France és annés 1661 & 1662. Kebec. September 18, 1662." In *The Jesuit Relations and Allied Documents . . . 1610–1791*, edited by Reuben Gold Thwaites, vol. 47 (1661–63/1899): 125–245. Cleveland: Burrow Brothers, 1899.

Lalemant, Jerome (also Hierosme), Jean de Brébeuf, Paul Ragueneau, Jean de Quen, and others. 1632–57/1899. "Catalogve des Bienfaictevrs de N. Dame de Recouurance de Kebec. Kebec, 1632–1657." In *The Jesuit Relations and Allied Documents . . . 1610–1791*, edited by Reuben Gold Thwaites, vol. 42 (1632–57/1899): 268–90. Cleveland: Burrow Brothers, 1899.

———. 1724. *Moeurs del sauvages amériquains, comparées aux moeurs des premiers temps.* 2 vols. Paris: Saugrain l'ainé y Charles Étienne Hochereau.

———. 1974–76. *Customs of the American Indians Compared with the Customs of Primitive Times.* Edited by W. N. Fenton and E. L. Moore. 2 vols. Toronto: Chaplain Society. Lalemant, Jerome (also Hierosme). 1639/1898a. "Relation de ce qvi s'es passé en la Nowelle France, en l'année 1639. [Chaps. iii–viii of Part II, completing the document.] Hierosme Lalemant; Ossossané, June 7, 1639." In *The Jesuit Relations and Allied Documents . . . 1610–1791*, edited by Reuben Gold Thwaites, vol. 17 (1639–40/1898): 7–217. Cleveland: Burrow Brothers, 1898a.

Lamana, Gonzalo. 2008. *Domination without Dominance: Inca-Spanish Encounters in Early Colonial Peru.* Durham NC: Duke University Press.

Lamberville, Jean de. 1682/1900. "Lettre à _____, Onnontagué, August 25, 1682." In *The Jesuit Relations and Allied Documents . . . 1610–1791*, edited by Reuben Gold Thwaites, vol. 62 (1681–83/1900): 54–107. Cleveland: Burrow Brothers, 1900.

Lastres, Juan B. 1947. "Dioses y templos Incaicos protectores de la salud." *Revista del Museo Nacional* 16:2–16.

Le Jeune, Paul. 1634/1897a. "Relation de ce qui s'est passé en La Novvelle France, en l'année 1634. [Chapters i–ix.] Maifon de N. Dame des Anges, en Nouuelle France, August 7, 1634." In *The Jesuit Relations and Allied Documents . . . 1610–1791*, edited by Reuben Gold Thwaites, vol. 6 (1633–34/1897): 91–318. Cleveland: Burrow Brothers, 1897.

———. 1634/1897b. "Relation de ce qui s'est passé en La Novvelle France, en l'année 1634 [Chapters x–xiii, completing the document]. Maifon de N. Dame des Anges, en Nouvelle France, August 7, 1634." In *The Jesuit Relations and Allied Documents . . . 1610–1791*, edited by Reuben Gold Thwaites, vol. 7 (1634–35/1897): 5–236. Cleveland: Burrow Brothers, 1897.

———. 1636/1897. "Relation de ce qui s'est passé en la Novvelle France, en l'année 1636. [Chapters iii–xi, completing Part I of the document.] Kebec, August 28, 1636." In *The Jesuit Relations and Allied Documents . . . 1610–1791*, edited by Reuben Gold Thwaites, vol. 10 (1636/1897): 5–304. Cleveland: Burrow Brothers, 1897.

———. 1637/1898. "Relation de ce qui s'est passé en la Novvelle France, en l'année 1637. [First installment, consisting of Chaps. i–ix of Part I.] Cap Rouge, August 31, 1637." In *The Jesuit Relations and Allied Documents . . . 1610–1791*, edited by Reuben Gold Thwaites, vol. 11 (1636–37/1898): 23–270. Cleveland: Burrow Brothers, 1898.

———. 1639/1898. "Relation de ce qvi s'est passé en la Novvelle France, en l'année 1639 [Chapters ii–xi, completing Part I of the document; and Chapters i, ii of Part II, being Lalemant's Huron report]; Sillery, September 4, 1639. Hierosme Lalemant; Ossossané, June 7, 1639." In *The Jesuit Relations and Allied Documents . . . 1610–1791*, edited by Reuben Gold Thwaites, vol. 16 (1639/1898): 7–254. Cleveland: Burrow Brothers, 1898.

———. 1640/1898. "Relation de ce qvi s'est passé en la Novvelle France, en l'année 1640. [Chaps. xi–xiii of Part I, and Chaps. i–viii of Part II.] Kébec, September 10, 1640. Des Hurons, May 27, 1640." In *The Jesuit Relations and Allied Documents . . . 1610–1791*, edited by Reuben Gold Thwaites, vol. 19 (1640/1898): 7–268. Cleveland: Burrow Brothers, 1898.

———. 1640–41/1898a. "Relation de ce qvi s'est passé en la Novvelle France, és annees 1640 et 1641. [Introduction, and Chaps. i–viii of Part I.] Kebec and Paris, undated." In *The Jesuit Relations and Allied Documents . . . 1610–1791*, edited by Reuben Gold Thwaites, vol. 20 (1640–41/1898): 107–300. Cleveland: Burrow Brothers, 1898.

———. 1640–41/1898b. "Relation de ce qvi s'est passé en la Novvelle France, és années 1640 et 1641. [Chaps. ix–xiii of Part I, and Part 2, concluding the document.] Kebec and Paris, undated, Jerome Lalemant; Ste. Marie aux Hurons, May 19, 1641." In *The Jesuit Relations and Allied Documents . . . 1610–1791*, edited by Reuben Gold Thwaites, vol. 21 (1641–42/1898): 19–267. Cleveland: Burrow Brothers, 1898.

———, ed. 1657/1899. "Relation de ce qvi s'est passé. . . . en la Novvelle France, és années mil six cens cinquante six & mil six cens cinquante sept. [Chaps. i–xvi—first installment of the document.] Au College de Clermont, December 1, 1657." In *The Jesuit Relations and Allied Documents . . . 1610–1791*, edited by Reuben Gold Thwaites, vol. 43 (1656–57/1899): 79–318. Cleveland: Burrow Brothers, 1899.

Le Mercier, François Joseph. 1637/1898. "Relation de ce qvi s'est passé en la Novvelle France, en l'année 1637. [First installment of Part II, the Huron Relation.] Ihonatiria, June 21, 1637." In *The Jesuit Relations and Allied Documents . . . 1610–1791*, edited by Reuben Gold Thwaites, vol. 13 (1637/1898): 5–268. Cleveland: Burrow Brothers, 1898.

———. 1652–53/1899. "Relation de ce qvi s'est passé en la . . . Novvelle France, depuis l'Eté de l'Année 1652. iufques à l'Eté de l'Année 1653. Quebec, October 29, 1653." In *The Jesuit Relations and Allied Documents . . . 1610–1791*, edited by Reuben Gold Thwaites, vol. 40 (1653/1899): 67–252. Cleveland: Burrow Brothers, 1899.

———. 1653–54/1899. "Relation de ce qvi s'est passé. . . . en la Novvelle France, es annees 1653. & 1654. François le Mercier, Quebec, September 21, 1654; Simon le Moine, July–September 1654." In *The Jesuit Relations and Allied Documents . . . 1610–1791*, edited by Reuben Gold Thwaites, vol. 41 (1654–56/1899): 25–203. Cleveland: Burrow Brothers, 1899.

———. 1664–65/1899. "Relation de ce qvi s'est passé en la Novvelle France, és années 1664 & 1665. [Chaps. i–v, first installment of the document.] Kebec, November 3, 1665." In *The Jesuit Relations and Allied Documents . . . 1610–1791*, edited by Reuben Gold Thwaites, vol. 49 (1663–65/1899): 183–268. Cleveland: Burrow Brothers, 1897.

———. 1668–69/1899. "Relation de ce qvi s'est passé en la Novvelle France, les années 1668. & 1669." [François le Mercie], n.p., n.d. In *The Jesuit Relations and Allied Documents . . . 1610–1791*, edited by Reuben Gold Thwaites, vol. 52 (1667–69/1899): 111–258. Cleveland: Burrow Brothers, 1899.

Le Petit [also Petet], Mathurin. 1730/1900. "Lettre au Père d'Avaugour, Procureur des Missions de l'Amerique Septentrionale, Nouvelle Orléans, July 12, 1730." In *The Jesuit Relations and Allied Documents . . . 1610–1791*, edited by Reuben Gold Thwaites, vol. 68 (1720–36/1900): 120–223. Cleveland: Burrow Brothers, 1900.

Le Roy, Claude Charles. 1753/1912. "History of the Savage Peoples who are Allies of New France." In *Upper Mississippi and Region of the Great Lakes*, translated and edited by Emma Helen Blair, vol. 2, 13–138. Cleveland: Arthur H. Clark.

Lescarbot, Marc. 1612/1896. "Relation Dernière de ce qui s'est Pass'e au Voyage du Sieur de Potrincourt; Paris, 1612." In *The Jesuit Relations and Allied Documents . . . 1610–1791*, edited by Reuben Gold Thwaites, vol. 2 (1612–14/1896): 119–92. Cleveland: Burrow Brothers, 1896.

Lévi-Strauss, Claude. 1966/1968. *The Savage Mind*. Chicago: University of Chicago Press.

Livingstone, David. 1874. *Livingstone in Central Africa*. 2 vols. London: John Murray.

Lizárraga Ibáñez, Manuel A. 2009. "Las élites andinas coloniales y la materialización de sus memorias particulares en los 'queros de la transición.'" *Boletín del Museo Chileno de Arte Precolombino* 14 (1): 37–53.

Lorandi, Ana María. 1995. "Señores del Imperio perdido, nobles y curacas en el Perú colonial." *Tawantinsuyu* 1:86–96.

Louis Armand de Lomd'arse, Baron de Lahontan. 1703/1790. *New Voyages to North America*. With introduction and glossary by Reuben Gold Thwaites. 2 vols. New York: Burt Franklin.

MacCormack, Sabine. 1991. *Religion in the Andes: Vision and Imagination in Early Colonial Peru*. Princeton NJ: Princeton University Press.

———. 1998. "The Incas and Rome." *Garcilaso Inca de la Vega: An American Humanist*, 8–31. Notre Dame IN: University of Notre Dame Press.

———. 1999. "Ritual, conflicto y comunidad en el Perú colonial temprano." In *Reproducción y transformación de las sociedades andinas, siglos 16–20*, compiled by Segundo Moreno Yañez and Frank Salomon, vol. 1, 47–67. Quito, Ecuador: Ediciones Abya-Yala.

———. 2001. "Cuzco, Another Rome?" In *Empires: Perspectives from Archaeology and History*, edited by Susan E. Alcock, Terence N. D'Altroy, Kathleen D. Morrison, and Carla M. Sinopoli, 419–35. Cambridge: Cambridge University Press.

———. 2003. "History, Language and Law in the Early Modern Spanish Empire: The Case of Peru." Paper presented at the Transatlantic Conference, City University of New York.

Macola, Giacomo. 2002. *The Kingdom of Kazembe: History and Politics in North-Eastern Zambia and Katanga to 1950.* Hamburg: Lit Verlag.

Mainga, Mutumba. 1966. "The Origins of the Lozi: Some Oral Traditions." In *The Zamesian Past: Studies in Central African History,* edited by Eric Stokes and Richard Brown, 238–47. Manchester: University of Manchester Press.

Mann, Charles C. 2005. "Unraveling Khipu's Secrets." *Science* 309 (5737): 1008–9.

Markham, Clements R. 1873/2016. *Narratives of the Rites and Laws of the Yncas.* London: Routledge.

Maršálek, Jan. 2011. "Innovations and Temporality: Reflections on Lévi-Strauss' 'Cold Societies' and Our 'Warming Science.'" In *Social and Cultural Dimensions of Innovation in Knowledge Societies,* edited by Jiří Loudin and Josef Hochgerne, 139–49. Prague: Filosofia.

Martínez Cereceda, José Luis. 1988. "Kurakas, rituales e insignias: Una proposición." *Histórica* 12 (1): 61–74.

———. 1995. *Autoridades en los Andes: Los atributos del señor.* Lima: Pontificia Universidad Católica del Perú.

———. 2009. "Registros Andinos al margen de la escritura: El arte rupestre colonial." *Boletín del Museo chileno de arte precolombino* 14 (1): 9–35.

Marston, Major Morrell. 1820/1912. "Letter of Major Marston to Reverend Doctor Morse." In *Indian Tribes of the Upper Mississippi Valley,* translated and edited by Emma Helen Blair, vol. 2, 139–82. Cleveland: Arthur H. Clark.

Mauss, Marcel. 1925/1967. *The Gift: Forms and Functions of Exchange in Archaic Societies.* New York: W. W. Norton.

Maxwell, Allen R. 2009. "Kadayan Personal Names and Naming." In *Naming Systems: 1980 Proceedings of the American Ethnological Society,* edited by Elisabeth Tooker, 25–39. Washington DC: American Ethnological Society.

Maxwell, Kevin B. 1983. *Bemba Myth and Ritual: The Impact of Literacy on an Oral Culture.* American University Studies. New York: P. Lang.

Maybury-Lewis, David. 2009. "Name, Person, and Ideology in Central Brazil." In *Naming Systems: 1980 Proceedings of the American Ethnological Society,* edited by Elisabeth Tooker, 1–10. Washington DC: American Ethnological Society.

Medinaceli, Ximena. 1995. "Nombres disidentes: mugeres aymaras en Sacaca, siglo XVII." *Estudios bolivianos* 1:321–42.

———. 2003a. "Identidad y localidad en los nombres personales indigenas: Sakaka en el siglo XVII." In *Los Andes: Cincuenta años después (1953–2003), Homenaje a John Murra,* edited by Ana María Lorandi, C. Salazar-Soler, and Nathan Wachtel, 207–28. Lima: Pontificia Universidad Católica del Perú.

———. 2003b. *¿Nombres o apellidos? El sistema nominativo aymara Sacaca, siglo XVII.* La Paz, Bolivia: Instituto Frances de Estudios Andinos. Medinaceli,

Ximena, and Silvia Arze. 1996. "Los mallkus de Charkas: Redes de poder en el norte de Potosí, siglos XVI y XVII." *Estudios Bolivianos* 2:283–319.

Megged, Amos. 2005. "Power and Memory: Indigenous Narratives of Past and Present in the Valley of Matalcingo, Mexico (1530–90)." In *Los buenos, los malos y los feos: Poder y resistencia en América Latina*, edited by Nikolaus Böttcher, Isabel Galaor, and Bernd Hausberger, 177–98. Frankfurt: Vervuert.

Mena, Cristóbal de. 1531–33/1938. "La conquista del Perú." *Los cronistas de la conquista*. Biblioteca de cultura peruana, Primera Serie, no. 2. Paris: Desclée, 307–28.

———. 1531–33/1967. "La conquista de la Nueva Castilla." In *Las relaciones primitivas de la conquista del Peru*, edited by Raul Porras Barrenechea, 79–101. Lima: Instituto Raul Porras Barrenechea. Meneses, Teodoro L. 1964. *Nueva Traducción de preces o himnos Quechuas del cronista Cristóbal de Molina, el Cusqueño*. Lima: Universidad Nacional Mayor de San Marcos.

Michelson, Gunther. 1991. "Iroquoian Terms for Wampum." *International Journal of American Linguistics* 57 (1): 108–16.

Miller, Joseph C. 1972. "The Imbangala and the Chronology of Early African History." *Journal of African History* 13 (4): 549–74.

———. 1976. *Kings and Kinsmen: Early Mbundu States in Angola*. Oxford: Clarendon.

———. 1979. "Kings, Lists, and History in Kasanje." *History in Africa* 6:51–96.

———, ed. 1980. *The African Past Speaks: Essays on Oral Tradition and History*. Folkestone, UK: W. Dawson.

Miller, Nathan. 1927. "Some Aspects of the Name in Culture-History." *American Journal of Sociology* 32 (4): 585–600.

Millet, Pierre. 1691/1900. "Lettre a Quelques Missionnaires du Canada, Onneitft, July 6, 1691." In *The Jesuit Relations and Allied Documents . . . 1610–1791*, edited by Reuben Gold Thwaites, vol. 64 (1689–95/1900): 66–107. Cleveland: Burrow Brothers, 1900.

Mitchell, J. Clyde. 1956. *The Yao Village*. Manchester: Manchester University Press for the Rhodes-Livingstone Institute.

Mitchell, Stephen. 2003. "Reconstructing Old Norse Oral Tradition." *Oral Tradition* 18 (2): 203–6.

Molina, Cristóbal de. 1570–84/1873. "An Account of the Fables and Rites of the Incas." In *Narratives of the Rites and Laws of the Yncas*, edited and translated by Clements R. Markham. New York: Burt Franklin.

Molina, el Chileno, Cristóbal. 1552/1943. "Relacion de muchas cosas acaecidas en el Perú . . . aquí trataré, mas se podrá decir 'Destrucción del Perú' que conquista ni población." *Las crónicas de los Molinas*. Los pequeños grandes libros de historia americana, Serie 1, Tomo 4. Lima: Editorial de Domingo Miranda.

Molina, el Cuzqueño, Cristóbal de. 1575/1916. *Relacion de las fabulas y ritos de los Incas.* In *Coleccion de libros y documentos referentes a la historia del Peru,* edited by Horacio H. Urteaga, vol. 1, 3–106. Lima: Imprenta y Librería Sanmartí y Ca.

Monteiro, Major José Maria Corrêa, and Captain Antonio Candido Pedroso Gamitto. 1831–32/1873. "Resume of the Journey of MM Monteiro and Gamitto." In *The Lands of Cazembe,* edited by R. F. Burton and translated by C. T. Beke, 245–57. London: John Murray.

Montesinos, Fernando de. 1644/1930. "Memorias antiguas historiales y politicas del Peru." In *Coleccion de libros y documentos referentes a la historia del Peru,* edited by Horacio H. Urteaga, Second Series, vol. 6. Lima: Libreria e Imprenta Gil, S.A.

Moore, Patrick. 2007. "Negotiated Identities: The Evolution of Dene Tha and Kaska Personal Naming Systems." *Anthropological Linguistics* 49 (3–4): 283–307.

Morgan, Lewis H. 1851. *League of the Ho-de-no-sau-nee or Iroquois.* Rochester NY: Sage and Brother.

———. 1851/1962. *The League of the Iroquois.* New York: Corinth Books.

———. 1851/1901. *The League of the Ho-de'-no-sau-nee or Iroquois.* 2 vols. New York: Dodd, Mead.

———. 1871. "Systems of Consanguinity and Affinity of the Human Family." *Smithsonian Contributions to Knowledge,* no. 17.

Moseley, Michael E. 1990. "Structure and History in the Dynastic Lore of Chimor." In *The Northern Dynasties: Kingship and Statecraft in Chimor,* edited by Michael E. Moseley and Alana Cordy-Collins, 1–41. Washington DC: Dumbarton Oaks Research Library and Collection.

———. n.d. "Structure and History in the Dynastic Lore of Chimor." Unpublished paper, copy in author's possession.

Moscovich, Viviana Ruth. 2011. "El khipu entre 1532–1650: De registro a historia." *Anuario de Estudios Bolivianos, Archivísticos y Bibliográficos* 17:443–61.

Motzafi-Haller, Pnina. 1994. "Historical Narratives as Political Discourses of Identity." *Journal of Southern African Studies* 20 (3): 417–31.

Moya, Ruth. 1986. "Los tejidos del norte andino: Símbolos y funciones." *Cultura: Revista del Banco Central del Ecuador* 8:545–63.

Mróz, Marcin. 1988. "Para cronología dinástica de los Incas según Guaman Poma de Ayala." In *Memorias del 45th International Congress of Americanists, Bogotá, Colombia, 1985,* compiled by Elizabeth Reichel, 65–78. Bogotá: Ediciones Uniandes.

Muller, Kathryn V. 2007. "The Two 'Mystery' Belts of Grand River." *American Indian Quarterly* 31 (1): 129–64.

Muñoz Arbeláez, Santiago. 2015. *Costumbres en disputa: Los muiscas y el Imperio español en Ubaque, siglo XVI.* Bogotá: Universidad de los Andes.

Murra, John V. 1968. "An Aymara Kingdom in 1567." *Ethnohistory* 15 (2): 115–51.

Murúa, Fray Martín de. 1613/1986. *Historia General del Perú.* Edited by Manuel Ballesteros. Madrid: Historia 16.

Mushikiwabo, Louise, and Jack Kramer. 2006. *Rwanda Means the Universe: A Native's Memoir of Blood and Bloodlines.* New York: St. Martin's.

Netherly, Patricia J. 1990. "Out of Many, One: The Organization of Rule in the North Coast Polities." In *The Northern Dynasties: Kingship and Statecraft in Chimor,* edited by M. E. Moseley and Alana Cordy-Collins, 461–87. Washington DC: Dumbarton Oaks Research Library and Collection.

Niles, Susan. 1999. *The Shape of Inca History: Narrative and Architecture in an Andean Empire.* Iowa City: University of Iowa Press.

Noble, William C. 1985. "Tsouharissen's Chiefdom: An Early Historic Seventeenth Century Neutral Iroquoian Ranked Society." *Canadian Journal of Archaeology* 9 (2): 131–46.

Ogburn, Dennis E. 2012. "Reconceiving the Chronology of Inca Imperial Expansion." *Radiocarbon* 54 (2): 219–37.

Ondegardo, Polo de. 1559/1916. "Los errores y svpersticiones de los indios, sacadas del tratado y aueriguación que hizo el Licenciado Polo." In *Colección de libros y documentos referentes a la historia del Perú,* edited by Horacio H. Urteaga, First Series, vol. 3, 3–43. Lima: Imprenta y Librería Sanmartí y Ca.

———. 1571/1917. "Del linage de los Ingas y como conquistaron." In *Colección de libros y documentos referentes a la historia del Perú,* edited by Horacio H. Urteaga, First Series, vol. 4, 45–94. Lima: Imprenta y Librería Sanmartí y Ca.

O'Phelan Godoy, Scarlet. 1993. "Tiempo inmemorial, Tiempo colonial: Un estudio de casos." *Procesos: Revista Ecuatoriana de Historia* 4:3–20.

Pachacuti Yamqui Salcamayhua, Juan de. 1613/1879. "Relación de antigüedades deste Reyno del Pirú." In *Tres relaciones de antigüedades peruanas,* 231–328. Madrid: Ministerio de Formento.

Pärsinnen, Martti. 1992. *Tawantinsuyu: The Inca State and Its Political Organization.* Helsinki: Societas Historica Finlandiae.

Patrón, Pablo. 1906. "La veracidad de Montesinos." *Revista Histórica* 1 (3): 289–303.

Pawlik, J. 1951. "Toponomástica: El problema del estudio de los topónimos." *Boletín de la Sociedad Geográfica* 68:51–57.

Pease, Franklin. 1969. "El mito de Manco Capac y la confereracion." *Boletín de arqueología del Instituto Riva Agüero* 2:82–90.

———. 1991. *Los ultimos Incas del Cuzco.* Madrid: Alianza Editoriales.

————. 1996. "Porque los Andinos son acusados de litigiosos?" In *Derechos culturales*, 27–37. Lima: Pontificia Universidad Católica del Perú.

Pearse, Adrian J., and Paul Heggarty. 2011. "Mining the Data on the Huancayo-Huancavelica Quechua Frontier." In *History and Language in the Andes*, edited by Paul Heggarty and Adrian L. Pearse, 112. New York: Palgrave Macmillan.

Peel, J. D. Y. 1984. "Making History: The Past in the Ijesho Present." *Man*, New Series, 19:111–32.

Perissat, Karine. 2000. "Los Incas representados (Lima: Siglo 18): Supervivencia o renacimiento?" *Revista de Indias* 60 (220): 623–49.

Perrot, Nicolas. 1700–1720/1911–12. "Memoir on the Manners, Customs, and Religion of the Savages of North America." In *Indian Tribes of the Upper Mississippi Valley*, translated and edited by Emma Helen Blair, vol. 1, 25–274. Cleveland: Arthur H. Clark.

Pinillos Rodríguez, Alberto. 1977. *Huacas de Trujillo: Derrotero Para una visita turística*. Trujillo: Ediciones Oro Chimu.

Pinto, Commander and Fr. Francisco João. 1798–99/1873. "Diary of the Expedition sent by Her Most Faithful Majesty to Explore the African Interior . . . by the Chaplain and Commander Fr. Francisco João Pinto in Continuation of the Diary of Dr. Francisco Jose de Lacerda e Almeida. . . ." In *The Lands of Cazembe*, edited by R. F. Burton, 107–64. London: John Murray.

Pizarro, Hernando. 1533/1964. "Carta a los oidores de la Audiencia de Santo Domingo." In *Tres Testigos de la Conquista del Perú*, edited by Conde de Canilleros, 14–30. Madrid: Editorial Espasa-Calpe, S.A.

Pizarro, Pedro. 1572/1978. "Relación del descubrimiento y conquista de los reinos del Perú. . . ." In *Colección de documentos inéditos para la historia de España*, edited by Martín Fernández de Navarrete, vol. 5, 201–388. Madrid: Imprenta de la Viuda de Calero.

Polia Meconi, Mario. 1996. "Siete cartas inéditas del Archivo Romano de la Compañía de Jesús (1611–1615)." *Antropológica* 15:209–59.

————. 1999. *La cosmovisión religiosa Andina*. Lima: Pontifica Universidad Católica del Perú.

Pomedli, Michael M. 1995. "Eighteenth-Century Treaties: Amended Iroquois Condolence Rituals." *American Indian Quarterly* 19 (3): 319–39.

Powers, Karen V. 1991. "Resilient Lords and Indian Vagabonds: Wealth, Migration, and the Reproductive Transformation of Quito's Chiefdoms, 1500–1700." *Ethnohistory* 38 (3): 225–49.

————. 1998. "A Battle of Wills: Inventing Chiefly Legitimacy in the Colonial Andes." In *Dead Giveaways: Indigenous Testaments of Colonial Mesoamerica and the Andes*, edited by Susan Kellogg and Matthew Restall, 183–214. Salt Lake City: University of Utah Press.

Prince, J. Dyneley. 1897. "The Passamaquoddy Wampum Records." *Proceedings of the American Philosophical Society* 36 (156): 479–95.

Quens, Jean de. 1655–56/1899. "Relation de ce qvi s'est passé en la Mission des Peres de la Compagnie de Iesvs, av pays de la Novvelle France, és Années 1655 & 1656. Kebec, September 7, 1656." *The Jesuit Relations and Allied Documents . . . 1610–1791*, edited by Reuben Gold Thwaites, vol. 42 (1632–1657/1899): 17–247. Cleveland: Burrow Brothers, 1899.

———. 1656/1899. "Journal des PP. Jésuites." In *The Jesuit Relations and Allied Documents . . . 1610–1791*, edited by Reuben Gold Thwaites, vol. 42 (1656/1899): 248–61. Cleveland: Burrow Brothers, 1899.

Quipucamayocs. 1542–44/1920. "Declaración de los quipocamayos a Vaca de Castro." In *Informaciones sobre el antiguo Peru (1535–75)*, edited by Horacio H. Urteaga, Second Series, vol. 3: 3–57. In *Informaciones sobre el antiguo Perú, Colección de libros y documentos referentes a la historia del Perú*. Lima: Imprenta y Librería Sanmartí y Ca.

Quiroga, Pedro de. 1560s/2009. "Coloquios de la verdad." In *El indio dividido: Fracturas de conciencia en el Perú colonial*, edited by Ana Vian Herrero. Madrid: Iberoamericana Vervuert.

Quiroga Zuluaga, Marcela. 2015. "Las políticas coloniales y la acción indígena: La configuración de los pueblos de indios de la provincia de Páez, siglos XVII y XVIII." *Anuario Colombiano de Historia Social y de Cultura* 42 (1): 23–50.

Rabasa, José. 2005. "On the History of the History of Peoples without History." *Humboldt Journal of Social Relations* 29 (1): 204–12.

Ragueneau, Paul. 1645–46/1898. "Relation de ce qvi s'est passé . . . en la Novvelle France, és années 1645 & 1646. [Chapters iv–viii, Part II, completing the document.] Des Hurons, May 1, 1646." *The Jesuit Relations and Allied Documents . . . 1610–1791*, edited by Reuben Gold Thwaites, vol. 30 (1646–47/1898): 17–145. Cleveland: Burrow Brothers, l'Ete de l'année1898.

———. 1648–49/1898. "Relation de ce qvi s'est passé en. . . . la Nouuelle France, és années 1648 & 1649; Saincte Marie aux Hurons, May 1, 1649." In *The Jesuit Relations and Allied Documents . . . 1610–1791*, edited by Reuben Gold Thwaites, vol. 34 (1649/1898): 67–236. Cleveland: Burrow Brothers, 1898.

———. 1651-52/1899. "Relation de ce qvi s'est passé av prays de la Novvelle France, depuis l'Eté de l'annee 1651 jufques à. L'Eté de l'année 1652. [Chapters viii–x, concluding the document.] Kebec, October 4, 1652; Marie de l'Incarnation, Kebec, 1652." In *The Jesuit Relations and Allied Documents . . . 1610–1791*, edited by Reuben Gold Thwaites, vol. 38 (1652–53/1899): 15–166. Cleveland: Burrow Brothers, 1899.

Rama, Angel. 1996. *The Lettered City*. Translated by J. C. Chasteen. Durham NC: Duke University Press.

Ramírez, Susan Elizabeth. 1996. *The World Upside Down: Cross-Cultural Contact and Conflict in Sixteenth-Century Peru*. Stanford CA: Stanford University Press.

———. 2005. *To Feed and Be Fed: The Cosmological Bases of Authority and Identity in the Andes*. Stanford CA: Stanford University Press.

———. 2006a. "From Person to Place and Back Again: 'Back Translation' as Decentering, an Andean Case Study." *Ethnohistory* 53 (2): 355–82.

———. 2006b. "Historia y memoria: La construccion de las tradiciones dinasticas andinas." *Revista de Indias* 236:13–56.

———. 2008. "Negociando el imperio: El estado Inca como culto." *Boletín del Instituto Francés de Estudios Andinos*, guest edited by Susan E. Ramírez and Chantal Cavaillet, 37 (1): 5–18.

———. 2014a. *Al servicio de Dios y Su Magestad: Los orígenes de las escuelas públicas para niños indígenas en el norte del Perú en el siglo XVIII*. Lima: Asamblea Nacional de Rectores.

———. 2014b. "Alternative Ways of Knowing: Place Names and Personal Titiles, an Andean Optic." *Revista Perspectivas Latinoamericanas*, Centro de Estudios Latinoamericanos, Universidad Nanzan (Japan), 10: 1–24.

———. 2016. "Land and Tenure in Early Colonial Peru: Individualizing the Sapçi: That Which Is Common to All." *The Medieval Globe* (Carol Symes, executive editor; Elizabeth Lambourn, guest editor) 2 (2): 33–71.

———. 2018. "Despedazando lo común: De testimonios orales a títulos escritos." In *Interpretando huellas: Arqueología, etnohistoria y etnografía de los Andes y sus tierras bajas*, 287–304. Cochabamba, Bolivia: Grupo Editorial Kipus.

Ramón Valarezo F., Galo. 1987. *Resistencia Andina: Cayambe 1500–1800*. Quito, Ecuador: Centro Andino de Accion Popular.

Ramos, Alcida R. 1974. "How the Sunumá Acquire Their Names." *Ethnology* 13 (2): 171–85.

Ramos, Gabriela. 2011. "Language and Society in Early Colonial Peru." In *History and Language in the Andes*, edited by Paul Heggarty and Adrian L. Pearse, 19–38. New York: Palgrave Macmillan.

Rappaport, Joanne. 1990. *The Politics of Memory: Native Historical Interpretation in the Colombian Andes*. Cambridge: Cambridge University Press.

Rappaport, Joanne, and Thomas Cummins. 2012. *Beyond the Lettered City: Indigenous Literacies in the Andes*. Durham NC: Duke University Press.

Read, Kay Almere, and Jason J. González. 2000. *Mesoamerican Mythology: A Guide to the Gods, Heroes, Rituals, and Beliefs of Mexico and Central America*. New York: Oxford University Press.

Reefe, Thomas Q. 1977. "Lukasa: A Luba Memory Device." *African Arts* 10 (4): 48–50, 88.

Richards, A. I. 1950. "Some Types of Family Structure amongst the Central Bantu." In *African Systems of Kinship and Marriage*, edited by A. R. Radcliffe-Brown and D. Forde, 207–51. London: Oxford University Press for the International African Institute.

Richter, Daniel K. 1983. "War and Culture: The Iroquois Experience." *William and Mary Quarterly* 40 (4): 528–59.

Rivière, Gilles. 1995a. "Caminos de los muertos, caminos de los vivos: Las figuras del chamanismo en las comunidades aymaras del altiplano boliviano." *Antropología, revista de pensamiento antropológicos y estudios etnográficos* 10:109–32.

———. 1995b. "Autoridades tradicionales y chamanismo en las comunidades aymaras (Bolivia)." Typescript, copy in author's possession.

———. 1997. "Tiempo, poder y sociedad en las comunidades aymaras del Altiplano (Bolivia)." In *Antropología del clima en el mundo hispanoamericano*, edited by M. Goloubinoff, E. Katz, and A. Lammel, vol. 2, 31–54. Quito, Ecuador: Ediciones Abya-Yala.

Roberts, Andrew. 1967. "Tippu Tip, Livingstone, and the Chronology of Kazembe." *Azania* 2:115–31.

Rojas y Silva, David de. 1981. "Los tocapus: Un problema de Interpretación." *Revista Arte y Arqueología* 7:119–32.

Romero Meza, Eddy. 2014. "Las sucesiones en el imperio de los incas." Accessed November 6, 2019. hahr-online.com/las-sucesiones-en-el-imperio-de-los-incas.

Rosaldo, Renato. 1984. "Ilongot Naming: The Play of Associations." In *Naming Systems: 1980 Proceedings of the American Ethnological Society*, edited by Elisabeth Tooker, 11–24. Washington DC: American Ethnological Society.

Rostworowski, María. 1961. *Curacas y sucesiones: Costa Norte*. Lima: Minerva.

———. 1970. "El repartimiento de Doña Beatriz Coya, en el Valle de Yucay." *Historia y cultura* 4:153–267.

———. 1984. "El baile en los ritos agrarios Andinos . . . siglo XVII." *Historia y cultura* 17:51–60.

———. 1997. "An Analysis of Historical Information in the *Royal Commentaries*." *Journal of the Steward Anthropological Society* 25 (1–2): 299–311.

———. 2003. "Peregrinaciones y procesiones rituales en los Andes." *Journal de la société des américaniste* 89 (2): 97–123. Roth, Christopher F. 2002. "Goods,

Names, and Silver: Rethinking the Tsimshian Potlash." *American Ethnologist* 29 (1): 123–50.

Rowe, John H. 1945. "Absolute Chronology in the Andean Area." *American Antiquity* 10 (3): 265–84.

———. 1946. "Inca Culture at the Time of the Spanish Conquest." *Handbook of South American Indians*, edited by Julian H. Steward, vol. 2, 182–330. Washington DC: Government Printing Office.

———. 1985. "Probanza de los Incas nietos de conquistadores." *Histórica* 9 (2): 193–245.

Sagard Théodat, Fr. Gabriel. 1632/1865. *Le grand voyage du pays des Hurons, situé en l'Amerique vers la mer douce, és derniers confines de la Nouvelle France, dite Canada*. Paris: Chez D. Moreav.

Sahlins, Marshall. 1981. *Historical Metaphors and Mythical Realities*. Ann Arbor: University of Michigan Press.

———. 1983. "Other Times, Other Cultures: The Anthropology of History." *American Anthropologist* 85:517–43.

———. 1985. *Islands of History*. Chicago: University of Chicago Press.

Sahlins, Peter. 1989. *Boundaries: The Making of France and Spain in the Pyrenees*. Berkeley: University of California Press.

Saignes, Thierry. 1987. "De la borrachera al retrato: Los caciques andinos entre dos legitimidades (Charcas)." *Revista Andina* 5 (1): 139–70.

Sala Vila, Nuria. 1989. "El cacicazgo de Lambayeque y Ferreñafe a fines de la colonia." *Boletín del Instituto Riva-Agüero* 16:123–33.

Salomon, Frank. 1986. *Native Lords of Quito in the Age of the Incas*. Cambridge: Cambridge University Press.

———. 1999. "Testimonies: The Making and Reading of Native South American Historical Sources." In *Cambridge History of the Native Peoples of the Americas*. Vol. 3. *South America*, edited by Stuart Schwartz and Frank Salomon, 19–95. New York: Cambridge University Press.

———. 2004. *The Cord Keepers: Khipus and Cultural Life in a Peruvian Village*. Durham NC: Duke University Press.

Salomon, Frank, Carrie J. Brezine, Reymundo Chapa, and Victor Falcón Huayta. 2011. "Khipu from Colony to Republic: The Rapaz Patrimony." In *Their Way of Writing: Scripts, Signs, and Pictographies in Pre-Columbian America*, edited by Elizabeth Hill Boone and Gary Urton, 353–78. Washington DC: Dumbarton Oaks Research Library and Collection.

Salomon, Frank, and George L. Urioste. 1991. *The Huarochiri Manuscript*. Austin: University of Texas Press.

Sancho de la Hoz, Pedro. 1534/1938. "Relación para S.M. de lo sucedido en la conquista y pacificación de estas provincias de la Nueva Castilla." In *Los cronistas de la conquista*. Biblioteca de cultura peruana, Primera serie, no. 2, 117–93. Paris: Descelée de Brauwer.

———. 1534/1917. "Relación de lo sucedido en la conquista del Perú." In *Las relaciones de la conquista del Perú*, edited by Horacio H. Urteaga. In *Colección de libros y documentos referentes a la historia del Perú*, vol. 5, 124–202. Lima: Imprenta y Librería Sanmartí y Ca.

Santo Tomás, Fray Domingo de. 1560/1951. *Lexicon: Vocabulario de la lengua general del Perv*. Lima: Universidad Nacional Mayor de San Marcos, Instituto de Historia.

Sarmiento de Gamboa, Pedro de. 1572/1942. *Historia de los Incas*. Buenos Aires: Emecé Editores.

———. 1572/1965. *Historia indica*. In Biblioteca de autores Españoles, vol. 135, 195–279. Madrid: Ediciones Atlas.

———. 1572/1988. *Historia de los Incas*. Madrid: Miraguano Ediciones.

———. 1572/1999. *History of the Incas*. Mineola NY: Dover.

Schottman, Wendy. 2000. "Baatɔnu Personal Names from Birth to Death." *Africa* 70 (1): 79–106.

Scott, Duncan C., and the Committee of Chiefs. 1911. "Traditional History of the Confederacy of the Six Nations." *Proceedings and Transactions of the Royal Society of Canada*, Third Series, 5:195–246.

Scott, James C., John Tehranian, and Jeremy Mathias. 2002. "The Production of Legal Identities Proper to States: The Case of the Permanent Family Surname." *Comparative Study of Society and History* 44 (1): 4–44.

Sheridan, Thomas. 1988. "How to Tell the Story of a 'People without History': Narrative versus Ethnohistorical Approaches to the Study of the Yaqui Indians through Time." *Journal of the Southwest* 30 (2): 168–89.

Shimony, Annemarie A. 1994. *Conservatism among the Iroquois at the Six Nations Reserve*. Syracuse NY: Syracuse University Press.

Sica, Gabriela. 2008. "El papel y la memoria: Medios de construcción de los procesos de identificación local en los puelbos de indios de Jujuy, siglo XVII." *Andes: Antropologia e Historia*, 19:327–44.

Sica, Gabriela, and Sandra Sánchez. 1994. "Entre águilas y halcones." *Estudios atacameños* 11:65–77.

Silva, María Isabel. 1984. "Agricultural and Fishing Communities of Coastal Ecuador." Unpublished paper, copy in author's possession.

Silverman, Gail P. 1994. "Iconografía textil Q'ero vista como texto: Leyendo el rombo dualista 'Hatun Inti.'" *Boletín del Instituto Francés de Estudios Andinos* 23 (1): 171–90.

Smith, Daniel Scott. 1985. "Child-Naming Practices, Kinship Ties, and Change in Family Attitudes in Hingham, Massachusetts, 1641–1880." *Journal of Social History* 18 (4): 541–66.

Snow, Dean R. 2007. "Searching for Hendrick: Correction of a Historic Conflation." *New York History* 88 (3): 229–53.

Snyderman, George S. 1954. "The Functions of Wampum." *Proceedings of the American Philosophical Society* 98 (6): 469–94.

———. 1961. "The Function of Wampum in Iroquois Religion." *Proceedings of the American Philosophical Society* 105 (6): 571–608.

Solano, Francisco de. 1991. "Los nombres del Inca Garcilaso: Definición y identidad." *Histórica* 15 (1): 93–120.

Spalding, Karen. 1984. *Huarochiri*. Stanford CA: Stanford University Press.

———. 2006. "Introduction." In *Royal Commentaries of the Incas and General History of Peru*, translated by Harold V. Livermore and edited by Karen Spalding. Indianapolis: Hackett.

Speck, Frank G. 1949. *Midwinter Rites of the Cayuga Longhouse*. Philadelphia: University of Pennsylvania Press.

Stefaniszyn, B. 1954. "African Reincarnation Re-examined." *Journal of African Studies* 13 (3–4): 131–46.

Stoller, Paul. 1994. "Embodying Colonial Memories." *American Anthropologist*, New Series, 96 (3): 634–48.

Strachey, William. 1612/1849. *The Historie of Travaile into Virginia Britannia*. London: Hakluyt Society.

Street, Brian V., ed. 1993. *Cross-Cultural Approaches to Literacy*. New York: Cambridge University Press.

Suzman, Susan M. 1994. "Names as Pointers: Zulu Personal Naming Practices." *Language in Society* 23 (2): 253–72.

Szeminski, Jan. 1997a. *De las vidas del Inka Manqu Qhapaq*. Trujillo, Cáceres, Spain: Ediciones de la Coria.

———. 1997b. *Wira Quchan y sus obras: Teología andina y lenguaje, 1550–1662*. Lima: Instituto de Estudios Peruanos.

———. 2001. "Como el pensamiento de los investigadores modernos les impide entender las imagenes del pasado [Caso del Imperio Inca, siglos II–XVIII]." Conferencia magistrales plenarias: Plenary Lectures, in *Actas del 50 Congreso*

International de Americanistas, edited by Andrzej Dembicz and Dorota Olen-
jniczak, 163–77. Warsaw: Center for Latin American Studies.

———. 2013. "Tradición oral, Montesinos y los reyes de Tiwanaku." *Aportes multi-
disciplinarios al estudio de los colectivos étnicos Surandinos*, edited by Ana María
Presta, 397–418. Lima: Instituto Frances de Estudios Andinos.

Tanodi de Chiapero, Branka María. 1994. "Escrituras americanas precolombi-
nas de los Andes centrales." *Historia. Instituciones. Documentos* 21:453–71.

Taylor, G. 1987/1999. *Ritos y tradiciones de Huarochirí del siglo XVII*. Lima: Instituto de Estudios Peruanos.

———. 2000. *Camac, camay y camasca . . . y otros ensayos sobre Huarochirí y Yauy-
os*. Cusco, Peru: IFEA.

Tebbenhoff, Edward H. 1985. "Tacit Rules and Hidden Family Structures: Naming Practices and Godparentage in Schenectady, New York, 1680–1800." *Journal of Social History* 18 (4): 567–85.

Thompson, Paul. 1978. *The Voice of the Past*. Oxford: Oxford University Press.

Thornton, John. 1993. "Central African Names and African-American Naming
Patterns." *William and Mary Quarterly*, Third Series, 50 (4): 727–42.

Thurman, Melburn D. 1984. "'Covering the Dead' and Arikara Mortuary Practices." *Plains Anthropologist* 29 (103): 61–63.

Thwaites, Reuben Gold. 1639–40/1898. "Notes." In *The Jesuit Relations and Allied
Documents . . . 1610–1791*, edited by Reuben Gold Thwaites, vol. 17 (1639–
40/1898): 239–42. Cleveland: Burrow Brothers, 1898.

———. 1649/1898. "Notes." In *The Jesuit Relations and Allied Documents . . . 1610–
1791*, edited by Reuben Gold Thwaites, vol. 34 (1649/1898): 245–57. Cleveland:
Burrow Brothers, 1898.

———. 1681–83/1900. "Notes." In *The Jesuit Relations and Allied Documents . . .
1610–1791*, edited by Reuben Gold Thwaites, vol. 62 (1681–83/1900): 271–76.
Cleveland: Burrow Brothers, 1900.

———, ed. 1896–1900. *The Jesuit Relations and Allied Documents . . . 1610–1791*. 72
vols. Cleveland: Burrow Brothers.

Tilsley, George Edwin. 1929. *Dan Crawford, Missionary and Pioneer in Central Africa*. London: Oliphants.

Titu Cusi Yupangui, Diego de Castro. 1570/1916. *Relación de la conquista del Perú
y hechos del Inca Manco II*, edited by Horacio H. Urteaga, vol. 2. In *Colección
de libros y documentos referentes a la historia del Perú*. Lima: Imprenta y Librería Sanmartí y Ca.

Tooker, Elizabeth. 1970. "Northern Iroquoian Sociopolitical Organization." *American Anthropologist*, New Series, 72 (1): 90–97.

Torero, Alfredo. 1993. "Fronteras lingüísticas y difusión de culto: El caso de Huari y de Contiti Viracocha." In *Religions des Andes et Langues indigènes*, compiled by Pierre Duviols, 219–33. Provence: Université de Provence.

Townsend, Camilla. 2014. "The Concept of the Nahua Historian: Don Juan Zapata's Scholarly Tradition." In *Indigenous Intellectuals: Knowledge, Power, and Colonial Culture in Mexico and the Andes*, edited by Gabriela Ramos and Yanna Yannakakis, 132–50. Durham NC: Duke University Press.

Travassos Valdez, Francisco. 1861. *Six Years of a Traveller's Life in Western Africa*. 2 vols. London: Hurst & Blakett.

Turner, Victor. 1975. *Dramas, Fields, and Metaphors: Symbolic Action in Human Society*. Ithaca NY: Cornell University Press.

Tweedie, Ann. 1966. "Towards a History of the Bemba from Oral Tradition." In *The Zambesian Past: Studies in Central African History*, edited by Eric Stokes, 197–225. Manchester: Manchester University Press.

Tylor, E. B. 1987. "The Hale Series of Huron Wampum Belts." *Journal of the Royal Anthropological Institute of Great Britain and Ireland* 26:248–54.

Urban, Matthias. 2015. "The Massa Connection: An Onomastic Link between the Peruvian North and the Far North in a Multidisciplinary Perspective." *Indiana* 32:179–203.

Urteaga, Horacio H. 1621/1920. "Notes." In Pablo José Arriaga, S.J., *La extirpación de la idolatría en el Perú*. In *Colección de libros y documentos referentes a la historia del Perú*, edited by Horacio H. Urteaga, Second Series, vol. 1. Lima: Imprenta y Librería Sanmartí y Ca.

———. 1919. *El Perú: Bocetos históricos*, Second Series. Lima: Casa editorial E. Rosay.

Urton, Gary. 1998. "From Knots to Narratives: Reconstructing the Art of Historical Record Keeping in the Andes from Spanish Transcriptions of Inka Khipus." *Ethnohistory* 45 (3): 409–38.

———. 2002. *Toasts with the Inca: Andean Abstraction and Colonial Images on Quero Vessels*. Ann Arbor: University of Michigan Press.

———. 2003. *Signs of the Inka Khipu*. Austin: University of Texas Press.

———. 2006. "Padrones poblacionales pre-Hispánicos y coloniales tempranos en los khipu Inka." *Revista Andina* 42:153–96.

———. 2011. "Khipu Typologies." In *Their Way of Writing: Scripts, Signs, and Pictographies in Pre-Columbian America*, edited by Elizabeth Boone and Gary Urton, 319–52. Washington DC: Dumbarton Oaks Research Library and Collection.

Urton, Gary, and Carrie J. Brezine. 2005. "Khipu Accounting in Ancient Peru." *Science* 309:1065–67.

———. 2013. "Khipu Typologies." In *Their Way of Writing: Scripts, Signs, and Pictographies in Pre-Columbian America*, edited by Elizabeth Boone and Gary Urton, 319–52. Washington DC: Dumbarton Oaks Research Library and Collection.

Urton, Gary, and J. Quilter. 2002. *Narrative Threads*. Austin: University of Texas Press.

Valera, Blas. 1596/1879. "De las costumbres antiguas de los naturales del Pirú." In *Tres relaciones de antigüedades Peruanas*. Spain: Ministerio de Fomento.

———. 1596/1945. "Las costumbres antiguas del Perú y la historia de los Incas." In *Los pequeños grandes libros de historia Americana*, edited by Francisco de Loayza, First Series, vol. 8. Lima: n.p.

Valladares Huamanchumo, Percy. 2013. "El apellido quingnam en Huanchaco." *Perspectivas Latinoamericanas* 10:47–55.

Vansina, Jan. 1965. *Oral Tradition*. London: Routledge & Kegan Paul.

———. 1966. *Kingdoms of the Savanna*. Madison: University of Wisconsin Press.

———. 1985. *Oral Tradition as History*. Madison: University of Wisconsin Press.

Vargas Ugarte, Ruben. 1951–54. *Concilios Limenses (1551–1772)*. 3 vols. Lima: Talleres Gráficos de la Tipografía Peruana, S.A.

Varón Gabai, Rafael. 1997. *Francisco Pizarro and His Brothers: The Illusion of Power in Sixteenth-Century Peru*. Norman: University of Oklahoma Press.

Vecsey, Christopher. 1986. "The Story and Structure of the Iroquois Confederacy." *Journal of the American Academy of Religion* 54 (1): 79–106.

Velasco, Pedro Xavier. 1805/1873. "Letter of the Chief Sergeant Pedro Xavier Velasco to the Home Government, November 14, 1805." In *Lands of the Cazembe*, edited by R. F. Burton, 164. London: John Murray.

Vellejo, Santiago. 1957. "Nombres de lugares y cosas que sobreviven de la autoctonía en Trujillo y sus valles." *Perú indígena* 6:88–94.

Vickers, Ovid. 1983. "Mississippi Choctaw Names and Naming: A Diachronic View." *Names* 31 (2): 117–22.

Villagómez, Pedro de. 1649/1919. *Exortaciones e instruccion acerca de las idolatrias de los indios del arzobispado de Lima*. Lima: Sanmartí y Cia.

Villamarín, Juan A., and Judith E. Villamarín. 1975. "Kinship and Inheritance among the Sabana de Bogotá Chibcha at the Time of the Spanish Conquest." *Ethnology* 14:173–79.

Vimont, Barthelemy. 1642/1898. "Relation de ce qvi s'est passé en la Novvelle France en l'année 1642. [Part I and Chap. 1 of Part II.] Kebec, October 4, 1642. Hierosme Lalemant; Ste. Marie aux Hurons, June 10, 1642." In *The Jesuit Relations and Allied Documents . . . 1610–1791*, edited by Reuben Gold Thwaites, vol. 22 (1642/1898): 19–312. Cleveland: Burrow Brothers, 1898.

———. 1642–43/1898. "Relation de ce qvi s'est passé en la Novvelle France, en l'année 1642 & 1643. [Chaps. iv–xii, second installment of the document.] Undated." In *The Jesuit Relations and Allied Documents . . . 1610–1791*, edited by Reuben Gold Thwaites, vol. 24 (1642–43/1898): 19–308. Cleveland: Burrow Brothers, 1898.

———. 1643–44/1898. "Relation de ce qvi s'est passé en la Novvelle France en années 1643 & 1644. [Chaps. ix–xiv of Part I and Chaps. i–v of Part II, being the second installment of the document.] Kebec, September 5, 1644. Hierosme Lalemant; September 21, 1643, 17–314." In *The Jesuit Relations and Allied Documents . . . 1610–1791*, edited by Reuben Gold Thwaites, vol. 26 (1643–44/1898): 7–314. Cleveland: Burrow Brothers, 1899.

———. 1644–45/1898. "Relation de ce qvi s'est passé en la Novvelle France, és années 1644 & 1645. [Chaps i–xi]. Quebec, October 1, 1645." In *The Jesuit Relations and Allied Documents . . . 1610–1791*, edited by Reuben Gold Thwaites, vol. 27 (1642–45/1898): 123–306. Cleveland: Burrow Brothers, 1898. Weeks, David. 1947. "European Antecedents of Land Tenure and Agrarian Organization of Hispanic America." *Journal of Land and Public Utility Economics* 23 (1): 50–75.

Whiteley, Peter. 1992. "*Hopitutungwni*: 'Hopi Names' as Literature." In *On the Translation of Native American Literatures*, edited by Brian Swann, 208–27. Washington DC: Smithsonian Institution.

Whiteley, W. H. 1950. *Bemba and Related Peoples of Northern Rhodesia: Ethnographic Survey of Africa, East Central Africa*, part 2. London: International African Institute.

Wieschhoff, Heinz. 1937. "Names and Naming Customs among the Mashona in Southern Rhodesia." *American Anthropologist*, New Series, 39 (3): 497–503.

Williams, Robert A. Jr. 1994. "Linking Arms Together: Multicultural Constitutionalism in a North American Indigenous Vision of Law and Peace." *California Law Review* 82 (4): 981–1049.

Wilson, Richard. 1995. "Shifting Frontiers: Historical Transformations of Identities in Latin America." *Bulletin of Latin American Research* 14 (1): 1–7.

Wolf, Eric. 1982. *Europe and the Peoples without History*. Berkeley: University of California Press.

Worby, Eric. 1994. "Maps, Names, and Ethnic Games: The Epistemology and Iconography of Colonial Power in Northwestern Zimbabwe." *Journal of Southern Africa Studies* 20 (3): 371–92.

Worsley, Peter. 1984. Review of *Europe and the People without History*. *American Ethnologist* 11 (1): 170–75.

Wright, Pablo G. 1983–84. "Notas sobre gentilicios Toba." *Relaciones de la Socie-dad Argentina de Antropología*, New Series, 16: 225–34.

Wrong, George M., ed. 1939. *Father Gabriel Sagard: The Long Journey to the Coun-try of the Hurons.* Toronto: Chaplain Society.

Xerez, Francisco de. 1534/1917. "Verdadera relación de la conquista del Perú y provincia del Cuzco. . . ." In *Las relaciones de la conquista del Perú*, edited by Horacio H. Urteaga, vol. 5, 1–123. In *Colección de libros y documentos referente a la historia del Perú.* Lima: Imprenta y Librería Sanmartí y Ca.

Yaya, Isabel. 2012. *The Two Faces of Inca History: Dualism in the Narratives and Cos-mology of Ancient Cuzco.* Leiden: Brill.

———. 2015. "Sovereign Bodies: Ancestor Cult and State Legitimacy among the Incas." *History and Anthropoloy* 26 (5): 639–60.

Zevallos Quiñones, Jorge. 1974. "La ropa de tributo de las encomiendas Trujilla-nas en el siglo XVI." *Historia y cultura* 7:107–27.

———. 1989. *Los cacicazgos de Lambayeque.* Trujillo, Peru: Graf. Cuatro.

———. 1992. *Los cacicazgos de Trujillo.* Trujillo, Peru: Grafica Cuatro, S. A.

———. 1994. *La cronica de Ocxaguaman.* Trujillo, Peru: Ediciones de la Funcación "Alfredo Pinillos Goicochea."

Zuidema, R. Tom. 1964/1966. "El calendario Inca." *Actas y memorias*, 36th Con-greso Internacional de Americanistas, vol. 2, 25–30. Seville: Editorial Católi-ca Española.

———. 1967. "El origen del imperio Inca." *Revista de la Universidad de Huaman-ga* 3 (9): 8–11, 21.

———. 1977. "The Inca Calendar." In *Native American Astronomy*, edited by A. F. Aveni, 219–59. Austin: University of Texas Press.

———. 1982. "Myth and History in Ancient Peru." In *The Logic of Culture: Ad-vances in Structural Theory and Methods*, edited by Ino Rossi, 150–75. South Hadley MA: J. F. Bergin.

———. 1983. "Hierarchy and Space in Incaic Social Organization." *Ethnohisto-ry* 30 (2): 49–75.

———. 1985. "Dynastic Structures in Chimor and Tahuantinsuyu." Paper pre-sented at the Dumbarton Oaks conference on "The Northern Dynasties: Kingship and Statecraft in Chimor," Washington DC, October 12–13, 1985. Unpublished paper, copy in author's possession.

———. 1989. "A Quipu Calendar from Ica, Peru, with a Comparison to the Ce-que Calendar from Cuzco." In *World Archaeoastronomy*, edited by A. F. Ave-ni, 341–51. Cambridge: Cambridge University Press.

———. 1990. "Dynastic Structures in Andean Culture." In *The Northern Dy-nasties: Kingship and Statecraft in Chimor*, edited by Micael E. Moseley and

Alana Cordy-Collins, 489–505. Washington DC: Dumbarton Oaks Research Library and Collection.

———. 1992. "Inca Cosmos in Andean Context." In *Andean Cosmologies through Time*, edited by Robert V. H. Dover, Katherine E. Seibold, and John H. McDowell, 17–45. Bloomington: University of Indiana Press.

———. 1997. "Cosmovisión Inca y astronomía en el Cuzco: Nuevo año agrícola y sucesion real." In *Pensar America: Cosmovisión mesoamericana y andina*, compiled by A. Garrido Aranda, 249–70. Córdoba: Ayuntamiento de Montilla.

———. 2002. "La organización religiosa del sistema de panacas y memoria en el Cuzco incaico." In *Incas e indios cristianos: Elites indigenas e identidades cristianas en los Andes colonials*, edited by Jean-Jacques Decoster, 19–37. Cusco, Peru: Centro de Estudios regionales Andinos Bartolome de las Casas.

———. 2004. "La identidad de las diez panacas en el Cuzco Incaico." *Boletín de Arqueología* 8:277–87.

———. 2008. "El Inca y sus curacas: Poliginia real y construcción del poder." *Bulletin de l'Institut français d'études andines* 37 (1): 47–55.

———. 2011. "Chuquibamba Textiles and Their Interacting Systems of Notation: The Case of Multiple Exact Calendars." In *Their Way of Writing: Scripts, Signs, and Pictographies in Pre-Columbian America*, edited by Elizabeth Hill Boone and Gary Urton, 251–76. Washington DC: Dumbarton Oaks Research Library and Collection.

———. 2015. "Guaman Poma on Inca Hierarchy, before and in Colonial Times." In *Unlocking the Doors of the Worlds of Guaman Poma and His Nueva Corónica*, edited by Rolena Adorno and Ivan Boserup, 441–69. Copenhagen: Royal Library and Museum Tusculanum.

———. n.d. "The Casana Dress in Guaman Poma's Drawings: Function and Meaning in Inca Textiles." Unpublished paper, copy in author's possession.

Index

Because many of the native peoples discussed in this book were preliterate, the spelling of their names varies by author. I have respected the various spellings, as appropriate, throughout the book.

Shades of Gray: Writing the New American Multiracialism
by Molly Littlewood McKibbin

The Limits of Liberty: Mobility and the Making of the Eastern U.S.-Mexico Border
by James David Nichols

*In Praise of the Ancestors: Names, Identity, and Memory in Africa
and the Americas*
by Susan Elizabeth Ramírez

Native Diasporas: Indigenous Identities and Settler Colonialism in the Americas
edited by Gregory D. Smithers and Brooke N. Newman

Shape Shifters: Journeys across Terrains of Race and Identity
edited by Lily Anne Y. Welty Tamai, Ingrid Dineen-Wimberly,
and Paul Spickard

*Scars of War: The Politics of Paternity and Responsibility for the
Amerasians of Vietnam*
by Sabrina Thomas

*The Southern Exodus to Mexico: Migration across the Borderlands
after the American Civil War*
by Todd W. Wahlstrom

To order or obtain more information on these or other University of Nebraska Press
titles, visit nebraskapress.unl.edu.

CPSIA information can be obtained
at www.ICGtesting.com
Printed in the USA
LVHW020301190422
716595LV00004B/423